DETROIT DIVIDED

DETROIT DIVIDED

REYNOLDS FARLEY
SHELDON DANZIGER
HARRY J. HOLZER

A VOLUME IN THE MULTI-CITY STUDY OF
URBAN INEQUALITY

RUSSELL SAGE FOUNDATION | NEW YORK

The Russell Sage Foundation

Library of Congress Cataloging-in-Publication Data

Farley, Reynolds, 1938–
    Detroit divided / Reynolds Farley, Sheldon Danziger, Harry J. Holzer.
        p. cm.
    "A volume in the Multi-City Study of Urban Inequality."
    Includes bibliographical references and index.
    ISBN 0-87154-243-9
    1. Detroit (Mich.)—Economic conditions. 2. Detroit (Mich.)—Social conditions. 3. Detroit (Mich.)—Race relations. I. Danziger, Sheldon, 1957– II. Holzer, Harry J. III. Title
    HC108.D6F37 2000
    306'.09774'34—dc21   99-087514

Text design by Suzanne Nichols.

RUSSELL SAGE FOUNDATION
112 East 64th Street, New York, New York 10021
10 9 8 7 6 5 4 3 2 1

The Multi-City Study of Urban Inequality

The Multi-City Study of Urban Inequality is a major social science research project designed to deepen the nation's understanding of the social and economic divisions that now beset America's cities. It is based on a uniquely linked set of surveys of employers and households in four major cities: Atlanta, Boston, Detroit, and Los Angeles. The Multi-City Study focuses on the effects of massive economic restructuring on racial and ethnic groups in the inner city, who must compete for increasingly limited opportunities in a shifting labor market while facing persistent discrimination in housing and hiring. Involving more than forty researchers at fifteen U.S. colleges and universities, the Multi-City Study has been jointly funded by the Ford Foundation and the Russell Sage Foundation. This volume is the second in a series of books reporting the results of the Multi-City Study to be published by the Russell Sage Foundation.

Contents

About the Authors

REYNOLDS FARLEY is Otis Dudley Duncan Collegiate Professor of Sociology, University of Michigan, and research scientist at the Population Studies Center of the Institute for Social Research.

SHELDON DANZIGER is Henry J. Meyer Collegiate Professor of Social Work and Public Policy and director of the Center on Poverty Risk and Mental Health at the University of Michigan.

HARRY J. HOLZER is professor of economics at Michigan State University.

Acknowledgments

The authors of this volume thank the Russell Sage Foundation, the Ford Foundation, and the Fannie Mae Foundation for their support of this volume. In particular, we wish to thank Eric Wanner, president of the Russell Sage Foundation, for his support and comments, Suzanne Nichols, associate director of publications, for her editorial assistance, and Nancy Casey for her organizational aid. At the University of Michigan, we wish to thank Nancy Collins, Jess Reaser, and Jen Tracey for their research assistance, and especially Judy Mullin for her artistic assistance, organizational help, and preparation for the figures and tables.

REYNOLDS FARLEY
SHELDON DANZIGER
HARRY J. HOLZER

1

Introduction: Three Centuries of Growth and Conflict

THE CENSUS OF 1990 counted seventy-seven U.S. cities with 200,000 or more residents. Detroit, the ninth largest, ranked 76th in terms of population growth in the 1980s—it lost one resident in six during that decade. It ranked first in terms of poverty, with one-third of its residents living in households reporting cash incomes below the poverty line. It also ranked first for percentage of households receiving public assistance payments, and it was the only large city in which the majority of family households were headed by a single parent. Detroit ranked 73rd of the seventy-seven cities in median income, and 75th in the percentage of adults with college diplomas. As for the worth of its owner-occupied homes, Detroit ranked at the very bottom, with a median home value of only $25,600. The comparable figure for the city of Boston was $161,400 and for Los Angeles, $244,500 (U.S. Department of Commerce 1994, table 3).

Detroit, the Motor City, was once the symbol of our national industrial prowess, the home of an innovative automobile industry that played a key role in the development of the modern middle class. Its engineers created the production line, and its firms soon dominated the world in the manufacturing of cars and trucks. Because of its specialization in the production of heavy equipment during World War II, the city earned the sobriquet Arsenal of Democracy. Thousands of trucks, jeeps, tanks, planes, and weapons built on Detroit's assembly lines helped bring the Allies to victory. Throughout the post–World War II boom, Detroit was known as a city where blue-collar workers of all ethnic and racial backgrounds could prosper, largely by working at tough, but high-paying, jobs in auto plants—jobs that came along with membership in a powerful union that successfully fought for high pay, generous fringe benefits, and good working conditions. Especially for the thousands of African Americans who migrated northward from the fields and towns of the Deep South, Detroit offered opportunities for full-time employment at good wages—and the right to vote.

Detroit no longer symbolizes industrial might or technological innovation. Rather, the city is frequently seen as leading the nation in
unemployment, poverty, abandoned factories, empty office buildings,
high crime, and bitter racial strife. Instead of offering great hopes and
opportunities for its African American residents, today Detroit's blacks
are frequently viewed as poor and disconnected from the mainstream
economy. No longer is Detroit a place where blue-collar workers of all
racial and ethnic groups can prosper together. It seems to have become
the quintessential underclass city, and attracts only a sliver of the great
stream of immigrants now coming to the United States from Latin
America and Asia. One resident of eight in metropolitan Los Angeles in
1997 had migrated to the United States earlier in the 1990s. In New
York, the figure was also one in eight. In Detroit, just one in one hundred was a new arrival (U.S. Department of Commerce 1998). Nor does
Detroit any longer attract migrants from the rural Midwest or South. In
population terms, the city has been declining in size while metropolitan
Detroit has been stagnant. The Census counted 4.2 million for its three
counties (Macomb, Oakland, and Wayne) in 1970, and the Census Bureau estimated 4.1 million in 1998, or a *drop* of 3 percent. In the same
span, the nation's population grew by 32 percent.

The important counterpoint to emphasize—one that will come up
again and again in this book—is that Metropolitan Detroit is not an
impoverished place. When one takes into account the overwhelmingly
white suburban ring, one finds that the Detroit metropolitan area is
among the nation's most prosperous. In terms of the earnings of employed men and women, Detroit ranked 7th out of 281 metropolises in
1990; in terms of per capita income, it was 24th of 281. In 1997, the
average income of families in metropolitan Detroit was 13 percent
above the national average. In that year, families in metropolitan Detroit had average incomes of $56,000, far above the $49,500 of metropolitan New York and the $47,600 of metropolitan Los Angeles (U.S.
Department of Commerce 1993, table 3; 1998). As the nation's major
retailers know, Detroit's suburban ring is a good place to do business
because of its highly-paid residents.

Metropolitan Detroit continues to be a high-wage, high-income location, even though the city's poverty rate remains elevated. The stark
inequality between poor blacks living in the central city and the more
affluent whites in the suburbs makes metropolitan Detroit unusual. A
few numbers convey this polarization. In 1990, the city's population was
76 percent African American; the suburban ring was only 5 percent African American. The poverty rate for the city was 32 percent; for the ring,
6 percent. The economic disparity is even greater among children, with
just under half (47 percent) of the city's population under the age of

eighteen living in impoverished households, compared with 10 percent in the suburban ring (U.S. Department of Commerce 1993). Detroit's extreme segregation is a recipe for racial tension.

How did this come to pass? What barriers are keeping African American residents of Detroit from pursuing better housing, steady employment, good earnings, and effective schools for their children? Is Detroit different from other cities? Do jobs go unfilled in the suburbs while unemployment remains high in the city? Is there a skills mismatch—lots of unfilled jobs for high-tech workers but much unemployment among the unskilled? Are there any processes under way that will address the city's decline, especially its poverty and unemployment? If so, will these processes provide more equal racial opportunities in the short run and declining black-white differences in the longer run?

Journalists, historians, and urban affairs experts have told the story of Detroit's fall from grace in many contexts. To present his provocative views about the causes and consequences of Detroit's polarization, Ze'ev Chafets (1990) focused on the unique—and fortunately contained—Detroit tradition of burning down hundreds of abandoned homes and garages the night before Halloween. He boldly labeled Detroit the nation's first Third World city. To portray her understanding of the black-white gulf, Tamar Jacoby (1998, pt. 2) focused on the bitter city-suburban controversy over integrating the area's public schools by busing both central-city black and suburban white children to the same classrooms—a plan stopped by an authoritative U.S. Supreme Court decision in 1974 (*Milliken v. Bradley*). Thomas Sugrue (1996) scrutinized employment and housing in the post–World War II era and described the contentious and often violent opposition blacks faced when they tried to move into the city's white neighborhoods.

In this volume, our goal is to discuss the economic and social processes that caused metropolitan Detroit to become so polarized, with an eye toward understanding how this situation might change in the future. We apply the concepts and research methods of the social sciences to answer questions about race, space, employment, and living standards in Detroit. As economists, demographers, and policy analysts, we analyze historical trends and examine information from censuses and data from surveys we administered to representative samples of Detroit residents and employers in the mid-1990s.

This key issue we address is why metropolitan Detroit became racially, economically, and geographically polarized. Similar political and economic forces were at work in most of metropolitan America, but we explain why they had such severe consequences in Detroit. But this is not only a look backward. We describe the trends and forces that are shaping metropolitan Detroit as it enters the new century. Some of them suggest a continuation of today's polarization, others offer hope for change.

We focus on the entire Detroit area. A large part of our story tells how poor blacks came to comprise a large share of the central city's population and why the overwhelming majority of whites chose to leave the city and settle in the surrounding suburbs. The extent to which the geographic segregation of whites and blacks is due to social and economic forces, as opposed to being an independent factor that itself contributes to racial inequalities, will receive a large share of attention.

Our Surveys and Sources of Information

Several sources provided the information we analyzed to describe the social, economic, and demographic changes in Detroit. The University of Michigan's Detroit Area Study has gathered data from a random sample of residents of the metropolis every year since the early 1950s. The 1976 Detroit Area Study focused on racial attitudes: how blacks and whites view each other and the causes of continued racial residential segregation. The 1992 Detroit Area Study also investigated these topics and included an additional array of questions about employment, earnings, job search, and how people thought they were treated when they sought work.[1] Because African Americans make up only one-fifth of metropolitan Detroit's population, both surveys oversampled neighborhoods with many black residents in order to give us a larger sample and greater confidence in our findings. In 1976, 1,134 adults were interviewed; in 1992, 1,543.

Interviewing Detroit-area residents provided extensive information about racial beliefs and about the supply side of the labor market, including where blacks and whites looked for employment. Our investigation is unique, since we simultaneously carried out a survey with a random sample of 800 metropolitan Detroit employers, whom we interviewed by telephone between May 1992 and March 1993. This employer survey focused on those jobs that did not require a college degree, thereby providing a clear picture of the demand side of the labor market that minorities and less-educated workers now face. This survey gives us detailed information about what kinds of jobs are being filled, whether those jobs are located in the city or in remote suburbs, what skills employers demand, how long it takes them to fill their openings, and how employers screen candidates and put chosen applicants on their payrolls. (See Holzer 1996 for further discussion of this survey.)

In addition to the household and employer surveys, we analyzed data gathered by the Bureau of the Census and other state and federal statistical agencies to explain the origins of Detroit's racial and economic polarization and to understand what policies might be effective in the future.

This study is one component of the Multi-City Study of Urban Inequality, supported by the Russell Sage Foundation and the Ford Foundation, to investigate why racial gaps remain large in urban America. The civil rights revolution of the 1960s and many programs implemented by federal and local governments at that time promised great racial progress and an eventual elimination of the gaps that separated whites and African Americans. In the subsequent decade, many indicators of poverty, income, and educational attainment revealed a diminution of those gaps as traditional barriers were eradicated and the black middle class grew. But by the 1980s, it became apparent that within most large metropolises, a significant minority of African Americans were making little progress. To some observers, it seemed that the civil rights revolution had stalled. The term "urban underclass" was frequently used to describe minority populations living in highly segregated, low-income neighborhoods where crime rates were high and opportunities for upward mobility rare (Wilson 1987).

The Multi-City Study addresses a number of questions related to this population: Are the problems of the urban poor due largely to changes in the nation's labor market, to their own reluctance to take advantage of available opportunities, or to racial discrimination? Four metropolises were selected for analysis. Interviews were conducted with nearly 9,000 household residents and 3,200 employers in the four sites to assess racial attitudes, the causes of continued residential segregation, and how labor market processes are linked to racial and gender differences in employment, occupational achievement, and earnings.

Two of the cities chosen for the study, Boston and Detroit, are in the North; one, Atlanta, is in the South; and one, Los Angeles, is in the West. Two (Atlanta and Detroit) have populations that are primarily white and African American, whereas Los Angeles is much more heterogeneous in its racial and ethnic composition. Two (Atlanta and Los Angeles) are characterized by high rates of recent population growth, while Boston has grown slowly and Detroit has stagnated. Immigration from Asia and Latin America has played a great role in changing neighborhoods and labor markets in Los Angeles, a modest role in Atlanta and Boston, and nearly no role in Detroit.

How Detroit Got Where It Is

The racial, economic, and spatial divides that have become entrenched in metropolitan Detroit result from the long-term interplay of four basic processes: historical trends, changing labor markets, persistent residential segregation, and pervasive racial animosity and mistrust.

Historical Trends

First, there is the heavy hand of history. Chapter 2 recounts the development of the city since the arrival of Antoine de Lamothe Cadillac on the banks of the Detroit River in July 1701, stressing those economic and political decisions that made the metropolis what it is today. In the mid-nineteenth century, it was already evident that those few blacks who moved to Detroit from the South or the East Coast were treated very differently from the European and Canadian immigrants arriving at the same time. In the twentieth century, Detroit's destiny was governed by the rise of the automobile industry, symbolized by the inventions of Henry Ford and his 1908 production line—the first mass production of what came to be, next to housing, the world's favorite consumer durable. If there had been no automobile industry, Detroit would now resemble a dozen other medium-sized Midwestern manufacturing towns.

The demands of World War I produced a tremendous increase in Detroit's output of trucks. The building of roads, and then an explosion in automobile production, followed. Quickly, Americans came to depend upon Detroit's vehicles for transportation. By the 1920s, Detroit—home to the nation's fastest-growing major industry—was the nation's fastest-growing large city. This growth spurt distinguished Detroit from other American metropolises: its employment structure depended primarily on vehicle production and closely linked manufacturing industries. Detroit, more highly specialized than other large cities, thus never became a dominant center for trade, financial services, higher education, entertainment, or government. As demand for automobile workers soared in the 1920s, restrictive immigration laws forced auto firms to recruit workers from the American South rather than from Italy or Eastern Europe. As a result, the racial composition of the population began to shift. Today, metropolitan Detroit is distinguished from other Northern and Midwestern metropolises for its relatively large African American population: 22 percent in 1990, about twice the national average.

By concentrating thousands of men in one plant and tens of thousands of men in linked plants within the same city, Detroit's automotive industry provided a unique opportunity for industrial unions to organize workers. They were successful in the late 1930s, when shifts in the nation's economy led to a limited demand for cars one year and a large increase the next. By sitting down on the job, workers effectively stopped production and forced management to negotiate with unions and meet their demands. This process was encouraged by the New Deal's labor policies. In the years just before and after World War II, unions and auto firms fought over how the company's revenues would be divided between workers and shareholders. After numerous bitter postwar strikes, management and the union signed the Treaty of Detroit in 1948, which made auto workers the nation's blue collar elite, enjoying generous fringe benefits and guaranteed wage increases (Lichtenstein 1995, chap. 13). Indeed, their benefits became a model for the demands of other unions around the country. When employers agreed to these demands, millions of blue-collar Americans and their families were shifted from hovering just above the poverty line into the prosperous middle class.

Detroit's unions played a major role in the creation of America's middle class. In the 1930s, Detroit's union leaders feared that management would hire black men to replace the striking white men. As a result, the United Auto Workers stressed the principle of equal pay and equal opportunities for blacks and whites. This meant that no other American city had such a cadre of highly paid unskilled and skilled workers organized into an effective union that endorsed equal racial opportunities for its members.

The choice of where rail lines and huge factories are put, and whether neighborhoods are filled with wooden workingmen's houses or large brick homes on quarter-acre lots, has a great deal to do with who will live where for the next century or so. We generally don't tear down large sections of cities and replace them, or move railroads and expressways. Factory districts tend to remain unattractive long after the plants close and production moves to the suburbs or overseas.

Decisions about jurisdictional boundaries—county boundaries, city boundaries, and city-suburban lines—shape political battles for decades. In Detroit, they influence city-suburban struggles over dozens of issues, including who pays what for water, how much the city may tax suburban residents who work in Detroit, where public transit goes, and even where Detroit's major league sports teams play their games. For half a century or more, Lansing's legislative halls have been the battlegrounds for debates about whether the state of Michigan's spending would disproportionately benefit the city or the surrounding ring.

A more subtle way in which history shapes the present is in its effect on both styles of conflicts and the issues that become conflicts. In Detroit, the struggles between organized labor and management and conflicts over racial issues continue. In this era, when a firm's management is judged a success or a failure on the basis of every quarterly earnings report, United Auto Workers leaders know that by shutting down a crucial plant for just a week or ten days, they can still turn a balance sheet from black to red. But race, not class, is at the heart of the most controversial issues: the assertions by Detroit blacks that they are profiled for arbitrary stops by police if they drive into white suburban neighborhoods; the 1998 fight to grant one of three licenses for casino gambling in the city to an African American entrepreneur or black firm. A well-developed history of political, economic, and racial conflicts continues to be played out in metropolitan Detroit, and the persistent blockage of attempts to merge the city and suburban public transit systems.

Changing Labor Markets

Changes in the structure of the labor market loom large in our explanation of how Detroit got to be where it is today and where it is heading. Three chapters in this volume are devoted to labor market trends including globalization, technological changes, and the subsequent decline in employer demand for less-skilled workers. Much of this discussion is based on our survey of Detroit's employers and what they seek from potential workers, and some on our household survey of the skills of Detroit's residents.

When the great boom in the automobile industry occurred, production was concentrated in huge, multistoried plants, many of them built within the city of Detroit or in the contiguous suburbs. Jobs were geographically close to city neighborhoods where whites and blacks lived. The increased demand for production in World War II led to the building of suburban plants, including the nation's leading bomber plant, about thirty-five miles away, in Ypsilanti. By the 1960s, Detroit's older plants had become technologically obsolete and, one after another, were closed: the Packard Motor Car plant, the Hudson Motor Car plant, the United States Rubber plant along the riverfront on Jefferson Avenue, Studebaker's Detroit plant, several Briggs Body plants, and, eventually, the Clark Avenue plant that had assembled Cadillacs for seven decades. Automobile firms and their suppliers shifted jobs, sometimes to the suburbs, sometimes to other parts of the United States or other countries. Because wage rates in Detroit were so high, plants that remained were retooled and modernized. Employment opportunities for unskilled workers declined dramatically, and by the mid-1960s, in-migration from the South had ceased.

In the early 1970s, Detroit's automobile industry was challenged as never before. German and Japanese producers sold high-quality vehicles at competitive prices and grabbed increasing shares of the American market. In 1973, oil prices skyrocketed, further curtailing the market for the larger American cars and trucks as the cost of gasoline doubled. The large automakers responded by redesigning their products and changing the way cars and trucks were made, especially by reducing wage costs through labor-saving processes and machinery and by outsourcing parts to smaller, sometimes nonunionized firms. Technological changes and the pressures of international competition created better job opportunities for highly trained and highly skilled workers, but fewer opportunities and lower wages for unskilled workers. Traditional black-white differences in educational attainment and the shift of blue-collar jobs from the city to outlying suburbs meant that whites were better able to adjust to these pervasive changes in Detroit's labor market than were African Americans. White workers with blue-collar jobs have suffered a great deal from labor market restructuring, but the burden on African Americans was far greater.

Persistent Residential Segregation

Ever since blacks started coming to Detroit in great numbers—during the World War I labor shortage—residential isolation has been the norm. A history of the city's neighborhoods in the twentieth century (told in chapter 6) shows that as blacks moved up the ladder economically, they sought better housing for their families—just as Italian, Polish, and Russian immigrants to Detroit had. But, with few exceptions, whites staunchly opposed the entry of blacks into their neighborhoods. In the two decades following World War II, a series of "turf wars" broke out in Detroit neighborhoods as blacks and whites contested who could live where. Gradually whites withdrew from the city, taking advantage of generous federal programs that allowed the nation to invade and conquer a "crabgrass frontier" (Jackson 1985). A four-day riot in 1967 (with forty-three fatalities), court decisions upholding the property rights of blacks, a number of racial confrontations within the city in the late 1960s and early 1970s, and demographic shifts led many whites to conclude that they were no longer welcome in the Motor City. They joined the well-established migration stream to the suburbs.

The city's white population fell dramatically, from 1,546,000 in 1950 to 222,000 in 1990—a drop of 85 percent. For whites, a move up the economic ladder typically meant a move to the suburban ring, but residential mobility was constrained for Detroit's African American residents, as most suburbs gave them the clear message that they were not welcome. Neighborhood segregation does not distinguish Detroit from Atlanta, Chicago, Boston, or New York. In all the nation's older metropolitan areas with substantial African American populations, blacks and whites seldom live in the same neighborhoods. But the thoroughness with which long-term social, economic, and racial trends produced an

African American central city in Detroit surrounded by an overwhelmingly white suburban ring makes Detroit unique.

Racial Animosity and Mistrust

Detroit has a long history of racial conflicts, often violent ones. Federal troops have been called out four times to put down black-white bloodshed: twice in the nineteenth century and twice in the twentieth. No other city has such a history. George Edwards (Stolberg 1998; chap. 6), a liberal Michigan Supreme Court justice who served as the city's police commissioner prior to the 1967 riots, tried to reform his force and make his officers sensitive to the city's immense racial divide. He accomplished little and pessimistically concluded that a "river of hatred" divided Detroit's whites from blacks.

The civil rights revolution of the 1960s was strongly supported by the United Auto Workers and by many Detroiters. Prior to the March on Washington, the greatest and most successful outpouring of support for Dr. Martin Luther King was a 1963 parade down Detroit's Woodward Avenue (Branch 1988, 842–43). Viola Liuzzo, from suburban Livonia, was one of two whites killed by extremists in the Voting Rights Marches in Selma, Alabama, in the spring of 1965 (Stanton 1998).

Our surveys of the racial attitudes of Detroit's residents (described in chapters 7 and 8) show much progress in the last two decades. Whites increasingly endorse the principle of equal racial opportunities and assert that they would not be upset by the arrival of an African American family in their neighborhoods. Many say that they would even consider moving into an integrated neighborhood if the number of black residents were low. It is difficult to imagine that Detroit will ever again see the battles over residential integration that raged into the 1960s. Yet our surveys also report that blacks and whites still have fundamentally divergent views of the importance of having black skin in metropolitan Detroit. With few exceptions, African Americans told us they believed that they frequently miss out on good jobs, promotions, and attractive homes and neighborhoods because of systematic and pervasive racial discrimination. Regardless of their educational attainment, income, or occupational achievements, Detroit's African Americans see extensive racial discrimination in all areas of public life. From their viewpoint, it is a color-coded metropolis with whites in control.

Whites certainly recognize the continued existence of frequent racial discrimination in the metropolis, but place much less emphasis on it as the primary cause of the problems of blacks. Instead, many whites endorse the idea that Detroit blacks are neither working very hard nor taking advantage of opportunities open to them. Whites have moved far beyond the racial ideas that made the Ku Klux Klan a potent force in Detroit municipal elections in the late 1920s, and far beyond the racial animosity that led the segregationist governor of Alabama, George Wallace, to a stunning victory in Michigan's 1972 Democratic party presidential primary. Racial views have changed. But when we asked whites questions about the modern racial stereotypes—that is, about racial differences in the tendency to be intelligent or the tendency to prefer to live off welfare rather than to work for a living—we found that a majority still endorse negative stereotypes.

One of the lingering consequences of decades of black-white conflict in Detroit is that the two races perceive racial issues extremely differently. African Americans see discrimination in many circumstances, whereas whites have their doubts about the intelligence of blacks, about their inclination to work hard, and about whether it is easy to get along with them. These views make whites reluctant to live with many African American neighbors and, perhaps, reluctant to add them on their payrolls. And those blacks who expect racial discrimination at every turn may overlook opportunities that really are open to them. These beliefs help explain continuing segregation and the large racial gaps in economic standing.

Although the current economic, geographic, and racial divides between whites and blacks are substantial, we describe herein several positive trends that might narrow those gaps. These include the consistent shift toward more egalitarian racial attitudes on the part of whites, the continued strength of the automobile industry, and a tight labor market in the late 1990s that seems to have benefited most residents.

How Detroit Could Move Forward

On June 11, 1805, a baker named John Harvey accidentally set his hay pile on fire and, within minutes, strong winds created a conflagration that destroyed almost all of the tiny village of Detroit (Conot 1973, 8). A few years later, the city's elders adopted the motto: "We Shall Rise Again from the Ashes. We Hope for Better Things." It is as appropriate now, as we approach Detroit's 300th anniversary, as it was when residents started to rebuild during the Jefferson presidency. This is an excellent time to analyze how the metropolis got to its present status and what will happen in the future. The city will celebrate its 300th anniversary in July 2001. This will be both a time to review the accomplishments of its citizens and industries across the three centuries and a time to look ahead.

A pessimist would stress three fundamental challenges for the metropolis as it enters the new century. First, unless there are dramatic reversals of demographic trends, metropolitan Detroit will become a smaller share of metropolitan America, and the city of Detroit will become a smaller fraction of metropolitan Detroit. Because city and suburban boundaries—and the political clout that goes along with independent units of government—are unlikely to change, continuing rivalries will produce winners and losers on a variety of public policy outcomes. Second, the area has been riven by racial conflict for so many decades that it seems unrealistic to believe that this will soon change. Finally, as manufacturing employment continues to shrink, metropolitan Detroit remains more of a manufacturing center than most metro areas. For example, in 1997, 22 percent of Detroit's employment was in durable goods manufacturing, compared with only 3 percent in New York, 9 percent in Atlanta, and 10 percent in Los Angeles (U.S. Department of Commerce 1997).

We do not believe that this pessimistic scenario is inevitable. Just a decade ago, one would have offered only gloomy predictions about Detroit's future. However, the long economic boom of the 1990s has had many beneficial effects and may be altering long-standing economic and demographic trends. Detroit remains the world headquarters of a now-thriving automotive industry. The rate of employment growth—after lagging far behind the national average for decades—has picked up. And, the city of Detroit is far from moribund. Indeed, the 1990s may prove to have been the years that mark the start of a turnaround. Chrysler constructed a large production facility in the city. General Motors—still the world's largest corporation—moved into the Renaissance Center, which undoubtedly will attract many high-paying jobs to the downtown. And, in 1999, the Compuware computer firm announced plans to build an 800 million dollars headquarters downtown. Thus, the city of Detroit will likely see further growth of highly-paid employees working at high-tech and professional jobs.

Efforts to make the city an entertainment and recreation center are under way. The new Comerica Park for the Detroit Tigers baseball club will attract several million fans downtown every summer. The city lost the Detroit Lions football team to the suburbs in 1974, largely because a state subsidy built the Silverdome in Pontiac, but the city won them back. They too will play their home games downtown in another new stadium. Three major casinos are open, and they are expected to put the city on the map of tourist destinations, and to provide many service-sector jobs for Detroit residents.

Along with the growing construction activity in the downtown area since the mid-1990s, there has been a dramatic drop in unemployment rates. In 1992, the unemployment rate in the city of Detroit was 17 percent—the highest of any major city in the country. By 1998, it was down to 7 percent—still above average for U. S. cities, but showing more improvement during this six-year period than any other major city (U.S. Department of Housing and Urban Development 1999). As we will argue, average earnings and employment levels in Detroit remain well below what they were in the 1950s and 1960s, but a good start has been made in rebuilding the local economy and generating jobs for city residents.

New stadiums, office buildings, and increased tourism are crucial if the city is to regain its vitality and prosperity. Even more important are the gradual reductions in racial tensions and improving city-suburban relations that seem to be under way.

Overview of the Book

The next chapter of this book describes key trends and turning points for Detroit over the last three centuries. In chapter 3, we summarize the recent history of Detroit's labor market, focusing on changes since the start of World War II. Chapter 4 describes the labor market of the 1990s from the perspective of the employer, while the next chapter describes the labor market from the views of workers and nonworkers. Chapter 6 analyzes the social and economic processes that produced the extremely high levels of racial residential segregation in metropolitan Detroit. The next chapter examines the willingness of blacks and whites to live in racially mixed neighborhoods. Chapter 8 describes the views and racial stereotypes that African Americans and whites hold of each other and discusses how each race evaluates programs and policies that might mitigate racial inequalities and divisions. The final chapter lays out various policy alternatives that flow from our study.

2

Detroit's History: Racial, Spatial, and Economic Changes

WHILE searching for a passage to Asia, Jacques Cartier discovered the St. Lawrence River in 1534 and sailed as far as the current site of Montreal. French missionaries followed his route, settled in Quebec, and then moved into the upper Great Lakes in hopes of converting Indians. By the 1630s, they established an outpost at Sault Ste. Marie—near Lakes Superior, Michigan, and Huron. Shortly after the missionaries, came fur traders seeking pelts for the European market (Dunbar and May 1995, chap. 3).

Antoine Cadillac arrived in New France from Gascony in 1683, went to Sault Ste. Marie, and prospered as a trader. The French in Upper Canada frequently fought the Indians, so Quebec administrators found it costly to staff and maintain the western forts. In 1696, Louis Frontenac, then governor of New France, curtailed the fur trade, but Cadillac sailed back to Paris in 1699 and sought King Louis XIV's approval to establish a new outpost for the fur trade. He got that permission and, fortunately for him, the Iroquois signed a peace treaty in 1701. Cadillac and a small band of followers left Montreal in June of that year, sailed up the Ottawa River, across Georgian Bay, down Lake Huron, and then through Lake St. Clair. On July 24, 1701, he found the ideal location for his trading post and thereby founded the city that he named Detroit (Hivert-Carthew 1994, chap. 2).

Antoine Cadillac encouraged the French from eastern Canada to move to Detroit but they were reluctant to go to such a remote place, so he encouraged Indians to settle around his trading post. Thus, from its beginning, Detroit has had a racially mixed population. Hurons, Ottawas, Miamis, and Chippewas lived close together, leading, inevitably, to marriages, since the French traders were men (Cleland 1993, 115; Dunbar and May 1995, 45–47). Living conditions were rustic, the fur trade unrewarding, and support from Paris lukewarm, so Cadillac left Detroit in 1711. (For an English translation of the annals of Cadillac, see Brown et al. 1976, 43–75.)

The French—and the British who followed them to Detroit—tolerated slavery, so there have been black residents for centuries. As whites pushed across the Alleghenies in the mid-1700s, Indians saw their hunting grounds threatened. From time to time, they attacked settlers, killing the whites but sometimes spared black slaves who could taken to posts, such as Detroit, and traded for guns and ammunition (Conot 1973, 120). We think of slavery as the peculiar institution of the American South, but from the 1770s to 1810, small numbers of bondsmen could be found in Detroit (Dunbar and May 1965, 103, 119; for a history of Indian and black slavery in Detroit, see Castellanos 1991).

Throughout the 1700s, the English and French contested control of North America, largely by arming different tribes of Indians. In November 1760, the French commandant at Detroit surrendered to the British. Little demographic change followed, and Detroit remained a small French-speaking village into the early nineteenth century. Even after the Revolutionary War, the international boundary between the United States and British Canada in the midwest remained subject to negotiation and warfare. The English continued to arm Indians, but American soldiers under the command of General Anthony Wayne, in 1794, defeated them in the Battle of Fallen Timbers near present-day Toledo (Gilpin 1970, 2). On July 11, 1796, British troops peacefully departed from Detroit when an American colonel, John Hamtramck, marched his regiment into the village (Dunbar and May 1995, 88–89).

Early in the next century, two key figures arrived. The first, Father Gabriel Richard, escaped from France and eventually made his way to Detroit. He founded the first school, brought in the first printing press, was elected as the territory's first representative to Congress and, in 1817, created the educational institution that became the University of Michigan.

In 1805, President Jefferson encouraged the organization of Michigan as a territory. He appointed five men to carry out the task, but only one of them, Judge Augustus Woodward from Virginia, threw himself vigorously into the job. He arrived in 1805, established the territory's capital, and hoped that the city would become the dominant mercantile center of the upper Midwest. Borrowing from Pierre L'Enfant's designs for Washington, Woodward laid out the radial boulevards, interlocking hexagons, and spacious plazas that still give Detroit's downtown a unique geography (Eckert 1993, 28).

The Detroit of Father Gabriel Richard and Judge Woodward was a village separated by several weeks' travel from any other population center. The Census of 1810 counted just 1,650 in Detroit (Gilpin 1970, 19). The growth of the city awaited two major developments. Most important, the area had to be made safe for white settlers. Much of the

15

nineteenth century was devoted to the national racial struggle over who would control land west of the Appalachians: Indians or European settlers. Just as the French and British had done, the Americans kept a military force in Detroit. Indians, under the leadership of Chief Tecumseh, fought alongside the British in the War of 1812. When the British-Indian forces overran Fort Detroit, most of the village was destroyed. But, in 1813, Commodore Perry defeated British ships on Lake Erie, while General William Henry Harrison defeated the British-Indian forces in battles in Ohio, Michigan, and Ontario (Dunbar and May 1995, chap. 7; Sugden 1997, chap. 22).

The American victory in the second war against England was the key to Indian removal from the Midwest. Two forts were built in Michigan, so that the military could control Indians: Fort Saginaw and Fort Brady at Sault Ste. Marie. Territorial governors negotiated with Indian leaders, typically promising to respect their land rights and give them an annual payment if they would restrict themselves to a particular locale. Backed by the military, whites were able to take over virtually all Indian lands in Michigan by the 1830s. Indians who survived either moved west or settled on reservations, seven of which remain in Michigan. Lewis Cass, the territorial governor who fought against Indians in the War of 1812 and then helped expel them from Michigan, summarized the racial perspective of his era in his essay, "Removal of Indians":

> Like the bear, and deer, and buffalo of his own forests, the Indian lives as his father lived, and dies as his father died. He never attempts to imitate the arts of his civilized neighbors. His life passes away in a succession of listless indolence, and of vigorous extortion to provide for his animal wants, or to gratify his baleful passions. . . . Efforts . . . have not been wanting to teach and reclaim him. But he is perhaps destined to disappear with the forest. [Quoted in Takaki 1979, 83]

The second crucial issue to spur growth in Detroit was access. The Census of 1820 counted almost 600,000 people in Ohio, but just 8,000 in Michigan. The completion of the Erie Canal in 1826 and Robert Fulton's application of steam power to boats explain the rise of Detroit. After 1827, agricultural products from the Midwest could be shipped from Detroit across Lake Erie to the Erie Canal, and eventually to New York City. Easterners who wished to come west could travel the same route. Enough settlers came so that by 1837, Michigan satisfied the population criterion for statehood (a minimum of 30,000). The state and federal governments soon began investing heavily in the development of the West. In Michigan, this meant draining swamps and building canals and, later, railroads. By 1848, a rail line west from Detroit reached Lake Michigan and seven years later, the Chicago to New York link was com-

TABLE 2.1   *Population of Michigan and City of Detroit in the Nineteenth Century*

| Year | State of Michigan | City of Detroit | | | Average Annual Growth Rates in Decade | |
		Total	Black	Percentage Black	State of Michigan	City of Detroit
1810	4,762	1,650	*n.a.*	*n.a.*	*n.a.*	*n.a.*
1820	8,896	1,422	67	4.7	+6.2%	−1.5%
1830	31,639	2,222	126	5.7	+12.7	+4.5
1840	212,267	9,102	193	2.1	+19.0	+14.1
1850	397,654	21,019	587	2.8	+6.3	+8.4
1860	748,113	45,619	1,402	3.1	+6.3	+7.7
1870	1,184,059	79,577	2,235	2.8	+4.6	+5.6
1880	1,636,937	116,340	2,821	2.4	+3.2	+3.8
1890	2,093,890	205,876	3,431	1.7	+2.5	+5.7
1900	2,420,982	285,704	4,111	1.4	+1.5	+3.3

Source: Ruggles and Sobek 1997.

pleted. It involved rail travel from Chicago to Detroit; a ferry across the Detroit River; a rail line across southern Ontario; a bridge into the U.S. near Buffalo; and finally a rail line across New York State. The city's population doubled in the 1840s and again in the next decade. Table 2.1 shows census counts for the nineteenth century.

Blacks and Whites in Nineteenth-Century Detroit

The same year the framers drafted the Constitution—1787—they enacted the Northwest Ordinance forever prohibiting slavery in the area that now includes Michigan. Local courts interpreted the ordinance to mean that those who owned slaves when the U.S. took over Michigan might continue to hold them, and slaves brought to Michigan from other states by their masters were still in bondage; but bondsmen coming to Michigan from Canada were free (Dunbar and May 1995, 103). The census of 1810 was the last to enumerate slaves when seventeen were counted in Detroit (Castellanos 1991).

Before statehood, the territorial legislature passed bills demonstrating that American blacks were to be treated as a different class of people. After the opening of the Erie Canal, the fear spread that numerous blacks would move from the East. As a result, the Michigan legislature enacted Black Codes. Ostensibly, these protected African Americans

17

against slave catchers who might sell free blacks into slavery, but these codes were put on the books to discourage in-migration. Blacks (but not whites) moving to Michigan had to present a court-attested certificate of freedom, register with the clerk of the local court, and post a bond of $500 guaranteeing good behavior. Sheriffs had the power to expel them from the state, but these codes were seldom enforced; there is only one recorded prosecution (Katzman 1973, 6–11; Litwack 1961, 70).

After Britain ended slavery throughout its empire in 1837, American slaves knew that once they crossed the Detroit River, they would be free: the Canadian authorities would not return them. As transportation improved, abolitionists in Michigan established an underground railway for escaping slaves. Windsor, Chatham, and neighboring Ontario communities just across the international boundary saw their black populations grow, as did two locations in Michigan: Detroit and Calvin Township in rural Cass County, where freedmen and fugitive slaves established many farms in the 1840s and 1850s (Hesslink 1968).

Escaped slaves in Michigan were at risk of being captured and returned, although many Northerners and sympathetic local courts tried to prevent it. The first Detroit racial riot was initiated by such an incident. Thornton and Ruth Blackburn fled from Kentucky in 1831 and lived within Detroit's small black community. In June 1833, slave catchers tried to return the Blackburns to their owners and requested help from Wayne County sheriff John Wilson. He took custody of the couple, but blacks from Detroit and southern Ontario surrounded the jail and demanded their release. They intended to spirit them across the Detroit River. Two black women entered the jail to console Mrs. Blackburn, but one of them switched places with her, and Ruth Blackburn escaped to Canada. The slave catchers demanded Thornton Blackburn, but the angry crowd threatened violence if the sheriff turned him over. Mr. Blackburn was taken from jail, but a compatriot had smuggled a gun to him, so he threatened to shoot anyone who tried to retain him. A melee ensued. Thornton Blackburn escaped to Canada but in the fighting, the sheriff was wounded and subsequently died.

Racial tensions remained high, since whites feared that blacks would burn the entire city. The mayor appealed to the secretary of war for federal troops—then garrisoned at Ft. Wayne within the city. They were dispatched and spent two weeks keeping Detroit's blacks and whites from violently attacking each other (Katzman 1973, 9–12; Conot 1973, 71; McRea 1991).

When Michigan became a state in 1837, it adopted a constitution that once again treated African Americans differently. It barred slavery, but denied African Americans the right to serve in the state militia and the right to vote (even though any alien who expressed an intention to become a citizen, as well as any "civilized" Indian, was granted suffrage). When the legislature authorized tax funding of public schools in 1842, it taxed blacks but limited school enrollment to whites (Litwack 1961, 123).

Population growth in Detroit in the middle nineteenth century was encouraged by the draining of swamps, thereby allowing settlement of the hinterland, and by federal funding that built the canal at Sault Ste. Marie (completed in 1855). Iron and copper ores from the Upper Peninsula could be shipped to the mills that eventually ringed the Great Lakes. There was a spurt in railroad building, so by the early 1880s, a rail network put all of the Lower Peninsula within a short journey of Detroit.

The Civil War witnessed the second racial riot in Detroit. With Union forces faring poorly against the Confederates, President Lincoln called for 300,000 more troops in 1862. Northern young men had the option of either paying $600 to the government or being drafted. Immigrants in northern cities could not afford to buy their way out of conscription, but they dreaded military service and blamed blacks for the war, as did many northern politicians who opposed president Lincoln. Racial riots pitted immigrants against blacks in numerous cities in 1863.

The riot in Detroit started with plans for a lynching. A black restaurant owner, William Faulkner, was accused of molesting two young girls and was jailed. On March 6, 1863, dock workers—primarily recent Irish, Dutch, and German immigrants—surrounded the jail and demanded Mr. Faulkner. The Wayne County sheriff called once again for federal troops from Ft. Wayne as well as from a newly established post in Ypsilanti. A crowd assembled to lynch Mr. Faulkner but the troops arrived to maintain order. The crowd attacked the soldiers with stones, prompting the troops to shoot into the crowd. One person was killed. The mob dispersed, but torched black-owned businesses and homes, killing two. The fire department stood by without taking action, fearing that their hoses and equipment would be destroyed by the angry rioters (Katzman 1973, 44–47).

Federal troops restored order and then remained in Detroit for several weeks to ensure the peace. Mr. Faulkner was convicted and served seven years in prison, but one of his accusers later admitted that the tale of molestation was a fabrication. He was released and Detroit's city council paid restitution for the business he lost in Detroit's second racial riot (Hendrickson 1991, 157–62; Katzman 1973, 45–47; Dunbar and May 1995, 335; Conot 1973, 96–98).

Detroit Today

Metropolitan Detroit today can best be understood by considering five crucial turning points, brief periods when great changes with long-lasting consequences occurred. Each shaped Detroit at later points and helps explain the character of the metropolitan area at the start of the twenty-first century.

The First Turning Point: Manufacturing and Detroit's Emergence as a National Metropolis

The emergence of Detroit as a national manufacturing center was encouraged by the Civil War's demand for armaments. Utilizing timbers from the pine forests of Michigan and capitalizing on its favorable location on the Great Lakes, Detroit's shops and factories produced wood products, railroad equipment, brass, aluminum and iron products, paint, varnish, and hundreds of industrial and pharmaceutical chemicals. As the need for labor increased, the city's population grew rapidly—just about doubling in the 1880s and then growing another 40 percent the following decade. Burgeoning manufacturing firms attracted workers from Canada, the rural United States, and, later, southern and Eastern Europe (Zunz 1982).

Effective public transit was yet to be invented, so late nineteenth century Detroit was a walking city. Workers had to live close to their jobs, so ethnic neighborhoods sprang up around factories throughout the city. Within or near those neighborhoods were built the beautiful and elegant houses of worship whose magnificent spires and domes still grace the city's skyline: St. Joseph's Catholic Church on Gratiot; the Gothic Woodward Avenue Baptist Church; the Romanesque St. Mary's Catholic Church in Greektown; and Temple Beth El, modeled after the Pantheon on Woodward (Meyer 1971; Eckert 1993). In the 1880s, the prosperous city hired the nation's leading landscape architect, Frederick Law Olmsted to design Belle Isle Park (Rybcznski 1999, 350–52).

The development of Detroit as a national manufacturing center had four lasting consequences:

- factories and chemical plants—and the rail lines to serve them— were built along the riverfront in an era of few zoning regulations and little concern for environmental issues
- a large stock of modestly priced, high-density housing was built for workingmen's homes
- immigrants from Canada, Eastern Europe, and the rural United States dominated the demographic composition
- the prosperity of Detroit's firms meant their owners amassed a great deal of capital, so the city had a prosperous economic elite to help finance the auto industry.

What about the city's tiny black population? For most of the nineteenth century, the black population grew at a lower rate than the white, so the proportion of African Americans fell from about 6 percent in 1840, when freedman and fugitive slaves were numerous, to about 1 percent in 1900 (see table 2.1). The census of 1900 enumerated just 4,000 blacks in a city of 290,000.

Sharp social class divisions apparently isolated a small group of highly educated elite blacks from a larger number of manual laborers. A few prosperous Detroit blacks lived in an integrated world—some of them professionals serving a white clientele—and they had strong connections to the Republican party. As early as 1892, one of the black elite, W. W. Ferguson, was elected to the Michigan legislature (Thomas 1992, 257). The Pelhams—descendants of free Virginia blacks who moved from Petersburg, Virginia to Detroit in 1862—were the most prominent African American family. Robert Pelham became one of the city's leading building contractors and his son, Benjamin Pelham, founded the city's first African American newspaper. Ben Pelham was appointed to a variety of offices by the Republican Party and, as clerk of the Wayne County Board of Supervisors, dominated county government for a decade shortly after the turn of the century. At that time, he was probably the nation's most powerful black political leader (Thomas 1992, chap. 7). A larger number of unskilled African Americans worked on Detroit's docks, although they gradually lost these jobs to European immigrants. Others labored at the traditional jobs black men held in northern cities until World War II: as waiters and porters in downtown hotels and restaurants. There also was a tiny middle class running small businesses in the neighborhood where many of the city's poorer blacks lived, an area just east of downtown that came to be known as Paradise Valley. But there was a striking absence of blacks from the early industrial jobs in Detroit (Zunz 1982, 222–23).

The Second Turning Point: Detroit Becomes the Motor City

In 1900, Detroit ranked 15th on the list of the nation's largest cities, but by 1920 it was 4th, trailing only New York, Chicago, and Philadelphia. This leap was attributable to a single development: the rise of the auto industry. Many Midwestern towns might have become the Motor City, because, until the Depression, most cities in the industrial heartland had several firms turning out vehicles. Automaking required engineering talent, access to wood and steel, some capital, and machine shops to turn out component parts. Detroit had those assets, but so did Cleveland, Chicago, and Pittsburgh.

What lifted Detroit to prominence as the world's motor capital were the innovators who used their creative ideas and drew on the skills of local craftsmen and the venture capital of Detroit's rich families to develop the automobile industry. Henry Ford, with his first assembly line and his principles of standardization and integrated production for the Model T, stands out, but many individuals from Michigan made great contributions to Detroit's major industry: Ransom Olds, Will Durant, Walter Chrysler, the Dodge Brothers, and Alfred Sloan.

Although early cars were unreliable and expensive, the market for them was expanding. U.S. producers turned out just 6,400 cars in 1908 but 78,000 four years later. The growth of the urban upper classes accounts for much of that rise. Cars were symbols of success, but more than that they were much cleaner and more convenient than horse-drawn coaches or slow-moving streetcars.

Selling cars to the upper classes would not have created modern Detroit. World War I contributed in a manner that no one could have foreseen. The war effort demanded the chemicals, steel, and industrial products Detroit had been making since the late nineteenth century—and also demanded motor vehicles. Getting armaments and munitions from the industrial Midwest to East Coast ports for shipment to Europe was a major challenge. The railroads were too congested and mismanaged to accomplish the task. The solution was trucks. Detroit turned out only 25,000 trucks in 1914, but 227,000 four years later (U.S. Department of Commerce 1975, 716). Shortly after World War I, trucks began to dominate the short-haul freight business, as states paved thousands of miles of highways, creating even more demand for Detroit's products.

Figure 2.1 describes the economic heart of twentieth-century Detroit: the number of motor vehicles produced each year since 1900. Several booms, and some deep troughs, are evident. Production soared in the two decades after Henry Ford opened his plant, but that trend plummeted with the Wall Street crash in 1929. There was a substantial—and unanticipated—recovery in the mid-1930s, but at the start of World War II, the government ordered an end to the production of cars. After 1946, production generally increased, reaching a peak in 1973. The sawtoothed nature of this figure points out another key factor in Detroit's economy: rapid fluctuations in production from one year to the next, depending on the business cycle. Manufacturers producing bread, milk, cheese, or computers never see their production fall by 40 or 50 percent in the course of a few years, only to rebound shortly thereafter. But that is de rigueur in motor vehicle manufacturing, leading to tremendous layoffs for Detroit workers one year and a shortage of labor soon afterward.

Between 1910 and 1920, the city's population more than doubled,

FIGURE 2.1 *Production of Motor Vehicles in the United States, 1900 to 1997*

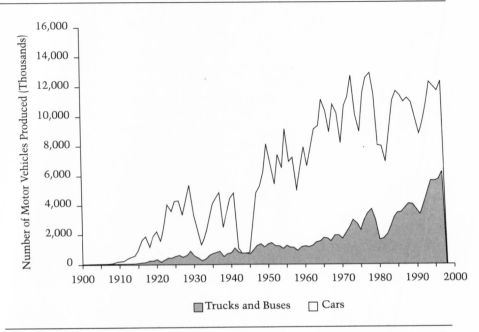

Source: U. S. Department of Commerce 1973b; Michigan Employment Security Commission 1997.

whereas the national population increased by just 21 percent. Detroit was the fastest-growing big city in the country. Shortly after the 1920 census, the city became a demographic millionaire, a status it maintained for seven decades. During the 1920s, the city's population grew another 60 percent—four times as rapidly as that of the nation—reaching 1.6 million in 1930, thus strengthening its claim as the nation's fourth largest and distinguishing itself in size from all Midwestern rivals except Chicago.

The emergence of the automobile industry produced the following important changes:

Shift in the Geography and Organization of Work In 1900, Detroit men worked in small factories with a modest number of other workers (Zunz 1982). While the work was labor intensive, men did a variety of tasks and the image of workers as craftsmen could be maintained. With the coming of the assembly line, the life of the working man changed. Production was broken down into simple, repetitive com-

23

The Fisher Building

In the 1920s, magnificent new office towers, such as the Fisher Building, reshaped prosperous Detroit's skyline. Photo reprinted with permission from the Detroit News Archives.

ponents requiring strength, but not much ingenuity. The innovation of the auto industry was to have thousands of men work in one location doing specific tasks, each closely integrated with every other task. Entrepreneurs needed great amounts of capital to build huge plants, then organize thousands of production line workers while keeping labor costs low but quality and productivity high.

Domination of Detroit's Employment and Economy by a Few Large Motor Vehicle Firms   At its peak in 1914, forty-three different manufacturers turned out new cars in Detroit (Davis 1988, table 20). With maturity came corporate amalgamations and the disappearance of small producers. By the early 1920s, the outlines of Ford, General Motors (GM) and Chrysler were in place, and by the end of that decade, just eight firms produced cars in Detroit. The development of these corporate giants—and their need for financial services—led to the building boom that gave Detroit many of its architectural treasures, including the GM Building (1922) and the Fisher Tower (1928). The city's nineteenth-century downtown financial district grew to a status commensurate with the city's national importance when the 1,200 room Book-Cadillac Hotel (1922), the 47-story Penobscott (1928) and 36-story Guardian building (1929) were erected.

Immense Housing and Transportation Problems for Blue-Collar Workers   Two problems bedeviled Detroit during its decades of explosive growth. There was a housing shortage for working men during World War I so hundreds of barns, stables, sheds, and garages were converted into uncomfortable and unsanitary living quarters (Conot 1973, 276). The city's tremendous building boom of the 1920s improved the situation since a wide range of housing units were constructed: the beautiful spacious homes in Palmer Park and along the great boulevards, middle-class housing including single family homes and flats throughout the city as well as thousands of small, wooden homes intended for low-paid workingmen and their families.

Even though many new neighborhoods were laid out in the 1920s, public transit was a major problem. Large factories were built throughout the city but there were no similar investments in modern transportation. The city's arteries became a congested mess of horse drawn wagons, slow streetcars, trucks, and cars, frequently at a standstill while a freight train pushed box cars into the factories. The city government tried to improve the inefficient streetcar system and, after a decade of bitter controversy, took over the Detroit Street Railways in the 1920s. Simultaneously, the city began developing plans for a superhighway system but the Depression and then World War II put those plans on hold (Eckert 1993, 39).

Setting the Boundaries of the City   In 1900, the city extended only a few miles back from the river. This changed with growth stimulated by the automobile industry and so annexation captured much of the growth this century. But the state adopted restrictive annexation laws in 1926 limiting the physical expansion of the city and ensuring that post–World War II growth would be in the suburbs (Thomas 1997, 30–33).

Two suburbs escaped annexation and survive as municipalities surrounded by the city of Detroit. The city tried to annex them in the 1920s but Ford Motor Company with its assembly plant in Highland Park and Dodge with its production facilities in Hamtramck feared the taxing powers of Detroit and preserved the independence of these enclaves.

Development of Detroit's Cultural Center   The city's wealth also contributed to the building of the Detroit Public Library (1921) and the Detroit Institute of Art (1927) both located along Woodward Avenue.

The Ford Rouge Plant in 1947

Detroit's automobile plants modernized industrial production by creating massive factories such as Ford's Rouge plant. Photo reprinted with permission from the Detroit News Archives.

The stretch of Woodward from the Hudson Department Store (1891) to the General Motors Building that anchored the New Center area became one of the nation's cultural capitals. Simultaneously, attractive venues for the performing arts were erected along this corridor: the Detroit Music Hall (1928), the Masonic Temple (1926), Orchestra Hall (1919), and the Fisher (1928) and Fox Theaters (1928) (Eckert, 1993: 77–88).

Suburbanization of Employment   Detroit differs from southern and western cities in its long history of suburban growth. Communities south of the city along the Detroit River—Ecorse, Wyandotte, and Trenton—became industrial centers in the late 1800s. They consisted, and still consist, of factories surrounded by modest homes. There were also numerous independent towns that became suburbs with the expansion of the automotive era. Henry Ford built Navy ships in River Rouge during World War I, bringing that city into the suburban ring. His ancestors had owned farms in Dearborn, influencing his decision to locate his

MAP 2.1   *Annexations to the City of Detroit*

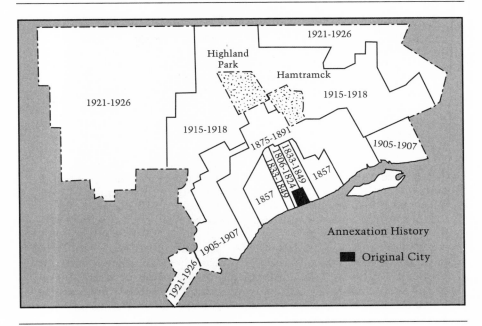

Source: City of Detroit 1985.

largest plant and his firm's headquarters there. The industrial center of Pontiac thrived as its automobile factories boomed. But the spread of population after World War II brought it into Detroit's suburban ring.

The Third Turning Point: The American South Replaces Europe as the Source of Detroit's Population Growth

Demographic shifts provoked by World War I began the process that eventually made metropolitan Detroit the quintessential "chocolate city, vanilla suburb" location (as the song heard on soul music stations in the 1970s put it). Just after World War I, Detroit was a city of European and Canadian immigrants. About 950,000 whites lived there, 30 percent of them having been born abroad and another 37 percent born in the United States but with one or both parents born outside the country. That is, two-thirds of the city's residents were either foreign-born or the children of immigrants (U.S. Department of Commerce 1921, table 17).

The Black Muslims and Father Charles Coughlin

Detroit was a center of religious and political innovation especially during the early decades of the Twentieth century. W. D. Fard arrived in the late 1920s and peddled goods door-to-door. He gradually founded an American version of Islam. From the Muslims, Fard borrowed many elements of his religion including devotion to the Koran. The nation's first mosque had opened in Highland Park in 1919. Influenced by Marcus Garvey, Fard encouraged blacks to depend upon their own resources and reject the white man's culture. Indeed, he taught that whites were incarnations of Satan and had imposed Christianity upon Africans to keep them enslaved and docile. From Henry Ford, he borrowed anti-Semitism and the idea that Jewish merchants exploited poor blacks. Fard called himself a prophet, organized what he called the Nation of Islam, founded a mosque and established the University of Islam in Detroit—really an elementary and secondary school. He named his security force the Fruit of Islam (Conot 1973, 355–60).

Fard mysteriously left Detroit in 1934 and Elijah Poole took over, eventually moving headquarters to Chicago where he became Elijah Mohammed. Until the 1960s, this religion's followers were primarily Detroit and Chicago residents. Then, Malcolm Little—a Michigan man who received some of his religious training at the mosque in Detroit—brought the nation's attention to the Black Muslim movement by stressing the ideas Fard enunciated four decades earlier (Smith 1999, chap. 2).

We are now familiar with preachers who attract large followings and raise money with messages that intertwine religion with conservative political values. This started in Detroit. Charles Coughlin, a young priest, was assigned the Herculean task of creating a new parish in the then almost empty suburb of Royal Oak in the 1920s. Realizing that he was a dramatic speaker, he sought to collect funds to build a church using a new medium—radio. Fortunately for him, a station in Detroit, WJR, needed to fill airtime. Coughlin's conservative political ideas were highly congruent with those of Eddie Rickenbacker—the World War I flying ace who had invested in the station.

By the fall of 1930, Father Coughlin made a weekly national broadcast and quickly developed an immense and loyal following. Audience surveys were in their infancy but they suggest that the only national figure reaching more listeners at the time was President Roosevelt. Father Coughlin mentioned generic Judeo-Christian values and spoke of traditional American virtues but increasingly he emphasized political issues. In 1932, he took credit for the election of President Roosevelt but shortly thereafter he became a leading—and exceptionally bitter—critic of the New Deal. As the Depression wore on, many sought a simple explanation for it and a simple solution. Father Coughlin was one of many offering both but he had a larger audience than his competitors. He joined Henry Ford and others in blaming the Depression on an international cabal of Jewish bankers who were manipulating finances for their own gains.

In 1936, Charles Coughlin intended to select the next president by uniting several factions of populists including the followers of Francis Townsend who propounded share-the-wealth ideas, the followers of Huey P. Long who, after his assassination, were led by Gerald L. K. Smith who moved his operation to Detroit and Coughlin's own large audience. It seemed possible the electorate might elect a populist, but as the year progressed their chances faded and Father Coughlin's candidate for president—Senator Lemke from North Dakota—carried nary a state.

Later in that decade, Coughlin's popularity waned but he still commanded an audience and raised funds. As Europe increasingly moved toward war, the Roosevelt Administration amassed information that suggested to them that Father Coughlin was supported by and espoused the ideas of our enemies in Germany and Italy. The Justice Department considered indicting him. Instead they went to his superior, Cardinal Mooney in Detroit. The hierarchy had been uneasy for years about having Charles Coughlin as the church's leading spokesperson but had never silenced him. When presented with the administration's evidence about Coughlin, Cardinal Mooney ordered him off the air. He complied and devoted himself to building an impressive array of religious buildings in Royal Oak. (Warren 1996; Brinkley 1983)

Of the city's 40,000 black residents, 87 percent were born outside Michigan, so they too were migrants, mostly from the South (U.S. Department of Commerce 1932, table 15).

Figure 2.2 shows the birthplaces of whites and blacks in metropolitan Detroit from 1920 to 1990. Among whites, the proportion of foreign-born fell steadily as the immigrants who came before World War I grew older. The proportion of whites born in the South increased, as automobile jobs became available, peaking at about 8 percent during World War II. After 1960, Detroit stopped attracting migrants, so the proportion born in Michigan rose steadily, reaching three-quarters by 1990.

Until recently, the majority of African Americans were in-migrants from the South, but their northward flow also stopped in the mid-1960s. A significant number of blacks in 1920 were foreign-born, from Canada—the descendants of fugitive slaves who lived for generations on the Ontario side of the river and who moved to Detroit when labor was in short supply.

Blacks were a small, but rapidly growing, fraction of the city's population, increasing from just 1 percent in 1910 to 4 percent in 1930. The social and economic processes set in motion at this time—especially

FIGURE 2.2 *Origins of the Population of Metropolitan Detroit, 1920 to 1990*

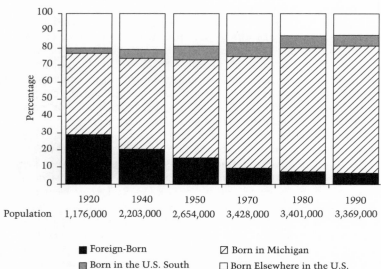

White Population

Population	1920	1940	1950	1970	1980	1990
	1,176,000	2,203,000	2,654,000	3,428,000	3,401,000	3,369,000

■ Foreign-Born   ▨ Born in Michigan
▥ Born in the U.S. South   ☐ Born Elsewhere in the U.S.

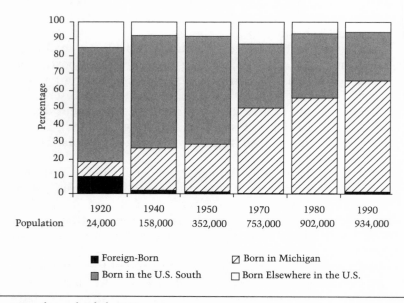

Black Population

Population	1920	1940	1950	1970	1980	1990
	24,000	158,000	352,000	753,000	902,000	934,000

■ Foreign-Born   ▨ Born in Michigan
▥ Born in the U.S. South   ☐ Born Elsewhere in the U.S.

Source: Ruggles and Sobek 1997.

Jim Crow policies in the housing market and on the shop floor—meant that metropolitan Detroit would be riven by race for decades to come. It is likely that employers shared widely held views that blacks were exceptionally unskilled and could not readily master factory work. It is also probable that employers feared that whites would not cooperate with black workers, so productivity would be enhanced when all employees were white. Nevertheless, Detroit differed from many other cities in that black men got industrial jobs. Coleman Young, the city's first black mayor, described the employment situation in his youth by recalling that Ford sent buses to the city's Black Bottom neighborhood every day to recruit factory hands (Bak 1996, 12–16). When the auto firms were hiring, the Detroit Urban League under the leadership of Forrester Washington and John Dancy served as an effective employment bureau (Thomas 1992, chap. 3). Their agents met trains and directed black men to an Urban League office where they were screened and sent to a factory for immediate employment.

Because of the booming auto industry, the black population of Detroit grew more rapidly than the black populations of Chicago, Cleveland, or other large northern cities in the 1920s. There were, however, no laws against racial discrimination in employment. Detroit firms varied in where they drew the color line, but all of them had one. Fisher Body did not hire any black workers, whereas Ford hired many (Levine 1976, 91–94). Within plants, occupations were racially coded, with blacks filling the dirtiest, least-skilled, but most hazardous jobs (Thomas 1992, chap. 2). Nevertheless, in the era from World War I to the Depression auto firms were more likely to put black men on their payrolls than other firms (Harris 1982, 60–62). With few exceptions, blacks were denied access to the skilled trades. The Urban League also found jobs for southern black women. Indeed, as the wages of white men went up, there was a tremendous demand for the labor of African American women: white women hired black women to do their domestic service. While the economy fluctuated in the years after World War I, they were basically prosperous ones for the industrial heartland. But the Depression ended Detroit's boom, and by 1932 automobile production was just *one-quarter* what it had been three years earlier. Smaller producers and their suppliers were bankrupt, so Detroit was home to a rather dormant industry. The Depression abruptly ended Detroit's building boom, and the shortage of jobs snapped its population growth. The city and state governments struggled to provide relief to impoverished residents. By 1933, more than one Michigan resident in seven drew a check from the Federal Emergency Welfare Relief Corporation (Conot 1973, 405). Municipal services were cut drastically as homeowners—and most businesses—could not pay their tax levies. Later that decade, President Roosevelt's Works Project Administration employed thousands of men on civic projects building streets, sidewalks, and parks. The city sought major infusions of federal funds for labor intensive projects and had some success. Public housing was built—on a racially segregated basis—but Chicago defeated Detroit in the competition to get federal funds for a subway system.

Developments in labor law during the 1930s restructured management-worker conflict. The Wagner Act (1935) allowed workers to organize and required managements to bargain in good faith with unions subject to the complex regulations of the National Labor Relations Board. So labor gained new power in negotiating wages and working conditions. As the Depression abated in 1936, no city revived as quickly as Detroit. Automobile production moved in lock step with overall economic trends and soared to 3.9 million vehicles in 1937, triple what it was in 1932. Management sought to compensate for years of losses by speeding up production to turn out as many cars as possible.

The employment of thousands of workers in one plant was advantageous to a union since, if workers are highly organized, a strike could quickly shut down production. The Wagner Act and the economic spurt of 1936 and 1937 created an eventually powerful United Auto Workers Union (UAW). This union adopted an innovative technique uniquely suited to the auto industry: the sit-down strike. Workers occupied the factory doing no work, but because they did not leave their jobs, they could not easily be replaced (Lichtenstein 1995, chap. 5; Widdick 1989, 67). And while managements often sought injunctions requiring strikers to leave, police forces found it challenging to go into plants and remove workers. By spring of 1937, this technique won recognition for the UAW at many GM and some Chrysler plants, but not at Ford, where opposition to the union was strongest.

Racial issues presented a challenge to the union movement. Some unions denied membership to all blacks, while others accepted black members, but set up Jim Crow locals. Because blacks worked in the auto industry when the United Auto Workers developed in the 1930s, union leaders had to make a key decision about race. They feared that if they organized white men only, management might quickly replace strikers with black men. So they adopted an integration strategy and became the strongest industrial union with such an egalitarian policy (Meier and Rudwick 1979, chap. 2; Lichtenstein 1995).

Within a short interval the major issue in Detroit switched from a shortage of jobs to a shortage of workers. By 1940, the domestic economy and automobile production boomed—going from 2.5 million vehicles in 1938 to 4.8 million in 1940. Of great importance to Detroit was President Roosevelt's lend-lease program, which called for American

The Fisher Sit-Down Strike

New labor legislation and a brief respite from the Depression helped make the sit-down strike a valuable weapon for union organizers. Photo reprinted with permission from the Detroit News Archives © 1937.

manufacturing firms to supply military equipment to England. So Detroit factories found a new market. After the U.S. entered World War II, firms switched production lines to turn out tanks, planes, jeeps, and munitions. Dozens of trains left Detroit factories every day with armaments to ship across the Atlantic and the Pacific. As an example of the creativity prompted by the national war effort, Detroit's favorite architect, Albert Kahn, designed a bomber plant for suburban Willow Run large enough to accommodate 100,000 production workers who could turn out a new B-24 every hour (Conot 1973, 482).

Employment in metropolitan Detroit soared from 857,000 in 1940 to 1,119,000 a decade later. Where did Detroit's employers find workers? Very quickly the unemployed got jobs, although white men fared better in the early days than African Americans. Then, private employers and the federal Department of Labor sent recruiters to rural areas, especially the South, to find men—and even women—who could help build tanks, jeeps, or guns. Young men could even get military deferments to work in certain defense jobs.

The Fourth Turning Point: Race
Becomes the Divisive Issue

The era from 1941 through 1973 was one of intense racial conflict—conflict over who would get which jobs, who could live where, whether public schools would be segregated or integrated, whether the city's police would primarily be a white force protecting white interests and which race would control the city's government. After three decades of struggle, a truce emerged, but it did not reflect the nation's highest ideals. Basically, it was a balkanization of the metropolis.

African American leaders insisted on jobs, occupational upgrading, access to housing, and equitable treatment from the police. Housing was a particularly explosive issue. The apartheid system had confined most blacks either to the traditional area east of downtown Detroit or to a more middle-class black area extending along Twelfth Street west of downtown, a largely Jewish area that blacks began to enter in the 1920s. When tens of thousands of blacks moved into Detroit for World War II, they had to live within overcrowded black neighborhoods. Restrictive covenants, the strong preferences of whites, and discrimination by real estate brokers kept them confined.

Because of Detroit's importance in the war, its industrial accomplishments, as well as its problems, were frequently scrutinized by the government and the national press. Race led the list of problems.

In Detroit, by World War II, not only the NAACP and Urban League but many new ad hoc organizations demanded jobs for black men—a demand that was backed up for the first time by federal power (Meier and Rudwick 1979, 115). As America mobilized for war, A. Philip Randolph, head of the Brotherhood of Sleeping Car Porters, realized that many white, but few black men, were getting defense industry jobs. He announced that 100,000 blacks and their supporters would march on Washington on Independence Day 1941 to insist that African Americans get their fair share of defense jobs. Fearing that whites would attack blacks at the very time when he was trying to garner support for a then unpopular war, President Roosevelt hastily signed Executive Order #8802, prohibiting racial discrimination in employment in defense industries and establishing a Committee on Fair Employment Practices. It was a timid order with weak enforcement mechanisms, but it provided black organizations backing from the federal government in the struggle for jobs and equal pay. In no place was its import greater than in Detroit, as the city's factories determined victory or defeat in the war.

In May 1945 the Allies defeated Axis forces in Europe, and in September Emperor Hirohito surrendered. The ramifications for Detroit's

The World War II Racial Riot

A federal agency with the prosaic name of Office of Facts and Figures investigated domestic conditions influencing the war effort. Their 1942 study concluded in extraordinarily unbureaucratic language that hell was likely to break loose in Detroit and other northern cities where black men competed with white men for jobs. The authors reported that Detroit's black men believed that if they were going to die fighting for democracy, it was far better to die fighting racism at home than overseas. In the same year, *Life* magazine stressed the military importance of the city, but the article, "Detroit Is Dynamite," predicted that the city would explode long before the war ended (Conot 1973, 486).

Those predictions were accurate. Belle Isle—Detroit's beautiful park designed by Frederick Law Olmsted in the 1880s—served as a major recreation spot during World War II. Thousands would visit to picnic, swim, fish, or play sports. Similar to parks in other northern cities, imaginary dividing lines separated the sections blacks were permitted to enjoy from those reserved for whites. Although black and white youths challenged each other and fought frequently at Belle Isle, the police usually controlled the situation. One such battle got out of hand on a hot Sunday, June 20, 1943, as crowds of young blacks and whites fought on the bridge linking Belle Isle to the city. Rumors spread in the east side black community that white youths had killed a black woman and her child by throwing them into the Detroit River. Fighting escalated as gangs of blacks and whites roamed downtown. By 4 A.M. on Monday morning, the Detroit police knew they could no longer contain the spreading racial violence, so Mayor Jefferies asked the governor to send in the Michigan State Troops—a home guard unit organized for the war effort (Shogan and Craig 1964; Shapiro 1988, 310–30; Capeci and Wilkerson 1991).

Throughout that Monday, violence increased as groups of young blacks and whites attacked each other. Because Detroit's defense plants kept up their production, black workers that day often rode streetcars through white neighborhoods, while whites drove through black neighborhoods, increasing the opportunities for racial violence. There is no clearer evidence of the racial nature of this riot than the death of Carrie Hackworth, a light-skinned black who, while driving through a black neighborhood, was mistaken for a white and killed (Shogan and Craig 1964, 53).

President Roosevelt moved federal troops to Detroit, but was extremely reluctant to call them out since they had been drafted to defeat the German and Japanese dictators, not to draw their guns in the Arsenal of Democracy. On Monday evening, with the riot out of control, the president ordered military police and infantry regiments to disperse gangs of rioters. They did so by using tear gas and marching toward crowds with their bayonets drawn. By midnight the fighting ended but with peace enforced by an occupying U.S. army and martial law. When the coroner completed his work, he counted thirty-four fatalities in that day and a half of violence.

White Mob Overturns Car on Woodward Avenue

In June of 1943, racial animosity flared into the nation's largest World War II urban riot, which led to the deaths of thirty-four Detroit residents. Photo reprinted with permission from the Detroit News Archives © 1943.

A fact-finding committee appointed by the governor blamed blacks for the violence, arguing that recent southern migrants were lawless and prone to use violence. The report condemned the city's African American leadership for failing to control the newcomers and for encouraging blacks to demand their rights too forcefully. But the NAACP, newspaper reporters and many civic officials were extremely skeptical of this one-sided explanation. The NAACP also investigated the riot and presented extremely different findings in a report written by Walter White, Executive Secretary of the national NAACP and by Thurgood Marshall, the future Supreme Court Justice. They stressed the continuing discrimination against African American men in defense factories, the absence of housing for blacks, the dearth of recreational areas and consistent police brutality (White and Marshall 1943). There were 3,400 men on the Detroit police force at the time of the riot, only 43 of them black (Conot 1973, 497). Twenty-five blacks died in the rioting, 17 of them shot to death by the city's police. President Roosevelt's Attorney General, Francis Biddle, offered a suggestion to prevent additional riots—use war powers to end migration of blacks to Detroit (Shapiro 1988, 319). This was a solution the president rejected. The bloody riot served as a catharsis in Detroit, as the remaining war years were marked by less black-white violence and by fewer hate strikes.

Racial Contentions in Post-War Detroit

For decades, a popular recreational activity for Detroiters was to board a steamboat at the foot of Woodward Avenue and sail down the river to Bois Blanc Island, where Bob-lo Amusement Park offered rides and entertainment. One afternoon in 1946, a black schoolgirl named Sara Ray showed up with twelve white classmates. Management enforced the Jim Crow rules (one day each week was reserved for black customers) and kept her off the boat while her classmates sailed away. Civil rights leaders promptly sued, pointing to a Michigan statute from the 1860s prohibiting racial discrimination by common carriers. The amusement park's owners asserted that the state law did not apply, as their craft plied international waters. Litigation made its way to the U.S. Supreme Court. The justices decided that an 1851 federal court ruling should take precedent, so they upheld the right of one black schoolchild in Detroit to take the steamboat to Bob-lo Park (*Bob-lo Excursion v. Michigan* 1948).

---

economy were immense, although few recognized it at that time. During the war, record high proportions of Americans worked for pay and received generous paychecks, but they spent little, since consumer durables were not produced for the domestic market. With the end of the war, Americans used their savings to buy cars, so Detroit's factories quickly switched back to motor vehicle production.

The National Defense Highway Act of the 1950s financed the largest construction project every undertaken in this country. Expressways connected distant suburbs to central cities, and 45,000 miles of interstate highways linked all corners of the nation. Families began to take their weekend trips and vacations by car, not train. Interestingly, this stimulus to the motor vehicle industry was justified on the basis of national security. The rationale was that warning systems would alert us to a Russian missile attack and we would then jump in our cars, drive away from the large metropolitan areas on the expressways and avoid nuclear destruction. Wars in Korea and in Vietnam also increased government spending without slowing down domestic automobile production—another huge boost in demand for the trucks and tanks rolled off Detroit's assembly lines.

Given the booming state of Detroit's economy in the postwar era, one might have expected that civic leaders would have taken steps to minimize the persistent racial conflict. But black-white conflict about all aspects of domestic policy continued in the postwar years:

(1) Neighborhoods: Where could blacks live without conflict?

(2) Public schools: Could they be integrated?

School Buses Burned and Bombed in Pontiac

Integrating schools generated conflict in the 1970s. Anti-integrationists burned this bus in suburban Pontiac to prevent transportation to racially integrated classrooms. Photo reprinted with permission from United Press International.

(3) Jobs: Would some or many of the traditional Jim Crow barriers be eliminated?

(4) City government: Which race would control local government, and would local agencies treat both whites and blacks fairly?

Racial conflicts over employment and neighborhoods are described in the next chapters. Here we discuss racial conflict over a related issue that helped to polarize Detroit: public schools.

Detroit's black residents had been fighting for educational opportunities since the state established whites-only schools in the nineteenth century. Blacks successfully appealed for their own school, and one was opened in Detroit in 1841 (Katzman 1973, 24). Following Emancipation, blacks in northern states litigated Jim Crow laws. Those in Detroit sued about segregated schools and the state's supreme court ordered integration. On October 11, 1869, black and white children sat next to each other in a Detroit classroom for the first time (Thomas 1992, 7–8; Wolf 1981, 11).

The Detroit Tigers and Racial Integration
_____

In 1948, Jackie Robinson became the first black man to play major league baseball, after sixty years of all-white teams. Within a couple of years, most teams drew on the highly talented pool of African Americans. Their success dispelled the stereotype that blacks lacked the physical and mental stamina to play major league sports. But the Detroit Tigers' owner, Walter Briggs, was well known for his unwavering opposition to blacks (Bak 1995, 211). In the summer of 1952, seven blacks graduating from Detroit high schools signed contracts to play professional baseball—none of them with the Tigers. By 1953, every team across the country except the Tigers had African Americans playing on their minor league teams. Detroit newspapers pointed out the team's unusual racial policy and civil rights leaders protested, but to no avail.

As the 1958 season began, only the Tigers and the Boston Red Sox upheld the Jim Crow principle. Representatives of the Michigan Association of Negro Trade Unions and pastors of several leading black churches called for a boycott if the Tigers remained all-white. They created an ad hoc civil rights organization called the Briggs Stadium Boycott Committee. Under pressure, the team's owners decided to "negotiate" and hastily traded for a black player, Ozzie Virgil, ending the threat of a boycott. In reality, the Tigers thwarted the pressures to hire a black by signing a dark-skinned Hispanic.

If Jim Crow ended on the field in 1958, it was slower to disappear in the grandstands. A *Detroit News* reporter experimented by ordering tickets by mail using different addresses. He found that fans with addresses in black neighborhoods were assigned less desirable seats than those with addresses in white neighborhoods (Harrigan 1997, 85).

A century later, the NAACP's litigation team came to Detroit. (For histories of this landmark litigation, see Hain 1978; Wolf 1981; and Mirel 1993, chap. 6.) Plaintiffs contended that residential segregation was due to deliberate policies that encouraged blacks and whites to live in different neighborhoods. The NAACP documented dozens of actions taken by city school officials just after World War II to maximize segregation, including the location of new schools, the redrawing of attendance boundaries to minimize white contact with black children, the selective busing of black children away from largely white schools, and transfer policies that permitted white children to exempt themselves from attending schools with blacks. Evidence in this trial revealed that school officials strove mightily to maintain white-only schools. While their efforts to segregate Jewish studies were not quite so obvious, there was a widespread belief that Mumford High was built to educate students who lived in northwest Detroit's neighborhoods, where Jews were concentrated. The evidence convinced Federal District Judge Roth, who concluded:

> The city of Detroit is a community generally divided by racial lines. Residential segregation within the city and throughout the large metropolitan area is substantial, pervasive and of long standing. Black citizens are located in separate and distinct areas within the city and are not generally to be found in the suburbs. While the racially unrestricted choice of black persons and economic factors may have played some part in the development of this pattern of residential segregation, it is, in the main, the result of past and present practices and customs of racial discrimination, both public and private, which have and do restrict the housing opportunities of black people. On the record, there can be no other finding.
>
> Government actions and inactions at all levels, Federal, State and local, have combined with those of private organizations, such as loaning institutions and real estate associations and brokerage firms, to establish and to maintain the pattern of residential segregation throughout the Detroit metropolitan area. The policies pursued by both government and private persons and agencies have a continuing and present effect upon the complexion of the community . . . as we know the choice of a residence is a relatively infrequent affair. For many years FHA and VA openly advised and advocated the maintenance of "harmonious" neighborhoods, that is, racially and economically harmonious. The conditions created continue. (*Bradley v. Milliken* 1971)

How could Detroit's schools be integrated? Even though the city's population was 44 percent black in 1970, its school-age population was 52 percent African American and rising rapidly (U.S. Department of Commerce 1973b, table 24). If white and black children were bused within the city to integrate schools, more whites would flee to the suburbs. Judge Roth eventually ordered the pooling of city and suburban students across the metropolis into seventeen moderately sized school districts, each containing largely white suburban areas and a slice of the increasingly black central city. Suburban communities strenuously fought this remedy, contending that the plaintiffs had not proven that the deliberate actions of individual suburbs had caused the unconstitutional segregation of white children from black. Although the Circuit Court of Appeals upheld metropolitan-wide busing, the Supreme Court in July 1974, by a 5–4 decision, agreed with suburban plaintiffs (*Milliken v. Bradley* 1974). The efforts of federal courts to fulfill the promise of *Brown* pretty much ended with this Detroit ruling, since they countenanced school segregation resulting from residential segregation. Eventually, a Detroit-only integration plan involving busing went into effect. As predicted, white enrollment in Detroit's schools dropped and, by 1990, only 10 percent of public school students were white. Justice Thurgood Marshall's comments in his 1974 dissent proved correct:

> Because of the already high and rapidly increasing percentage of Negro students in the Detroit system, as well as the prospect of white flight, a Detroit-only plan simply has no hope of achieving actual desegregation. Under such a plan, white and Negro students will not go to school together. Instead, Negro children will continue to attend all-Negro schools.

Another major area of racial conflict after World War II concerned control of the city's government and police. Throughout the twentieth century, many whites in Detroit have supported a strong and authoritative police force to protect them, but African Americans tended to see the police as consistently discriminating in favor of whites and using excessive violence against blacks, especially against young black men. Forrester Washington (1991) asserted that white police officers were far too ready to shoot or beat up black men: half of the more than fifty persons killed by Detroit's police in 1925 and 1926 were blacks, even though blacks made up only 8 percent of the population. As the African American population grew in the 1940s and 1950s, police officials continued to recruit officers from southern cities. Blacks assumed this was done deliberately to ensure that officers would be tough with African Americans.

Mayors of Detroit after World War II were challenged to do much more than just maintain streets and keep property taxes low. Their white constituents wanted the city to maintain white neighborhoods and white schools and minimize crime through stern policing. But mayors needed the support of the rapidly growing black electorate, as the white electorate was usually split across competing white candidates. To win, candidates had to take liberal stands on civil rights issues, so Detroit's politicians were much more likely than those in other large cities to espouse ideals of equal racial opportunity. But once in office, they hesitated to implement liberal policies.

The mayoralty election of 1961 produced a surprising result. Black voters joined with a minority of whites to elect an inexperienced politician, Jerome Cavanagh, who was distinguished by his dedication to the civil rights movement and to a belief that an activist government could solve most problems. He took office at an opportune time. The Kennedy administration symbolized a new approach to solving the nation's problems, so the federal government sent generous funds to Detroit for roads, urban renewal, and important but mundane issues such as rat control. The Cavanagh administration obtained as much as $360 million from the federal government for local needs including an imaginative Model Schools Program that sought to raise test scores and lower dropout rates. Detroit, in the mid-1960s, was the national testing ground to determine what federal support and a liberal mayor could do to revitalize an aging industrial city (Fine 1989).

Realizing the depth of tensions between blacks and the police, Mayor Cavanagh selected as his police chief Michigan Supreme Court Justice George Edwards—a former union organizer and liberal activist with a long history of promoting racial justice. Edwards dedicated himself to reforming the police department, but faced insurmountable challenges. The city's media stressed the threat that black crime posed to whites and, for the most part, white officers thwarted attempts at reform (Stolberg 1998, chap. 6). When Edwards resigned to accept President Johnson's appointment on the federal bench, he had accomplished only a few of his goals. During the Cavanagh administration, blacks were employed and promoted by the city's government in substantial numbers and funds were targeted to black neighborhoods, but the forces of racial conflict and economic changes were too great. Detroit became just the opposite of the Model City that Mayor Cavanagh, his supporters, and Presidents Kennedy and Johnson dreamed about. (For a description of the soaring hopes and then failures of the Cavanagh Administration, see Fine 1989.)

In the late 1960s, there were frequent confrontations between the police and young blacks, especially those in militant organizations. The New Bethel incident in 1969 later illustrated the continuing pattern of violent black-white confrontations in the Motor City. The Republic of New Africa—founded in Detroit in 1968—was a black nationalist organization demanding African American control of five states, with the threat to accomplish that by force if necessary. On March 29, 1969, they held a meeting in the New Bethel Baptist Church near the flash point for the July 1967 riot. As their meeting broke up close to midnight, two white patrolmen saw a dozen apparently armed members of the Republic of New Africa leaving the church. One officer stopped to question the men, but was shot to death before he could unholster his revolver; the other was shot and seriously wounded, but managed to call for reinforcements.

Police arrived and knocked on the door of the church. At this point, they asserted they were fired upon, so they forced their way into the church where, they claimed, they found a rifleman at the altar and a

The Racial Violence of the 1960s

In the 1960s, Fifth Precinct officers accused members of the Afro-American Unity Movement of crimes, arrested them and held them without indictment as long as possible. On the evening of August 8, 1966, four white officers charged seven young black men with loitering. Rather than submitting to arrest, the blacks started fighting with the officers. A crowd gathered, then began breaking windows and pelting the police with rocks and bottles. The department was exceptionally well prepared, and instantly deployed about 175 officers, who swept the streets with bayonets drawn. Although there was riot damage to stores along a stretch of Kercheval (this became known as the Kercheval mini-riot), Mayor Cavanagh immediately dispatched cleanup and repair crews to remove debris before dawn. Heavy patrolling by the police on subsequent evenings dispersed the crowds and minimized further rioting (Fine 1989, 135–39).

The riot of 1967 began early on July 23. (For descriptions, see Canot 1974, 679–719; Fine 1989, chaps 7 and 8; National Advisory Commission on Civil Disorders 1968, chap. 1, pt. 8.) A vice squad in the Twelfth Street neighborhood specialized in raiding "blind pigs"—that is, closing down establishments that offered gambling and sold liquor after hours. Running a blind pig was not an unusual occupation in Detroit nor a high-level crime, but vice squads were obligated to close quite a few of them. Owners were fined $100, while the patrons would be booked and then released. After raiding four blind pigs that evening, two undercover officers gained entry to one at 9125 Twelfth Street around 4:00 on Sunday morning. They expected to find a dozen customers, but a party of eighty-two was celebrating the return of two servicemen from Vietnam. The clients were rounded up, and held on Twelfth Street for more than an hour, as there were not enough police vans to take them in for booking. A large crowd gathered and taunted the police. By the time the last arrestees were removed, bottles were being thrown at the police and windows broken (Fine 1989, chap. 7).

Detroit officials recognized the potential for a major riot. By 7 A.M., Mayor Cavanagh mobilized the city's police force, alerted the State Police and Michigan National Guard, and informed federal officials. City officials, church leaders, and heads of local organizations were roused on Sunday morning and sent into the streets to preach calm. But rioting spread throughout the day and escalated after sunset. Crowds of blacks, and some whites, looted stores. There were 283 recorded incidents in which firefighters were prevented from doing their work because they were attacked.

On Monday, most residents stayed home because businesses and many factories were closed. Throughout the day, the city and state police and the Michigan National Guard Units patrolled the streets. After nightfall, there were numerous reports of snipers firing at the police, firefighters, and the National Guard. Shortly after 11 P.M., President Johnson ordered a thoroughly integrated unit of 2,700 army paratroopers into Detroit, many of them with combat experience in Vietnam. The President assigned his experienced troops to the relatively safer areas east of Woodward, while the state's National Guard Units were assigned the much more troubled areas west of Woodward. The National Guard had no training for riot duty, few of them had ever been fired upon, and they were largely white: blacks made up only 1.3 percent of their ranks (Conot 1973, 699).

Detroit, along with Newark, Harlem, and Oakland, was presumed to be a center for militant black organizations advocating violent changes. This led to the belief that many blacks armed with high power rifles who would use rioting as a cover to murder those who represented government authority. Therefore, the reports of sniper fire during the July 1967 riot seemed highly credible.

The presence of thousands of military personnel in Detroit's black neighborhoods and the virtual shutdown of the city reduced the looting, firebombing, and shooting. By Wednesday the major factories were back in operation. A total of forty-three died in the violence: thirty-three blacks and ten whites. Twenty-one had been killed by Detroit police officers, nine by Michigan's National Guard, and only one by federal troops. More than 7,200 were arrested, primarily for looting and property offenses. Within a few days, most of those arrested were released on their own recognizance. This was not reported because there was a strong and consistent effort to portray this violence—not as a racial riot—but as an attempt by looters to steal property from shopkeepers. Although there were many calls for heavy punishments, the justice system in Detroit simply could not process so many arrestees.

The Algiers Motel incident occurred as the riot was winding down and became the most discussed racially charged killing of that era (Hersey 1968). Before midnight on Tuesday, a National Guardsman and a private security officer who were protecting the Great Lakes Mutual Life Building on Woodward thought they were fired upon by snipers. They radioed for help and Detroit police, federal paratroopers, state police, and National Guardsmen responded. Thinking that the shots might be coming from the Algiers Motel, these forces entered the building through several doors.

There is no certainty about what happened next. Apparently nine or ten black men and two white women were taken from their rooms, lined up, and roughly questioned. When it became apparent that the suspects were not armed and offered no resistance, all personnel except three Detroit police officers apparently left. Sometime later these officers released the suspects and departed. Shortly thereafter, the motel's night clerk found the dead bodies of three of the black men (Fine 1989, chap. 11).

By Wednesday, word spread throughout the black community that white officers had shot three unarmed Detroit black men at close range. Within a day, the Police Department, the County Prosecutor, and Detroit's

> two newspapers began their own investigations, to be joined shortly there-after by the U. S. Department of Justice. While much evidence suggested that the men had been murdered, those involved—including the police officers and National Guardsmen—told conflicting stories about the events. The officers stated that one of the victims had been killed before they arrived, and that one other was shot while trying to grab an officer's gun. Three trials were held, but inconsistent testimony bedeviled the prosecution, and none of the officers were convicted. The Algiers Motel killings epitomized to many the state of urban race relations in the late 1960s.

sniper in the loft. After a brief exchange of fire, the police arrested 142 and confiscated 12 guns and ammunition.

New Bethel's pastor promptly called Recorder's Court Judge George Crockett, who by 6:00 A.M., had set up a temporary courtroom in the police station and began releasing many defendants on their own recognizance or on low bail. Subsequently, it turned out that he released three prisoners who had nitrate on their hands and one fugitive wanted for the attempted murder of three civil rights leaders.

This convinced many whites that Detroit was home to well-armed, black militants who were ready to kill whites, especially white police officers—and, if given the authority to do so, blacks would exonerate other blacks who killed white police officers. Detroit blacks had a different perspective and saw this as one of the few times African Americans thwarted Detroit's largely white police force.

The Fifth Turning Point: The City Suburban Divide Becomes a Racial and Economic Divide

Investigators failed to turn up convincing evidence that organized African American militants were targeting Detroit's whites or the city's police, but this idea reverberated through the white community for several years. Violence, however, was on the upswing, leading many to conclude that the city was a dangerous place, especially for white merchants doing business there or for whites traveling through the city.

There were only 97 recorded homicides in 1950 when the city's population approached two million but, the number steadily increased with a particularly sharp upturn in the years after the 1967 riot. In 1974, 750

FIGURE 2.3   *Number of Homicides in the City of Detroit and Estimated Homicides per 100,000 Residents, 1940 to 1998*

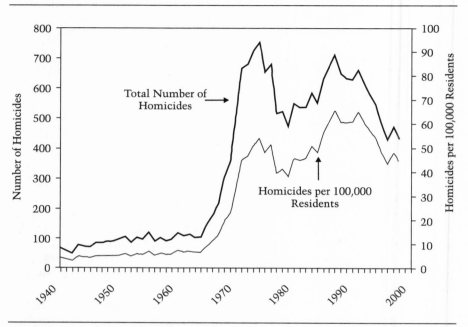

Sources: Conot 1973, appendix; U.S. National Center for Health Statistics, various years.

people were murdered in the city. Figure 2.3 shows the number of homicides and the estimated homicide rate for each year. The escalation in the rate from about 5 homicides per 100,000 in 1950 to more than 50 per 100,000 in the mid-1970s led critics to label Detroit the nation's murder capital.

Racial conflict was at the heart of the mayoral election of 1969. The white sheriff of Wayne County, Roman Gribbs, ran on a law-and-order platform, promising to use all necessary policing to forcefully crack down on crime. He won a narrow victory over the African American Wayne County auditor, Richard Austin. Mayor Gribbs's most memorable accomplishment was the creation of a STRESS (Stop Robberies, Enjoy Safe Streets) unit within the police. This was a largely white group of specially trained officers who worked in predominantly black neighborhoods. These officers killed twenty-two Detroit citizens before the first African American mayor, Coleman Young, ended the program.

The 1973 election also centered on race, crime, and policing. John Nichols, a former police commissioner, was the white candidate, but Coleman Young focused on the abusive way the police were treating blacks. Young, helped by the continuing exodus of whites, won easily and served for twenty years. He symbolized the racial, and the city-suburban, polarization of the 1970s and 1980s. Most whites thought he espoused the kind of black power they feared, as he consistently blamed whites and racism for the troubles of blacks and for Detroit's difficulties, especially for its increasing financial crisis. Whites thought he was unwilling to crack down on black crime, especially when it was black on white crime. Mayor Young's most discussed pronouncement came from his first inaugural address in which he said, "I issue a formal warning now to all the pushers, to all rip-off artists, to all muggers. It is time to leave Detroit for Eight Mile Road." The mayor may have intended to tell African American thugs to get out of town and stay out, but suburban whites—and the city's press—interpreted him as saying that black criminals should prey on suburban whites, not on Detroit's African Americans residents (Jacoby 1998, 298). In Young's first year in office, the Supreme Court issued the ruling that mandated busing to integrate the city's schools, but overturned city-suburban busing. This undoubtedly hastened the departure of more whites, since they knew that every central-city public school would have a substantial black enrollment, while the suburban schools would remain largely white.

Several other incidents at this time convinced many whites they were unwelcome and unsafe in Detroit. Ethnic festivals and rock concerts still attracted suburban whites to the city's waterfront in the 1970s. At one such event in August 1976, gangs of young black men set upon the participants, taking wallets, purses, and jewelry. The police were slow to respond, even though this was a large public event. Few of the muggers were arrested, and all charges were dropped the next day.

Many whites charged that Mayor Young and his colleagues engaged in criminal activities to enrich themselves. While there were regular reports that the mayor was the target of investigations and about to be indicted on federal charges, this never happened. Unfortunately, several prominent appointees were indicted for their participation in kick-back schemes and Mayor Young's Chief of Police—William Hart—served several years in federal prison for embezzling 2.6 million dollars from the city (Jacoby 1998, 347).

Detroit's black residents generally supported Coleman Young and his confrontational style. In their view, he wrested control of the city—

John Saber, One of the Last Residents of Poletown

In the 1970s, Detroit encouraged job creation even though it required demolishing neighborhoods, as was the case with GM's Poletown plant. Photo reprinted with permission from the Detroit News Archives © 1981.

especially control of the police—from white bigots. He never faced any serious challenges from other candidates in his twenty-year term, but spokespersons from low income neighborhoods frequently criticized Mayor Young for providing poor services. His administration—beset by financial crises, charges of corruption, and a dearth of jobs in the city— sought to improve opportunities for citizens by developing the downtown and by encouraging auto firms to build new plants in the city. Perhaps the most publicized controversy of his term focused around razing low-income neighborhoods in Hamtramck and Detroit so that General Motors could erect a huge new Poletown assembly plant. Mayor Young and his administration never wavered from their commitment to their Detroit Development strategy that called for building of plants for GM and downtown development. The prosperous owner of the Detroit Red Wings Hockey Team, Bruce Norris, declared he would move to the suburbs unless the city built a new arena for what was then and still is the most successful and profitable team in this sport.

FIGURE 2.4 *Percentage of the Three-County Metropolitan*
Population Living in the City of Detroit, 1900 to 1998

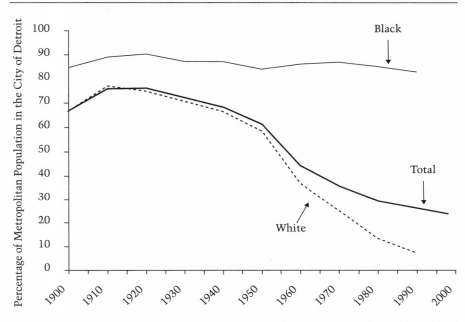

Source: Ruggles and Sobek 1997.

The Young administration agreed and used city resources to build the Joe Louis Arena on the waterfront (Thomas 1997, 156–57; Rich 1989, chap. 6).

The city could do nothing could turn the demographic tide of suburbanization. Figure 2.4 shows the percent of metropolitan-area blacks and whites who lived within the central city throughout this century. While the percent of whites in the city fell a bit between 1910 and 1940, massive suburbanization awaited the post–World War II boom. Two-thirds of metropolitan whites lived in the city in 1940, but only 14 percent in 1980, and then less than 10 percent in 1990. There has been no such suburbanization of blacks and, in 1990, the proportion in the city (83 percent) was not much different from what it was in 1930. In Detroit, geographic segregation went hand-in-hand with a growing city-suburban economic gap.

Figure 2.5 describes economic conditions in the city of Detroit and its suburbs in 1950 and 1990. With regard to the prosperity of residents,

FIGURE 2.5   *Economic Status by Place of Residence and Race,
              1950 and 1990 (in 1997 Dollars)*

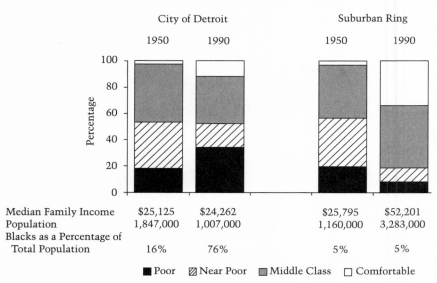

City-Suburban Income Trends

	City of Detroit			Suburban Ring	
	1950	1990		1950	1990
Median Family Income	$25,125	$24,262		$25,795	$52,201
Population	1,847,000	1,007,000		1,160,000	3,283,000
Blacks as a Percentage of Total Population	16%	76%		5%	5%

■ Poor   ▨ Near Poor   ▨ Middle Class   ☐ Comfortable

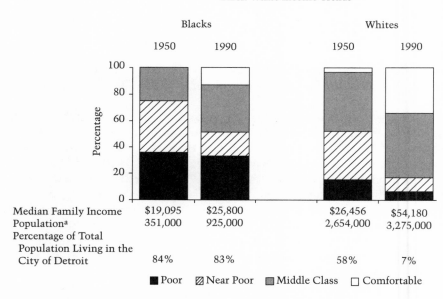

Black-White Income Trends

	Blacks			Whites	
	1950	1990		1950	1990
Median Family Income	$19,095	$25,800		$26,456	$54,180
Population[a]	351,000	925,000		2,654,000	3,275,000
Percentage of Total Population Living in the City of Detroit	84%	83%		58%	7%

■ Poor   ▨ Near Poor   ▨ Middle Class   ☐ Comfortable

Source: Ruggles and Sobek 1997.
[a]This reports the population for which the census determined poverty status.

there was not much difference between the city and the ring in the early post–World War II years. We show the percentage poor—that is, families reporting cash incomes below the poverty line. The near poor are those with incomes 100 percent to 199 percent of the poverty line. Next is the economic middle class—those with incomes two to five times the poverty line. And finally there are those we term economically comfortable, who reported cash incomes at least five times the poverty line. (In 1999, the poverty line was $17,500 for a family of four, so they needed an income exceeding $87,500 to be economically comfortable.)

In 1950, the poverty rate was actually a bit higher in the suburbs than in the city of Detroit, and median family incomes were about identical. But the poverty rate for Detroit just about doubled after 1950, while in the suburbs, it was cut in half. The purchasing power of the median central-city family fell by 3 percent in this interval, while in the suburbs, purchasing power doubled. One other significant change that occurred in the city was the polarization of the income distribution, since there was growth in the proportion of families below the poverty line and, simultaneously, growth of families with high incomes. The city's middle class declined.

The bottom panel shows similar information for the total black and white populations of the metropolis in 1950 and 1990. Here the story is one of rising incomes, but the reductions in poverty and gains in income were much greater for whites. The African American poverty rate in 1990 (33 percent) was just a bit lower than in 1950 (35 percent). But among whites, the poverty rate was cut in half. Despite a high poverty rate, the median income of black families rose by 35 percent, but among whites, it more than doubled. On all economic indicators, Detroit whites fared much better in the last half century than Detroit blacks. Note also the important shift in population distribution: the percent of metropolitan whites living in the city dropped from 58 to 7 percent. Among blacks it hardly changed, from 84 in the city to 83 percent.

Following the urban riots of the 1960s, the Kerner Commission bleakly described what they thought the future held if the government failed to address the nation's fundamental racial inequalities: a nation divided into largely black and impoverished central cities surrounded by largely white and prosperous suburban rings (National Advisory Commission on Civil Disorders 1968). They were wrong about New York, Los Angeles, Washington and other locations, since immigration from Asia and Latin America changed the composition of many central cities. And the Kerner Commission did not foresee the substantial shift of African Americans to the suburbs that began in the 1980s. But they were correct about Detroit: economic changes since 1970, combined with continuing racial polarization and the longstanding movement of whites—but not blacks—to the suburbs, make Detroit the polarized metropolis they predicted.

3

The Evolution of Detroit's Labor Market Since 1940

IN 1940, the Ford Motor Company employed 85,000 workers at its Detroit-area factories, 21 percent of them African Americans. *More than half* of all employed black men in metropolitan Detroit at that time drew their paychecks from Ford (Maloney and Whatley 1995, 470). Ford, however, was the exception. The Hudson Motor Car Company, with a payroll of 12,200, had just 225 black workers (Thomas 1992, 157). African Americans accounted for 9 percent of the city's population, but just 1 percent of the labor force of 30,300 employed by the municipal government (Sugrue 1996, 110).

Jim Crow practices accounted for the unusual representation of blacks on some payrolls but their absence from others. Black men held jobs at Ford not because they lived close to Ford plants or because their skills were especially suited to Ford's needs but because they were permitted to work there. Indeed, according to Thomas Maloney and Warren Whatley (1995), virtually the only Detroit African American men who earned enough to support their families at the start of World War II were those who worked at Ford plants. (For more about which firms did or did not hire blacks, see Weaver 1946, chap. 5; Bailer 1943.)

There were many favorable changes in Detroit's labor market in the subsequent three decades. Thanks to federal pressures, the insistence of the UAW, a World War II labor shortage, and a sustained push for opportunities by black leaders, jobs opened up during the 1940s. By the 1950s, employed adult black men in the metropolis who worked in the previous year reported median earnings of $19,095, or 81 percent as much as the $23,115 reported by white men. (Amounts are shown in 1997 dollars and refer to men age twenty-five to sixty-four.) The racial gap in earnings was smaller than in most other metropolitan areas, since there were few cities in which black men got so many good blue-collar jobs.

After the early 1970s, developments in Detroit's labor market were more often negative than positive, especially for less-educated workers. Indeed, the most popular explanation for the emergence of the black urban underclass, that of William Wilson (1987 and 1996), suggests that the decreasing demand for the labor of African American men, especially blacks who lacked college training, meant that black men could no longer count on stable blue-collar jobs in the factories of Chicago, Detroit, and Cleveland. Technological changes, the globalization of markets and production, and the push for greater labor productivity left many less-educated workers with dim labor market prospects (Kasarda 1985, 1993, and 1995).

Nonetheless, an African American economic elite has emerged in Detroit the last forty years. By 1990, about 12 percent of blacks were in households whose incomes exceeded five times the poverty line (see figure 2.5). Only 1 percent was that affluent forty years earlier. But poverty among blacks was just about as prevalent in 1990 as in 1950. On all economic measures, the gap between the typical white man and the typical black man was just as large—sometimes larger—in the 1990s as in the 1950s. In 1990, employed black men in metropolitan Detroit reported median annual earnings of $32,250, or just 71 percent of the white median of $45,150. And there was an important shift reflecting the changing labor market. Only 4 percent of adult black men reported not having worked at all in 1949, but for 1989, that figure was 28 percent. Among white men, the change was more modest: from 6 to 9 percent.

Key aspects of labor market trends, along with their implications for racial differences, are described in this chapter.

• Job growth in the metropolis
• Changes over time in the goods and services produced by Detroit's employers
• Where jobs are located
• Occupational changes
• Employment trends by race and gender
• Occupational achievement by race and gender
• Earnings trends by race and gender

Employment Growth: Did Jobs Disappear?

Detroit, to many, symbolizes a declining Rust Belt, implying a disappearance of jobs and declining employment opportunities for all who live there. Presumably, young people frequently move away from Rust

TABLE 3.1   *Number of Persons Holding Jobs in Metropolitan Detroit, 1940 to 1998*

Year	Employment in Metropolitan Detroit (Thousands)	Change over the Decade		Percentage of National Employment in Metropolitan Detroit
		Metropolitan Detroit	Total U.S.	
Data from Decennial Census for Three-County Metropolis				
1940	852			1.9
1950	1,205	+41%	+24%	2.2
1960	1,329	+10	+12	2.1
1970	1,571	+18	+20	2.1
1980	1,657	+5	+26	1.7
1990	1,716	+4	+20	1.4
Establishment Data for Six-County Metropolis				
1990	1,993			1.6
1999	2,128	+7	+12	1.6

Sources: Ruggles and Sobek 1997; U.S. Department of Labor 2000.

Belt centers when they complete their educations or lose jobs, while those who remain compete for fewer openings. But the facts are not consistent with such a pessimistic view. While numerous older manufacturing plants have been closed, metropolitan Detroit continues to be a place where employment increases. Until recently, the number of jobs grew at a slow pace compared to the national average, and at a very slow pace compared to the booming metropolises of the South and West. Manufacturing has not disappeared, even though its share of total employment has plummeted. And, Detroit remains the nation's largest metropolis with such a high proportion of workers in traditional manufacturing—about 25 percent of the employed labor force in the late 1990s.

In 1940, employment in Detroit totaled 852,000. Fifty years later, this had more than doubled, to 1,716,000.[1] Table 3.1 compares employment growth in Detroit to that across the nation, and figure 3.1 shows the average annual rate of job growth over the decades.

World War II and the boom thereafter propelled a great increase in employment, pushing the rate of job growth in Detroit up to one and one-half times the national average. Employment continued to surge in the early 1950s. The Korean War demanded many products from Detroit's factories but, equally important, consumers feared a long war and a cessation of auto production, so sales were given a short-run boost.

FIGURE 3.1   *Average Annual Change in Number of Employed*
             Persons, 1940 to 1998

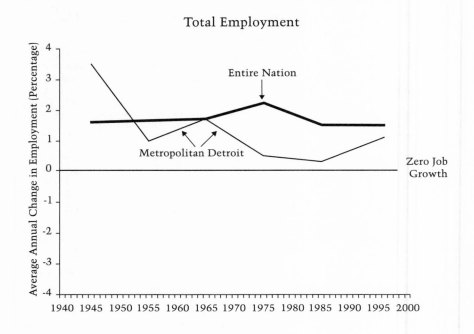

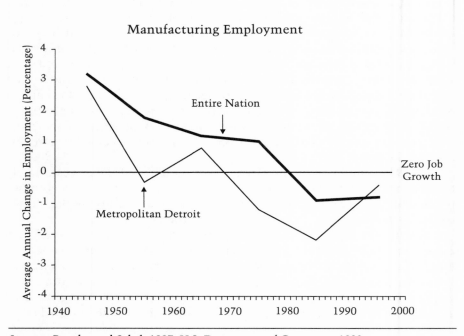

Sources: Ruggles and Sobek 1997; U.S. Department of Commerce 1998.

Hudson's Smokestack

The Hudson Motor Car Company was one of many auto-related firms that failed to survive the transition to the modern automobile era. Photo reprinted with permission from the Detroit News Archives © 1961.

Overall job growth persisted at a healthy rate, though it began to lag a bit behind the national rate. To be sure, there were massive employment shifts, and thousands of workers lost jobs as three auto makers—Hudson, Kaiser-Fraser, and Packard—went out of business. But new plants were built in the suburbs, so overall job growth in Detroit rivaled the national rate in the 1950s and 1960s.

The recession of 1969–1970 and the energy crisis of 1973 signaled an important turning point for Detroit's economic foundation. The sharp drop in the demand for large American cars combined with the success of foreign producers challenged American firms to improve quality and cut costs. Older plants were closed and automation increased. Chrysler would have ended up in bankruptcy if the federal government had not guaranteed its loans. In the 1970s and 1980s, job growth in metropolitan Detroit slowed to only about one-quarter of the national average rate. In 1950, metropolitan Detroit was home to 2.2 percent of the nation's jobs (see far right column of table 3.1); by 1990, this had fallen to 1.4 percent.

Figure 3.2 shows a quarter-century trend in estimates of jobs in six southeastern Michigan counties.[2] Before the energy crisis, in 1972, there were about 1.6 million jobs; a dozen years later there were still 1.6 million jobs. This was the era of stagnant wages and stagnant employment. But the economy began to recover in the first quarter of 1983, and jobs

FIGURE 3.2   *Total Jobs and Manufacturing Jobs in Metropolitan Detroit, 1972 to 1999 (Establishment Data for Six-County Metropolis)*

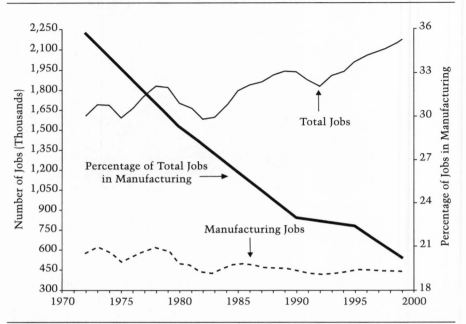

Source: U.S. Department of Labor 1987, 1994, 1999.
Note: These are establishment data and exclude self-employment. These data refer to the six-county Detroit Metropolitan Area.

have grown steadily since, increasing to an estimated 2.1 million in 1998. The economic expansion that began in the second quarter of 1991 has been beneficial for vehicle manufacturers in general and for metropolitan Detroit in particular. Job growth in metropolitan Detroit in the 1990s was more rapid than in the 1970s or 1980s—but at a rate below the national average. The percentage of all jobs in manufacturing fell steadily, from more than one-third to less than one-fifth over the past quarter-century.

Industrial Change in Metropolitan Detroit

Since its emergence as a national metropolis after the Civil War, Detroit has specialized in manufacturing durable goods: wood products, steel, railway equipment, and chemicals in the nineteenth century, and motor vehicles in the twentieth. Until the 1970s auto production was a labor-intensive industry, so employment soared when the demand for cars and trucks increased and declined quickly when demand slackened. But in the last couple of decades, automakers have introduced labor-saving technologies. Productivity has risen so rapidly that as the output of motor vehicles increased to record highs in the 1990s, the number of autoworkers actually declined. In Detroit, this helps account for slow growth of employment, and it kept the metropolitan population from growing since 1970. Table 3.2 summarizes changes in employment by industry in metropolitan Detroit from 1950 to 1990.

In addition to declines in auto employment, there was a geographic shift, so metropolitan Detroit's share of national automotive employment fell from 35 to 20 percent between 1950 and 1970. But from 1970 to 1990, automotive employment in Detroit declined at close to the national rate, so the metropolis held on to about one-fifth of the nation's jobs in this industry.

The Detroit area does not have a backup industry to make up for the downturn in motor vehicle employment. It is not a center for governmental employment, nor does it rival Boston in having dozens of colleges where young people seek advanced educations. Detroit has not captured any new or booming industries. While the computer field hires many Detroit workers, the metropolis does not rival San Jose or Seattle for the development of software and hardware. Detroit's financial sector has not carved out a unique niche, as Chicago's has with options trading. And Detroit has not become an entertainment mecca, such as Las Vegas, or a tourist destination, such as Orlando, Florida. More than most metropolises, Detroit's prosperity and employment continue to depend on producing durable goods.

Where Are the Jobs Located?

If there were an efficient and low-cost transportation system and if everybody had a wide selection of places to live, the changing location of jobs might make little difference in who gets which jobs and what they earn. But where jobs are located influences, to a greater or lesser degree, who gets them. Most people would commute a long way for an extremely good job, but would be willing to travel only a short distance for many moderate-wage jobs. Employers may also take place of residence into account when deciding whom to hire and, as chapter 5 reports, African Americans and whites differ in where they search for work.

For thirty years, "spatial mismatch" has been used to explain why black men fare poorly in the labor markets of urban centers of the

TABLE 3.2   *Industrial Distribution of Total Employed Persons in Metropolitan Detroit, 1950, 1970 and 1990*

Major Industrial Categories	Employment in Metropolitan Detroit (Thousands)			Percentage Change 1950 to 1970		Percentage Change 1970 to 1990	
	1950	1970	1990	Metropolitan Detroit	Total U.S.	Metropolitan Detroit	Total U.S.
Motor vehicle manufacturing	285	282	206	-1	91	-27	-31
Other manufacturing	223	282	258	26	28	-9	5
Retail and wholesale trade	216	304	417	41	41	37	56
Construction	54	65	89	20	17	37	52
Transportation and utilities	80	83	96	4	11	16	37
Finance, insurance, and real estate	36	72	120	100	97	67	107
Business and repair services	31	52	126	67	83	142	153
Personal services	56	56	48	0	3	-14	-1
Entertainment	5	8	12	57	21	64	46
Professional services	79	237	399	300	273	68	96
Public administration	40	62	77	55	62	24	51
Total employment	1,119	1,517	1,882	36	34	24	50

Source: Ruggles and Sobek 1997.
Note: Data are not shown for agriculture, mining or industry not reported.

A Communist and the Capitalists: Diego Rivera in Detroit

Among this nation's artistic treasures are the impressive murals the Mexican artist Diego Rivera painted for the Detroit Institute of Art (DIA) in the midst of the Depression—murals depicting the city's industrial might in a breathtaking array of colors and designs. They are often seen as a forceful message about how capitalism demeans, regiments, and exploits the workingman, turning him into an appendage of a machine. That is not surprising, given Rivera's enthusiasm for revolutionary political change. How did a citadel of capitalism wind up with a set of murals that could readily grace the masthead of a Communist newspaper?

The city's government took over the art institute in 1919 and, using both tax funds and generous donations from the elite, built a beautiful new gallery in the cultural center on Woodward. William Valentiner, the director, knew that Rivera was the most imaginative painter of the era, creating a new and distinctively American art form. But Rivera intertwined his art with his strongly held beliefs about the rejection of European influences in art and religion and his hopes that, with the fall of capitalism, a true proletariat art would emerge, built upon his own innovations. His ideas were so radical and his commitment to communism so fervent that the State Department sought unsuccessfully to keep him out of the country during the 1920s.

Rivera knew that Detroit was the home of America's proletariat, so he agreed to Valentiner's request that he paint murals representing Michigan themes in the most impressive area of the new gallery, The Garden Court. Rivera came to Detroit in the spring of 1932, just a few weeks after a Communist-led march of unemployed workers ended with the shooting deaths of four by Ford's security service (Conot 1973, 365).

On arrival in Detroit, the trustees of DIA escorted Rivera to the Wardell Hotel, just across the street from the art gallery. When he learned that the hotel accepted no Jews, he proclaimed loudly that he and his wife were Jewish (he had Portuguese Jewish ancestors) and would leave. Desperate for business in the midst of the Depression, hotel officials begged the world's most acclaimed artist to stay, and cut his rent. He agreed to remain only if the hotel changed its policy and agreed to accept Jewish customers, which it did (Marnham 1998, 241; Herrera 1983, 134).

Rivera spent several months immersing himself in Detroit, seeking inspiration. Edsel Ford, a financial backer of DIA, became fascinated with the artist, as did his father, Henry Ford. Both were generous to him and offered any assistance they could provide, including new cars and chauffeurs. Rivera asked to spend time at the Ford plant, and then devoted more than a month to sketching the workers and their machinery (Rivera 1960, 111). After many visits to the plants, he began painting a series of twenty-seven murals, with the largest and most dramatic depicting men doing dirty, dangerous work while supervisors and customers looked on, seemingly demanding more work from the laborers. High above his major murals, he painted smaller ones showing Michigan-inspired themes: men working in a chemical plant with so much protective clothing they looked

---

Continued

---

like animals, four large nudes simultaneously representing the races of mankind and the minerals of Michigan, and a Nativity-like scene (Hamill 1999, 152–59).

The murals provoked controversy, almost from the first brush strokes. Father Coughlin led the charge, using his popular radio program to denounce them as immoral, blasphemous, antireligious, obscene, and Communistic. (Rivera 1960, 118). Others called them a hoax Rivera had designed to embarrass his capitalist employers (Herrera 1983, 161). This, of course, delighted the artist. The newspapers were full of condemnations of the murals. Politicians, the leaders of civic clubs, and some voices in the press condemned them, and one member of city council wanted them whitewashed (Marnham 1998, 244). A group of Trotskyite and Communist workers came to the art gallery, met Rivera, and promised to guard his murals, an offer he found exceptionally gratifying (Rivera 1960, 121). The controversy about the murals not only added to Rivera's stature but also generated so much interest that the art gallery was patronized as never before.

Throughout the summer of 1932, Rivera increased his requests for support. He had originally agreed to a fee of $10,000, but this was raised to $25,000, with substantial expenses for his assistants. The DIA could offer little, since the city had cut its appropriation from $400,000 in 1928 to $40,000 in 1932 (Marnham 1998, 440). Although his personal portfolio had declined by $15 million in 1931 (in 1931 dollars), Edsel Ford complied with Rivera's requests for additional funds. So one of the nation's leading families of capitalists paid for the murals that many see as a dramatic portrayal of class struggle.

Northeast and Midwest. Supposedly, firms—especially manufacturing firms that once employed thousands of semiskilled workers at high wages—shut down their old, inefficient factories in central cities and moved to modern plants in the suburbs. At the same time, the expanding interstate highway system allowed shippers and warehouses to increasingly locate in the suburbs rather than in congested cities, and to shift more high-paying but moderate-skilled jobs to suburbs. But discriminatory practices in the housing market kept blacks confined to the city, so a spatial mismatch developed: more good jobs went to the suburbs, while African Americans remained in the city, farther from employment centers. Hence, their employment rates fell, they could not support their families, and poverty increased (Kain 1968 and 1992; for a current review of the spatial mismatch hypothesis, see Ihlanfeldt and Sjoquist 1998b). We return to this idea in later chapters.

Since 1960, decennial censuses have asked people where they worked, giving us valuable information—although comparisons over time are challenging, since different procedures were used and different employment locations have been identified. A national census of manufacturers has been conducted regularly since 1947, which also tells us about geographic changes, since firms report where their production and front-office personnel work. Of course, pinpointing place of employment is not easy, since some people work in several locations. Others, like construction workers, substitute teachers, and visiting nurses have no fixed place of employment.

Throughout World War II and for more than a decade thereafter, the city of Detroit offered many more jobs than its suburbs. The number of jobs in the city in 1960—about 700,000—exceeded suburban jobs by 170,000. But by the mid-1960s, suburban employment equaled city employment and, for the past quarter-century, has surpassed it. Between 1960 and 1990, employment in the central city was just about cut in half, and the city's share of metropolitan employment fell from 57 percent to 21 percent. Figure 3.3 shows the number of jobs in the city and the three-county suburban ring.

Job growth within the ring has differed by proximity to the city. In the 1980s, growth was modest within suburban Wayne County because that area includes the older suburbs, where open spaces are less plentiful than in outlying Macomb and Oakland counties. So in recent decades shopping malls, manufacturing plants, and machine shops needing vacant land have, for the most part, been built in outlying counties. Two major exceptions are GM's Poletown Plant and Chrysler's Jefferson Avenue plant, both built within the city of Detroit.[3]

Oakland County has been the focal point for job growth in recent decades: substantial increases in retail trade employment in its upscale malls, administrative jobs in Southfield, and high-tech jobs in the Auburn Hills area (which was, briefly, the world headquarters of the Chrysler Corporation before its merger with Daimler). In the early 1990s, only two counties in the country—Maricopa County, Arizona (Phoenix), and Clark County, Nevada (Las Vegas)—added more new jobs than Oakland County (U.S. Bureau of the Census 1996b). So even though overall job growth is modest in the metropolis, prosperous Oakland County—with its population of 1.2 million—is a national leader in employment growth.

The Census of Manufacturers reveals what happened to employment in Detroit's key industrial sector since World War II. In 1947, one-third of a million manufacturing jobs were located within the central city. The trend has been steadily downward since then, with the exception of the Korean War years. By 1992, the number of manufacturing

FIGURE 3.3   *Number of Jobs by Location for Metropolitan Detroit, 1960 to 1990*

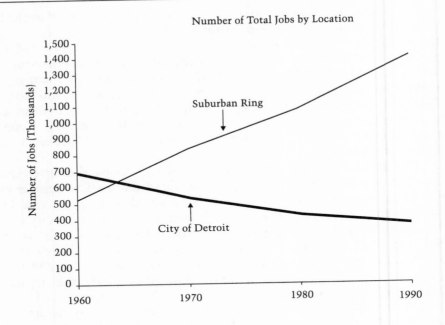

Number of Total Jobs by Location

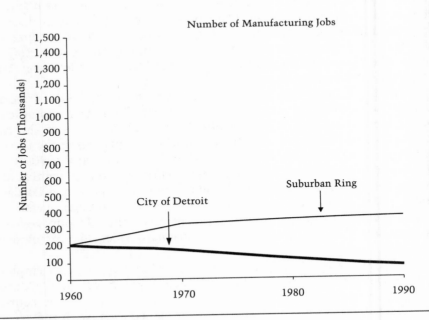

Number of Manufacturing Jobs

Source: Ruggles and Sobek 1997.
Note: These data were obtained by asking people enumerated in the census where they worked.

jobs in the city fell to 62,000, or just 20 percent what manufacturing employment had been after World War II.

Table 3.3 reports the number of manufacturing firms and manufacturing jobs in the metropolis since the end of World War II. The upper panel describes a rapid growth in the number of manufacturing firms until the early or mid-1960s. Since that time, the number has held steady at about seven thousand. However, there has been a suburbanization of firms, and the city's share has fallen from two-thirds to one-third. As new firms replace old ones, they are typically located in the suburbs.

Production jobs in manufacturing—those blue-collar jobs that once brought workingmen and their families securely into the middle class—declined greatly throughout metropolitan Detroit since the early 1970s. But the drop was more substantial in the city than in the outlying suburban counties. Put differently, blue-collar jobs in manufacturing were, in 1992, just about as numerous as in 1972 in outlying counties, but in the city of Detroit, about three out of four production jobs disappeared. It is easy to see why some observers think that a spatial mismatch explains the poverty of Detroit's African Americans and why Thomas Sugrue concluded that the city of Detroit was transformed from a magnet of opportunity to a reservation for the poor (Sugrue 1996, 4). African Americans stayed in the central city, but good-paying jobs left. And in suburban Wayne County, manufacturing jobs have also been declining for a quarter-century.

Increasing productivity in manufacturing was achieved primarily by cutting production workers. Between 1947 and 1972, white-collar jobs in manufacturing doubled in the Detroit area. The city held on to its employment of these workers throughout the post–World War II growth years, but the reorganization of manufacturing stopped the growth of front office employment. The number of such employees in metropolitan Detroit was about the same in 1992 as it had been twenty years earlier. And for these workers, too, there was a pronounced geographic shift—a decline of white-collar jobs in manufacturing in the city of Detroit and growth, especially in Oakland County, with its edge city employment nodes in Southfield and Auburn Hills. (See Garreau 1991, chap. 4.) The loss of highly paid administrative jobs in the auto industry within the city may be at its end. While the relocation of GM's world headquarters to the Renaissance Center may largely be a movement of jobs within the city, much additional employment may be generated downtown as various units of that company and the numerous firms consulting with GM seek office space near their corporate headquarters.

TABLE 3.3   Numbers of Manufacturing Establishments and Employees for the City of Detroit and the Suburban Ring, 1947 to 1992

Geographic Area	1947	1963	1972	1982	1992	Average Annual Rate of Change 1947 to 1972 Percentage	Average Annual Rate of Change 1972 to 1992 Percentage
Number of manufacturing establishments							
City of Detroit	3,272	3,370	2,398	1,518	1,061	−1.2	−4.1
Suburban Wayne County	600	1,176	1,404	1,498	1,506	+3.4	+0.4
Macomb County	326	1,098	1,483	1,821	2,102	+3.4	+1.7
Oakland County	567	1,379	1,839	2,449	2,587	+4.7	+1.7
Total	4,765	7,023	7,124	7,281	7,256	+1.6	+0.1
Total employees in manufacturing (thousands)							
City of Detroit	338	201	180	106	62	−2.5	−5.3
Suburban Wayne County	159	157	172	121	125	+0.3	−1.6
Macomb County	15	70	93	88	108	+7.3	+0.7
Oakland County	45	67	91	93	106	+2.8	+0.8
Total	557	495	536	408	401	−0.2	−1.4
Production employees in manufacturing (thousands)							
City of Detroit	282	141	125	59	32	−3.3	−6.8
Suburban Wayne County	135	99	109	62	61	−0.9	−2.9
Macomb County	13	41	57	53	61	+5.9	+0.3
Oakland County	37	49	63	56	60	+2.1	−0.2
Total	467	330	354	230	215	−1.1	−2.5
Managerial and administrative jobs in manufacturing (thousands)							
City of Detroit	56	60	55	47	32	−0.1	−2.7
Suburban Wayne County	24	58	63	59	61	+3.9	−0.2
Macomb County	2	29	36	35	48	+11.6	+0.3
Oakland County	8	18	28	35	46	+5.0	+2.5
Total	467	330	354	230	215	−1.1	−2.5

Sources: U.S. Department of Commerce, various years.

Which Jobs Remain in the City of Detroit?

Reading the preceding statistics, one might think that the only jobs left in the city of Detroit are in fast-food restaurants or with manufacturing firms that lacked the capital to buy new equipment and move to the outlying suburbs. That is not the case. Detroit has retained a substantial share of the area's most prestigious and rewarding jobs. And those who work in the city earn about as much as those who work in the suburbs. In the census of 1990, men working in the suburban ring earned an average of $21.20 per hour, or just 2 percent more than the average earnings ($20.80) for those working inside the city. Women working in the city of Detroit earned 9 percent more per hour than those working in the suburbs ($15.00 versus $13.70, in 1997 dollars).

Figure 3.4 describes the job picture in the city in 1990. Overall, one-fifth of the area's jobs were located in the city. The top panel classifies those jobs by pay level and then by their industrial sector. The vertical line shows the percent of total metropolitan jobs located in the city, while the horizontal bars show the percent of jobs in each category in the city. When classified by wage level, jobs in the city paid neither exceptionally well nor poorly. With regard to earnings, the highest proportion of city jobs were paying $10 to $15 at the time of the last census, while the minimum was for jobs paying $5 to $10 per hour. So the city does not have a concentration of the lowest paid jobs.

When jobs are classified by industrial sector, however, we find striking differences. For decades, J. L. Hudson's store dominated retail trade in southeastern Michigan. But it was closed in 1982, sat empty for seventeen years, and was then demolished. The demise of Hudson's symbolized the disappearance of retail trade from the city, a process that began with the opening of the innovative Northland Shopping Center in Oakland County in 1954. That was the first large, automobile-oriented comprehensive shopping mall in the United States. Its immediate and tremendous success set an example for the rest of the nation and led to the dramatic shifts in how and where the nation shops. In Detroit, the suburbanization of shopping means the central city retains no major retail stores.

With the building of expressways and the emergence of air freight for valuable commodities, wholesaling also left the city. Figure 3.4 reports that only a minuscule fraction of metropolitan employment in trade is located in the city. But there are several key industrial sectors where a substantial share of employment remains in the city and will continue to remain there. The presence, and recent growth, in the city's medical centers helps explain the high proportion of professional service

FIGURE 3.4   *Percentage of Metropolitan Jobs Located Within the City of Detroit, 1990*

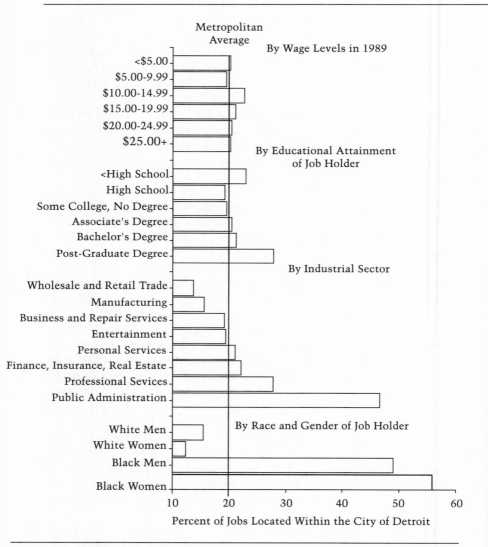

Source: U.S. Department of Commerce 1993.

sector employment in the city. Even more concentrated is governmental employment, since the state and federal government continue to have major offices in the city—including a regional postal center that employs thousands.

Jobs may also be classified by the characteristics of their incumbents. Figure 3.4 shows the representation of employed persons in six educational groups in the city. Here there is strong evidence for a polarization of jobs in the city of Detroit. Occupations low in skill (requiring less than a high school education) or high in skill (requiring a postgraduate degree) are overrepresented in the city. If the relocation of GM's headquarters stimulates Detroit as a center for office employment, this overrepresentation of the highly educated in the city's labor force will likely increase.

There is a large racial difference in the location of workplaces: many whites go from suburban homes to central-city jobs, while African Americans go in the opposite direction. Just 8 percent of metropolitan whites lived in the city in 1990, but 14 percent worked there. There is a counterbalancing flow of central-city blacks to the suburbs: only 17 percent of blacks lived in the ring, but 50 percent of those with jobs worked there. Blacks and whites drive past one another every day in a massive racial exchange that goes almost unnoticed—in 1990, 150,000 suburban whites commuted to jobs in the city, while 91,000 blacks left the city for jobs in the ring. Figure 3.4 also reports a great gender difference in commuting: suburban white women were much less likely than suburban white men to make the journey into the city for a job.

The Changing Occupational Distribution of Detroit's Jobs

Between 1950 and 1990, total employment in metropolitan Detroit went up 60 percent, but the number of blue-collar jobs declined. As a consequence, there is an occupational mismatch: shortages of engineers, financial managers, nurses, and math teachers, but a surplus of men and women who lack specialized training.

Several challenges crop up in studying changes over time in occupations. One is a measurement issue. Censuses ask people to give their job titles or describe in a few words what they do at work. A coding expert reads the responses and assigns the employee to a specific job category using an occupational classification system. This assumes the person accurately describes his or her job in a few words and that the coder can readily interpret that information and assign the correct job title. Another challenge is that the occupational system itself is constantly

FIGURE 3.5   *Distribution of Employed Persons Aged Twenty-Five to Sixty-Four in Metropolitan Detroit by Major Occupational Group, 1940 to 1990*

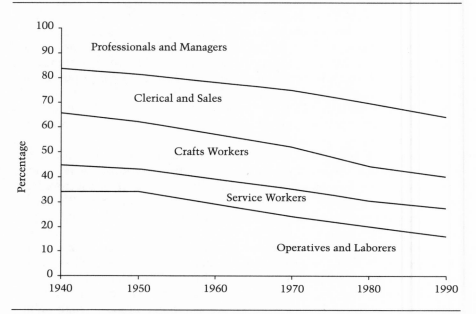

Source: Ruggles and Sobek 1997.

changing. Some jobs, like milkman and streetcar motorman, disappear; others, like computer programmer and television newscaster, emerge. In a few cases the occupational title stays the same but the content of the work shifts—such as teamster and insurance adjuster. (In this book, we rely on occupational codes used in the Integrated Public Use Microdata Sample. Occupational reports given by persons enumerated from 1940 through 1990 were coded into a classification system involving about 500 job titles, and then these were grouped into inclusive categories such as professional workers, crafts workers, or laborers.)[4]

Figure 3.5 classifies jobs into four broad occupational categories. Professional and managerial workers, shown at the top, typically have some college credentials and are more highly paid than other workers. Clerical and sales personnel work at many different types of jobs. Some of them, such as those in the financial sector, require advanced training but others, including those in retail trade, do not. Manufacturing industries traditionally offered high pay to recruit the most accomplished blue-collar workers: those in the crafts such as millwrights and toolmakers. Thus, crafts occupations make up the third category. Finally, jobs represented toward the bottom of the figure—operatives and laborers— are typically semiskilled or unskilled positions like machine operators, laborers, or service workers such as janitors, porters, and waiters.

Clearly established trends are evident. Detroit's employers now need relatively more engineers, doctors, designers, lawyers, and personnel managers, but fewer men and women to work on assembly lines, unload rail cars, or process paper in offices. The share of professional and managerial employment more than doubled, to about 33 percent, in this fifty-year span, while the share accounted for by operatives and laborers fell from 46 percent to 29 percent.

Information showing how the restructuring of employment changed what people did at work is presented in table 3.4. Eight occupational categories are used. Some occupations (professional and service jobs) increased rapidly in Detroit throughout the period. Managerial jobs, on the other hand, grew rapidly in the 1970s and 1980s, but not so rapidly earlier. And then there are the jobs whose numbers either grew slowly over the decades or declined: the crafts trades, machine operators, and laborers.

The downsizing of good blue-collar occupations in Detroit occurred primarily after 1970. In 1950, 214,000 Detroit men (175,000 white and 39,000 black) worked as machine operators or laborers in durable goods manufacturing industries. Only 22 percent of them had high school diplomas, but they earned an annual average: $19,400 (in 1997 dollars). By 1970, many of these jobs had shifted from the city to the suburbs, but their number declined only moderately: 178,000 Detroit men (125,000 white and 53,000 black) drew paychecks from such jobs, and their average earnings had gone up to $35,700 per year. But then the labor market changed. In 1990, only 104,000 men (81,000 white and 22,000 black) were employed as machine operators or laborers by manufacturing firms. And their annual earnings had increased at only a moderate rate, to $40,100. While good blue-collar jobs certainly did not disappear in Detroit and never will, they are becoming harder to find. After 1970, vehicle manufacturers kept a substantial share of their production in the Detroit area, but dramatically shifted the occupational composition of their labor forces. In 1950 in Detroit, auto producers employed just 26 white-collar workers for every 100 blue-collar workers. By 1990, it was 63 white-collar per 100 blue-collar.

Table 3.4 also compares occupational change in Detroit to the nation. From 1950 through 1970, employment in metropolitan Detroit grew at or above the national rate, but from 1970 through the 1990s, job growth in Detroit dipped far below the national rate in every broad occupational category.

TABLE 3.4   *Occupational Distribution of Total Employed Persons in Metropolitan Detroit, 1950, 1970, and 1990*

| Broad Occupational Category | Employment in Metropolitan Detroit (Thousands) | | | Percentage Change in Employment | | | |
| | | | | 1950 to 1970 | | 1970 to 1990 | |
	1950	1970	1990	Detroit	Total U.S.	Detroit	Total U.S.
Professional workers	98	238	392	142	135	65	100
Managers	98	103	229	5	19	122	143
Clerical	177	283	365	60	91	29	56
Sales	86	116	131	36	40	12	38
Crafts workers	192	221	216	15	30	−2	16
Machine operatives	292	305	233	4	18	−24	−2
Service workers	112	187	243	68	64	30	56
Laborers	58	59	67	2	−8	14	43
Total employment	1,119	1,517	1,882	36	34	24	50

Source: Ruggles and Sobek 1997.
Note: Data are based on occupational reports given in the censuses and reclassified into broad occupational categories by the Integrated Public Use Microdata Sample project. Information for farm workers is not shown. Metropolitan Detroit refers to Macomb, Oakland, and Wayne counties.

Employment: Racial and Gender Differences

Industrial changes and occupational shifts altered Detroit's labor market. But there are key questions about who gets employed in the first place, what positions they fill if they are hired, and how much they earn. Economic gaps continue to distinguish the races largely because black and white men fare differently in Detroit's labor market now, just as they did sixty years ago. A crucial difference is that in the late 1990s, only two-thirds of Detroit's African-American men aged twenty-five to sixty-four are employed; 87 percent of white men are.

Historians who describe race and employment in Detroit—August Meier and Elliott Rudwick (1979), Thomas Sugrue (1996)—report that until the 1960s, some Detroit employers refused to hire any blacks; others put modest numbers of African Americans on their payrolls but kept them in menial jobs; a few hired many blacks. They suggest that most employers and white workers strongly endorsed the idea of restricting employment to whites, but African American groups—and the UAW—fought for years to get jobs for blacks. A few individuals made key decisions. Henry Ford was willing to hire blacks, and Mayor Jefferies allowed blacks to get city jobs in the early 1940s. To the extent that Detroit's employers discriminated on the basis of skin color, African Americans paid higher search costs to find jobs, had longer spells of unemployment, and, presumably, worked fewer hours during the year than whites. Employment trends are, of course, strongly influenced by the nation's business cycles, but also influenced by widely-held norms about who should or should not work at which jobs and by federal policies including the Fair Employment Practices Committee during World War II and Title VII of the 1964 Civil Rights Law.

Figure 3.6 summarizes what happened to blacks and whites in metropolitan Detroit's labor market. (These and subsequent data in this chapter refer to the Macomb, Oakland, Wayne County metropolis.) Information from decennial censuses is used, along with data from large surveys carried out by the Census Bureau in 1996, 1997, and 1998. We merged data for these three years and identify them with 1997. All information in this figure refers to persons aged twenty-five to sixty-four. The first panel shows trends over time in the employment-to-population ratio; that is, the number of employed persons at the time of the census or survey per 1,000 total population. Persons holding public emergency jobs created by the government in the Depression—18 percent of the adult black male labor force in Detroit in 1940, but only 2 percent of the white—were counted among the employed.[5]

Several trends are evident. At all dates a much smaller proportion of African American men than white men held jobs. Even in the booming post–World War II economy, race apparently made a difference since, in 1950, 84 percent of black men were employed compared with 92 percent of white. Second, after 1970 there was a dramatic fall in the employment of black men, and thus racial differences in employment-to-population ratios grew large. Surveys and censuses since 1970 find that no more than about 65 percent of adult black men were employed at any one point—a labor market issue that helps explain the racial gap in economic status.

The data for women remind us that prior to the 1960s, relatively few women were employed. Even though many men were unemployed or on public emergency jobs during the Depression, women could not readily find work. Indeed, a convincing illustration of how norms have changed is that federal and state regulations in the 1930s called for laying off married women so that men could support their families (Goldin 1990, 166). Unfortunately, we do not have information about employment during World War II, when a shortage of labor apparently led Detroit's manufacturers to hire many black women. But they left those jobs when the servicemen returned.

In the three most recent decades, women have joined the labor force

FIGURE 3.6   *Indicators of Labor Force Status of Black and White Men and Women Aged Twenty-Five to Sixty-Four, Metropolitan Detroit, 1940 to 1997*

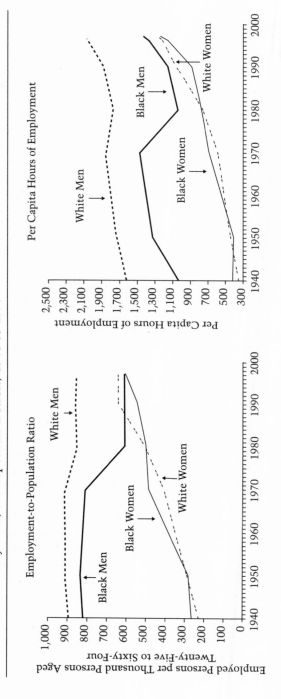

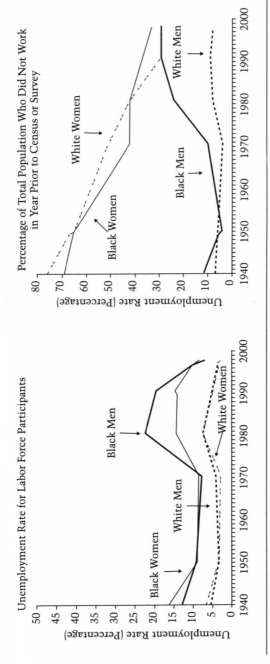

Source: Ruggles and Sobek 1997; U.S. Department of Commerce 1996, 1997, 1998.
Note: Estimates for 1997 are from pooled data from 1996, 1997, and 1998.

in great numbers, so much so that we can now ask whether there will soon be a time when employment-to-population ratios will be much the same for men and women. In metropolitan Detroit, as across the nation, the pace of increasing employment among women has been quite similar for whites and African Americans.

The second panel in figure 3.6 reports per capita hours of employment in the year prior to the census or survey—a measure highly sensitive to the business cycle. If a person works forty hours per week for fifty weeks, he or she would put in 2,000 hours. Once again, there is evidence that African American men have always been at a substantial disadvantage. However, there was a particularly sharp fall in hours of employment for black men after the energy crisis of the 1970s restructured employment. The booming 1990s witnessed a sharp rise in the hours of male employment, but no diminution of the racial gap. The per capita hours reported by white men in 1997—2,100—helps explain why a major issue in recent labor-management conflict in the auto industry concerned compulsory overtime. Faced with a great demand for vehicles, management found it cheaper to pay overtime than to hire new workers. Among women, per capita hours spent at work just about tripled between 1950 and the late 1990s. An extrapolation of recent trends implies that white women will soon work as many hours each year as black men.

The unemployment rate is the most frequently cited index of whether the national economy is doing well or poorly and whether groups of workers are prospering or suffering. The national statistical system defines the labor force to include persons at work, persons about to start or resume a job they have, and those without jobs who made efforts in the last four weeks to find employment, but failed in their search. The unemployment rate equals those whose search was futile as a percent of the total labor force. Several findings are apparent from the trends in unemployment shown in the third panel. First, the major difference is a racial one, not a gender one. African Americans in Detroit have generally had unemployment rates two and one-half to three times those of whites in both prosperous and lean years. There is no evidence of either an increase or decrease in this large racial gap. Second, when Detroit's major industries went through the painful era of adjustment, the consequence was much higher unemployment for all groups. Third, although the sample sizes are modest, surveys from the late 1990s imply real and substantial improvements in the employment situation for labor force participants. The sustained economic boom lowered the unemployment rate of white men to about 3 percent and that of black men to about 7 percent. While these are surprisingly low rates given the previous twenty years of extensive unemployment, Detroit's African Americans still lag behind whites when it comes to success in the search for work.

Finally, figure 3.6 presents a measure that appears often in the underclass debate: the percentage of adults who did not work at all in the year before the census or survey. Some analysts, especially John Kasarda (1985, 1993) and William Julius Wilson (1987, 1996), interpret the high proportion of black men with no employment in a year to mean that they lack the skills to find any work at all in the restructured labor force. To others, especially Lawrence Mead (1986), it suggests that many individuals are now unwilling to accept low-level jobs, perhaps because they can obtain welfare or work in the irregular economy. The census and Census Bureau survey asks several probing questions about employment. Those who work irregularly, the self-employed, those who work off the books, and those who labor at illegal occupations should be counted among the employed, but underreporting of employment may be widespread.

Lines for women in this panel show the secular trend: the percent who did not work in a year steadily declined. During the Depression year of 1939, about three-quarters of Detroit's women reported no employment; by 1979, that number had fallen to 42 percent. Since then, white women have joined the labor force even more rapidly than black women, so on this indicator white women are getting more labor market experience than black women. That is, in the late 1990s, about 29 percent of white women, but 39 percent of black, reported no employment in the previous year. It is probable that welfare reform will narrow the black-white gap in employment among women. The census of 1990 found that 20 percent of adult black women in metropolitan Detroit who did not work in 1989 and 8 percent of white women who did not work obtained cash public assistance payments. The TANF (Temporary Assistance for Needy Families) program that has replaced traditional welfare will likely increase labor force participation by women, presumably more so among African American women.

A familiar pattern is evident among men: after 1970, African American men increasingly reported no employment at all during the year, but among white men the rise was modest. Comparing panels in this figure reveals an important finding about Detroit's economic boom in the 1990s: it has substantially increased the average hours of employment for men who work and substantially decreased the unemployment rate for labor force participants, but it has not drawn men into the force. *The percent of men—both white and black—who did not work during a year was as high in the labor-tight late 1990s as in the labor-surplus year of 1980.*

Who's Who Among Men Who Did Not Work at All for a Year?

The common assumption is that men will work most of the time from their mid-twenties to their mid-sixties, earning salaries to support themselves and their families while saving for retirement. But more than one-quarter of Detroit's adult black men and 9 percent of the white men reported no employment at all during 1989. The decennial census asks a few pertinent questions, giving us insight into this not-so-small population. In brief, few of these men are house-husbands, college students, or imprisoned, but many are disabled or lack the educational credentials now required for most jobs.

Table 3.5 shows that disability is an important factor of those who did not work. Forty percent of white and 34 percent of black men reported on their census forms that they had a physical or mental condition lasting at least six months that prevented them from doing any work. An additional 8 percent said they had a condition that limited the amount or type of work they could do. More than 4 in 10 men who did no work in 1989 reported a disability. Another substantial fraction—more than 40 percent of whites and just over one-half of blacks—faced the challenge of getting a job in the absence of a high school diploma or GED.

Since the late 1940s, UAW negotiators have successfully sought company-paid pensions that might be taken after thirty years of service or after the employee turns fifty-five. Early retirement is common among men in Detroit, but there is a huge racial difference. One in three nonworking white men, but only one in ten African American men, was fifty or over and obtained at least $10,000 in retirement or Social Security income during 1989.

Rather small minorities of not-employed men appear to be prime candidates for jobs, and explaining their absence from work is a challenge. That is, about one-sixth of the white men and one-quarter of the black men were under age fifty, reported a complete secondary school education, and had no physical or mental disability. These are the men we would expect to be drawn into the booming Detroit labor market of the 1990s, but apparently they were not.

Are the Employment Differences Really Racial Differences?

Large racial differences in labor force participation and unemployment are evident and persistent. To what extent are these differences primarily racial differences? Whether or not you find a job is strongly influenced by your training, since many employers insist on educational credentials and others use schooling as an index for skills and abilities. Age is also important. Early in their careers, workers often experiment with

TABLE 3.5   *Characteristics of Detroit-Area Men Aged Twenty-Five to Sixty-Four Who Were Not Employed at All in 1989*

	White Men	Black Men
Total number who did not work at all in 1989	65,721	54,406
Percentage of total male population aged twenty-five to sixty-four who did not work in 1989	9	29
Characteristics of Nonworkers	Percentage of Nonworking Men	
Disabled and impaired		
Percent who were unable to work because of a physical or mental condition lasting six months or more	40	34
Percentage able to work, but with a physical or mental condition lasting six months or more that limits the type of work they can do	8	7
Lacking in skills		
Percent with no high school diploma or GED	42	53
Early retirees		
Percentage over age 49 with at least $10,000 in retirement income in 1989 (amount in 1989 dollars)	33	10
Homemakers		
Percentage who are living with a wife and with a child or children	14	9
College students		
Percentage enrolled in college or a graduate program	5	5
Coupon clippers		
Percentage with dividend, interest, and net rental income in 1989 exceeding $10,000 (amount in 1989 dollars)	7	< 1
Incarcerated		
Percentage enumerated in institutions in 1990	3	3
Prime candidates for employment		
Percentage under age fifty with a high school diploma or GED and no work-limiting disability	16	23

Source: U.S. Department of Commerce 1993.

different jobs to see which one fits best, so people in their twenties generally have higher unemployment rates than those in their forties. Marital status also makes a difference. Married men are more likely to be employed and work longer hours each year than those who are not married. In 1999 in Detroit, for instance, married-spouse-present men aged 25 to 64 averaged 2,132 hours on the job, but for men who had never married, it was only 1,837 hours. Although the situation is changing rapidly, married women generally participated much less in the paid labor force than single or divorced women.

African Americans and whites differ on these determinants of employment. In 1999, 20 percent of Detroit's blacks aged twenty-five to sixty-four had college diplomas, but among whites, it was much higher: 34 percent. Those differences suggest that whites "should" have lower unemployment rates than African Americans. And blacks, as a group, were somewhat younger than whites, meaning they had less experience, on average, in the labor force. If we take these demographic characteristics into account, will we find that black-white differences are much smaller than those displayed in figure 3.6?

Per Capita Hours of Employment   The answer is a clear no. Although demographic factors explain some of the black-white gaps, when we take educational attainment, age, and marital status into account, we still find large differences. And we find little, if any, evidence that the net racial gap in employment itself is declining.

Let's consider how many hours men, on average, worked in the year prior to the census or survey. Here we focus on per capita hours of employment with the age range limited to twenty-five to sixty-four, to eliminate most full-time students and many early retirees. Table 3.6 reports those hours, the gross racial difference, and the net difference.[6]

White men have a great advantage over black men on this employment indicator, an advantage that has grown much larger since the 1970s. But this advantage is not solely because white men spent more years in classrooms and have more labor market experience. Race makes

TABLE 3.6   *Racial Differences in Per Capita Hours Worked, 1940 to 1997*

Year of Census or Survey	Per Capita Hours Worked		Gross Racial Difference	Net Racial Difference
	White Men	Black Men		
1940	1,613	1,027	−586	−522
1950	1,722	1,317	−405	−310
1970	1,837	1,456	−381	−227
1980	1,756	1,028	−728	−495
1990	1,852	1,144	−708	−466
1997	2,106	1,431	−675	−511

Source: Ruggles and Sobek 1997.

a difference. The column of net differences tells us how much African American men fell behind white men once we have taken into account education, age, and marital status. In every case, these numbers have a smaller absolute value than the gross racial differences, revealing that demographic factors help to explain the rather few hours black men spent on the job. The net racial difference numbers would be zero if age, educational, and marital status accounted for the entire black-white gap in this employment indicator. The fact that the net differences are so large implies that even if African American men had characteristics identical to those of white men, they would work many fewer hours: about 500 hours less per year in the 1980s and 1990s. At $15 per hour, this translates into a loss of $7,500 per year for the typical African American man.

Unemployment   What about unemployment? Is there a net racial difference, or is the gross racial difference largely the result of blacks and whites differing in their characteristics, especially education? In table 3.7, we see that back in 1940, about 7 percent of white men in Detroit's labor force and 13 percent of blacks looked for work but could not find it. The odds of being unemployed were roughly .07 to 1 for whites and .15 to 1 for African Americans, meaning the relative gross odds of unemployment were 2.14. That is, the odds of being unemployed, given that you were in the labor force, were more than twice as great for black men as for white. If unemployment rates were identical for both races, the gross odds ratios would be 1.

Gross and net odds ratios are shown for each year in the table. The net ratio reports what the relative odds of unemployment would be if there were no racial differences in education, age, and marital status. If race made absolutely no difference in the job search process, this net relative odds ratio would also equal 1. Gross odds ratios should be compared to net ratios to detect the consequences of race. In every case, the net ratio is smaller than the gross ratio, implying that demographic variables explain some of the elevated unemployment rates of Detroit's African Americans but the net odds ratios are far above 1.0 suggesting that race still makes a difference in who is employed or unemployed. We cannot, of course, control all the factors relevant to employment. We do not know what grades people earned in school, how articulately they speak, or anything about their deportment in job interviews. If we had information about those variables, we might find the net odds ratios to be even smaller. But the available data indicate that blacks have been much less successful than whites in their search for jobs. And, disappointingly, there is no evidence of improvement over time. These net odds ratios imply that in eras of both high and low unemployment, African Americans have a harder time than whites getting employers to hire

TABLE 3.7 *Unemployment Rates for Labor Force Participants by Race and Gender, and Relative Odds of Unemployment, Metropolitan Detroit, 1940 to 1997*

	Percentage of Labor Force Unemployed		Gross Relative Odds Ratio	Net Relative Odds Ratio
	White	Black		
Data for men				
1940	6.7	13.3	2.14	1.88
1950	3.8	9.2	2.57	2.11
1970	3.0	7.6	2.66	1.80
1980	7.7	22.0	3.38	2.35
1990	5.1	19.2	4.45	2.75
1997	2.8	6.9	2.54	1.88
Data for women				
1940	5.5	16.2	3.32	2.51
1950	3.4	9.0	2.81	2.50
1970	4.2	8.2	2.02	1.80
1980	7.3	14.2	2.10	1.80
1990	5.1	14.5	3.16	1.90
1997	3.2	8.3	2.71	2.37

Source: Ruggles and Sobek 1997; U.S. Department of Commerce 1996, 1997, 1998.
Note: The net relative odds ratio was estimated from a logistic regression equation with the log of odds of employment as its dependent variable and indicators of educational attainment, age, marital status, and race as independent variables. All the estimated net effects of race are significant at the .01 level.

them. With regard to finding a job, Detroit's African Americans in the 1990s apparently face as many hurdles as did African Americans forty or fifty years ago.

Occupational Achievement: Racial and Gender Differences

There is a long history of employers believing that one racial group is appropriate for some jobs, but not for other jobs. Similarly, organizations of workers—be they craft unions, bar associations, or the American Medical Association—determine admission criteria for their occupations and these often favor one group over another. In addition, there are widely held values about who should be hired for specific jobs. If a powerful group keeps minorities and women out of a job category, that group will face less competition and thereby protect its occupational advantage. In every era, a few individuals become widely known for breaking the rules and becoming the first of their group to enter a previously closed occupation: Brandeis, O'Connor, and Marshall on the Supreme Court; Kennedy in the White House; Perkins and Weaver in the Cabinet; Robinson in baseball; O'Rea in hockey.

Detroit's history is replete with struggles over whether African Americans could fill specific jobs. Whites frequently dominated occupations, blacks fought for opportunities, and, for the most part, white workers and employers strongly resisted the occupational advances of African Americans. In 1897, a committee of Detroit blacks sought to get industrial and service-sector jobs for their race, arguing that since African Americans made up one-fifteenth of the city's population, they should get one-fifteenth of the jobs. They had little success, but did get the street railway company and one stove factory to hire a few blacks (Washington 1991, 254).

In the early years of the Depression, Detroit's public schools enrolled in excess of 200,000 students and had nearly 6,000 teachers on the payroll. Forty of those instructors were blacks, but they were assigned exclusively to elementary schools with African American enrollments. The Detroit Civic Rights Committee protested the "rule" that prevented blacks from teaching in high schools. Finally, in September 1934, the first black man, Lloyd Cofer, was appointed to teach at a secondary school (Mirel 1992, 187). The same group later insisted that blacks be hired as firefighters. After four years of struggle, Mayor Reading agreed to appoint three African Americans. When they showed up for work in a white neighborhood, however, local residents surrounded the firehouse and would not let them enter. After more confrontations, including strong protests from the firefighters' union, they were allowed to work—but were assigned separate living quarters and toilet facilities (Thomas 1992, 152).

Important changes occurred in a brief interval with regard to occupational opportunities for black men in Detroit's manufacturing plants. In June 1941, A. Philip Randolph pressured President Roosevelt to issue Executive Order #8802, prohibiting racial discrimination in the defense industry. Shortly thereafter, Detroit's firms began converting to war work. These jobs typically demanded greater skills and paid a little more than the traditional automotive jobs. With the exception of Ford, blacks employed in Detroit's plants in 1941 worked as janitors, polishers, foundry laborers, and maintenance men. They expected to get some of the better defense jobs but were turned down. As early as August 1941, African American men at a Dodge foundry were striking in protest. The next month, whites at Packard went on strike when a few black polishers were transferred to defense work. After this, management at several firms expressed their intentions to comply with the executive order, but asserted they could not because white men halted production whenever blacks were moved up the occupational ladder. Early in 1942, union leaders and management agreed that striking white workers should be fired, but apparently few were. White supremacist organizations, including a revived Ku Klux Klan, encouraged whites to hold the line.

In June 1942, Hudson's management announced that African Americans would be advanced to better jobs in their naval ordnance plant. White workers shut down production on the morning of June 18. By noon, Secretary of the Navy Frank Knox telegrammed management and union leaders, pointing out that the plant produced munitions only, that the production was supervised by naval personnel, that the government owned the plant, and that it was designed as a military reservation for the duration of the war. He stressed that striking workers were violating an executive order and declared that if they did not return to work immediately, they would be fired—and, because of their disloyalty in a time of war, could never again be hired by a defense contractor. White men returned to work that afternoon (Weaver 1946, 55–63; Meier and Rudwick 1979, chap. 3). While this did not end the hate strikes, it broke the back of white resistance. For the first time, black men were hired for an array of high-paying blue-collar jobs in Detroit's factories.

Although African American men got many unskilled jobs, white men continued to dominate the craft trades after World War II. In 1960, the United States Civil Rights Commission held hearings about racial differences in job opportunities in Detroit, and obtained employment data from the Big Three. Blacks made up 15 percent of the metropolitan labor force at that time. At General Motors, only 67 of 11,125 skilled tradesmen were black; at Chrysler, just 24 of 7,425; and at Ford, approximately 250 of 7,000 (Widdick 1989, 148). African Americans accounted for 60 percent of the men working at Chevrolet's forge plant, but only one-tenth of 1 percent of those working at GM's Technical Center (Sugrue 1996, table 4.1).

Censuses document where changes have occurred with regard to occupational achievements. They report an overall upgrading of Detroit's occupational structure, reflecting the trend away from manual labor and the rise of professional jobs, especially in recent decades. But they also reveal substantial and continuing racial differences, so, at every date, whites held a much more favorable array of jobs than blacks.

Among the most desirable occupations are professions and managerial jobs. In 1990, 51 percent of Detroit's professionals and managers had a college degree. The top panel of figure 3.7 shows the percent of employed workers who held these highly ranking jobs. Back in 1940, only 16 percent of white men were employed as professionals or managers. But, at that time, just a tiny fraction of African Americans got into the professions or worked as managers—less than 3 percent. Undoubtedly many of them served a black clientele, such as staffing the Jim Crow proprietary hospitals then found in Detroit's African Ameri-

FIGURE 3.7   *Indicators of the Occupational Status of Black and*
White Men and Women Aged Twenty-Five to
Sixty-Four, Metropolitan Detroit, 1940 to 1990

Percent of Employed Workers with Professional or Managerial Jobs

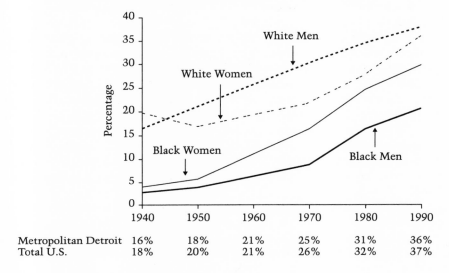

	1940	1950	1960	1970	1980	1990
Metropolitan Detroit	16%	18%	21%	25%	31%	36%
Total U.S.	18%	20%	21%	26%	32%	37%

Average Socioeconomic Occupational Index for Employed Persons

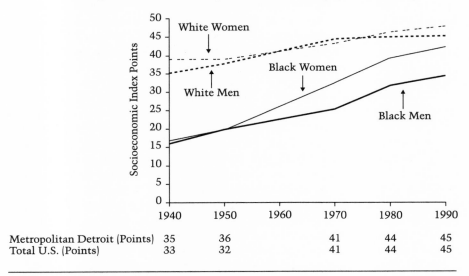

	1940	1950	1960	1970	1980	1990
Metropolitan Detroit (Points)	35	36		41	44	45
Total U.S. (Points)	33	32		41	44	45

Source: Ruggles and Sobek 1997.

can community (Thomas 1992, 180–84). Each decade saw a rise in the proportion of men employed as professionals or managers, but the racial gap remained large. By 1990, the proportion with these highly ranked jobs among blacks was equivalent to what it was among white men during the Truman presidency.

Through the 1950s, domestic service was the most common job for black women. But thereafter they moved into more rewarding occupations, so the occupational achievements of black women improved more rapidly than those of white women. Any extrapolation of recent trends implies the eventual disappearance of a racial difference in the jobs Detroit-area white and black women hold.[7]

Numbers underneath the top panel, contrast the occupational distribution of Detroit to that of the nation. Despite the automobile industry with its large blue-collar work force, at all dates Detroit had close to the national average in terms of workers with professional or managerial jobs.

There are widely shared views about which jobs are desirable and which should be avoided. Parents encourage their children to pursue the training needed to become professionals, but discourage them from setting their sights on low-paying jobs such as day laborer or short-order cook. For decades social scientists have used scoring systems to rate the prestige of jobs, thereby allowing a comparison of different groups with regard to their overall occupational achievement. These systems were developed on the basis of how national samples actually ranked specific jobs, along with information about the educational attainment and earnings of the incumbents of each occupation (Duncan 1961). The scoring scheme used in this analysis assigns a favorable 93 occupational prestige points to lawyers and judges, but only 6 points to domestic servants and farm laborers.

The lower panel of figure 3.7 utilizes occupational prestige scores to describe the overall trend toward better jobs in metropolitan Detroit, a trend evident among men and women of both races. The typical employed white man in 1940 had an occupational index of 35 points—the value assigned to plumbers and pipefitters. Fifty years later, this increased to 45 points—the score assigned to inspectors on construction projects. For employed black men, the improvement was from the average occupational prestige score assigned to men who operated machines in steel fabrication plants to that of an auto mechanic. Despite the obvious occupational improvements, African American men in 1990 worked at jobs that were less prestigious than those white men typically held in 1950. The shift away from domestic service helps explain the steadily rising occupational prestige of African American women and the gradual decline in the black-white gap.

After fifty years of occupational change, which are the occupational niches where many blacks are found and in which are almost none found? Starting with the list of 503 specific jobs, we selected those that had 2,000 or more incumbents in metropolitan Detroit in 1990. Those occupations were ranked by their representation of blacks, keeping the analysis separate by gender, since men and women continue to work at different jobs.

The occupations where blacks were most numerous were civil service jobs—social workers, police officers, mail carriers—or unskilled blue-collar occupations: stamping press operators and assemblers. African American women have benefited, in recent years, from expanded expenditures for health care and were highly represented in the bottom-level jobs in that industry: practical nurses, orderlies, and health aides. Geography helps explain why five-eighths of women sorting mail in the metropolis were African Americans. The large postal center just south of downtown Detroit provides good jobs for central-city women, but is not enough of a draw to attract white women from the suburbs.

Given the large African American population in Detroit and the authoritative laws proscribing racial discrimination, there are few occupations with virtually no blacks, but many where blacks were greatly underrepresented. These include jobs that require much technical training—mechanical engineers and computer systems analysts—as well as the most highly paid blue-collar jobs: toolmakers and carpenters. Decisions about investments in education may be one reason why there are so few blacks in some of the highest-paying jobs, but table 3.8 implies that race may be an important consideration. Blacks are underrepresented in occupations serving white customers: sales representatives, financial managers, dental assistants, and waitresses. Commenting on similar findings at the national level, Andrew Hacker (1992, 110) commented:

> The suspicion arises that proprietors of restaurants and lounges may feel that their white clientele do not want their food and drinks handled by black employees. Perhaps most revealing of all is the small number of black dental hygienists. While white patients seem willing to be cared for by black nurses, they apparently draw the line at having black fingers in their mouths.

Are There Net Racial Differences in Occupational Achievement?

The number of professional workers is growing rapidly in Detroit, just as it is across the nation. In 1970, 34,000 men and women were employed as engineers in Detroit; in 1990, the number was 51,000. The

TABLE 3.8   Detailed Occupations in Which Blacks Were Most Highly or Least Represented, Metropolitan Detroit, 1990

	Men			Women		
Occupation[a]	Total Workers	Percentage Black	Occupation[a]	Total Workers	Percentage Black	
Most Highly Represented						
Nursing aides	2,196	44	Postal clerks	3,356	62	
Private security guards	7,262	42	Licensed practical nurses	4,536	49	
Social workers	2,744	40	Orderlies	15,191	48	
Miscellaneous machine operators	27,114	35	Social workers	7,735	43	
Stamping press operators	3,360	35	Assemblers	11,280	41	
Janitors	16,472	32	Public administrators	2,067	40	
Welders and cutters	8,877	31	Telephone operators	2,335	38	
General office clerks	2,560	26	Maids	5,267	38	
Police officers	6,662	26	Health aides	2,744	35	
Mail carriers	2,543	25	Child care workers	3,173	35	
Least Represented						
Tool and die makers	9,679	5	Dental assistants	2,034	10	
Construction supervisors	5,105	5	Physicians	2,480	10	
Lawyers	8,507	4	Family child care providers	2,833	9	
Carpenters	9,551	4	Financial managers	3,596	8	
Sales representatives	17,593	4	Computer systems analysts	2,336	7	
Mechanical engineers	14,502	3	Miscellaneous sales occupations	2,708	7	
Printing press operators	3,091	3	Sales representatives	5,125	5	
Financial managers	5,066	3	Real estate sales	4,450	5	
Engineers, not elsewhere classified	5,627	3	Waitresses	11,011	5	
Dentists	2,599	2	Designers	3,696	4	

Source: U.S. Department of Commerce 1993.

[a] These data refer to detailed occupations with 2,000 or more employed persons in the three-county Detroit area in 1990. There were 91 such occupations for men and 71 for women. Occupational titles from the Census of 1990 are used in this analysis.

TABLE 3.9   *Average Socioeconomic Occupational Index*

Year	Whites	Blacks	Gross Difference	Net Difference
Data for men				
1940	35	16	−19	−16
1950	38	20	−18	−16
1970	43	25	−18	−11
1980	45	32	−13	−7
1990	45	34	−11	−6
Data for women				
1940	39	17	−22	−16
1950	39	20	−19	−17
1970	43	32	−11	−8
1980	46	39	−7	−6
1990	48	42	−6	−6

Source: Ruggles and Sobek 1997.

number of lawyers soared from 4,900 to 13,100; physicians from 6,500 to 10,300; nurses from 18,600 to 34,800. If you do not have the requisite educational credentials, you cannot design new vehicles, pass the bar exam, or get a license to practice medicine. Perhaps the substantial racial gaps in occupational status displayed in figure 3.7 are largely the result of black-white differences in demographic characteristics, especially educational attainment. Table 3.9 shows average occupational prestige scores for employed persons from 1940 to 1990, the gross racial difference in occupational, and then the net difference.[8]

There are signs of racial progress here, implying a gradual change toward racial convergence. The average occupational index for employed black men rose from 16 points in 1940 to 34 points in 1990—a gain of 18 points. But the average occupational index for employed white men went up only 10 points, so the racial gap narrowed in that half-century. Recall that many low-ranking jobs have disappeared from Detroit's labor market, and blacks were more likely than whites to hold those jobs. The occupational distribution of African Americans has been upgraded a little more rapidly than that of whites, albeit an upgrading that has left about one-quarter of adult black men out of the labor force. The gross racial gaps in occupational scores have declined among both men and women.

Using a model to take racial differences in age, education, and marital status into account, we estimated net racial differences in the occupational index. If these demographic variables accounted for all the differences in occupational achievement, the net difference would be zero.

In every comparison of the gross and net differences except one, the net was smaller, implying that racial differences in education, age, and marital status help explain why blacks worked at less prestigious jobs than whites.

The net differences, however, are not zero, but they have declined substantially over time. Among employed adults, race has clearly become less important in determining who gets what jobs. Blacks still typically work at jobs with less prestige and lower pay than those of whites, but the many efforts to root out discrimination in Detroit's labor market apparently had beneficial effects, since blacks and whites with ostensibly similar qualifications are increasingly likely to be working at similar jobs.

Earnings in Detroit: Racial and Gender Differences

Surprisingly, the earnings of black and white men were quite similar in the late 1940s and 1950s in Detroit, but a large earnings gap developed after 1970 as white men shifted more rapidly than black into the more rewarding occupations. Among employed women, the opposite trend occurred: a large racial difference decades ago gradually declined and then disappeared.

This section lays out racial and gender differences in earnings. It is restricted to persons aged twenty-five to sixty-four who reported wage or salary earnings during the year prior to the census or survey; thus, it excludes self-employed persons and those who did not work for pay. Over time, a higher percent of adult women but fewer men report wage and salary earnings. The census of 1950 found that one-third of adult women in Detroit reported cash earnings, but by the late 1990s this was up to 70 percent. Among men, especially black men, the shift was in the other direction: 98 percent reported earnings in 1949, but by the late 1990s only about 70 percent.

Before we examine racial and gender differences, several important dimensions of Detroit's labor market should be stressed. First, it is a high-wage area. The top panel shows median annual earnings for men and women in Detroit and in the entire metropolitan United States since the end of the Depression. Detroit men have traditionally earned about 20 percent more than men in other metropolises. Even the slack labor markets of the 1970s and 1980s failed to lower Detroit's wage rates to the national average.

Second, earnings—as indexed by the median—rose rapidly in Detroit from 1940 into the 1970s, just as they did across the nation. Since then earnings have gone up little if at all. A more detailed examination of trends implies that male earnings peaked about 1972 and then stagnated or declined into the 1990s, while in the same interval the wages of women went up, but at a modest rate.

Third, in Detroit as throughout the nation, earnings inequality increased substantially. Those toward the top end of the earnings distribution have come through the economic restructuring of recent decades quite well, since their wages held steady or increased a bit while those at the bottom end lost ground. In Detroit, the man at the 80th percentile point in 1970 reported annual earnings of $61,400. By 1980, this increased to $66,600 and then was at $63,000 in the later 1990s. But the man at the 20th percentile point saw his earnings—in constant 1997 dollars—plummet from $31,200 in 1969 to $21,900 in 1989, with a modest recovery to $23,400 in 1997. Thus the gap between the top and bottom of the earnings distribution grew much bigger in both absolute amount and relative terms, as shown in table 3.11. In 1950, the man at the 80th percentile earned 1.78 times as much as the man at the 20th percentile; in 1990, he earned almost three times as much. And yet, as you can see by comparing 80th to 20th ratios for Detroit to those for the metropolitan United States, earnings distributions in Detroit have been and continue to be more nearly egalitarian than those in other places, since the gap between the top and bottom of the earnings distribution is even bigger elsewhere.

However you assess it, economic inequality has increased in Detroit from 1970 through the 1990s. The figures in table 3.10 show the share of total male earnings obtained by the bottom quintile and the top quintile of earnings, and then the share of total family income received by the poorest and the richest quintile of families.

Earnings inequality was at a minimum in the 1960s, when the lowest one-fifth got 8 percent of total earnings, but this fell to about 5 percent in the 1990s. Those at the top did well, since the share of earnings

TABLE 3.10 *Share of Earnings or Income Received by the Top and Bottom Quintiles, Metropolitan Detroit, 1940 to 1997*

	Earnings of Adult Men		Income of Families	
	Bottom 20 Percent	Top 20 Percent	Bottom 20 Percent	Top 20 Percent
1940	6%	38%	n.a.	n.a.
1950	8	34	8%	37%
1970	8	36	5	41
1980	7	36	4	42
1990	5	41	4	46
1997	6	44	3	47

Sources: Ruggles and Sobek 1997; U.S. Department of Commerce 1996, 1997, 1998.

TABLE 3.11 Median Earnings by Gender for Persons Twenty-Five to Sixty-Four, and Indicators of Trends in Earnings Inequality, Metropolitan Detroit and Metropolitan United States, 1940 to 1997 (in 1997 Dollars)

	Data for Men			Data for Women		
Year	Metropolitan Detroit	Metropolitan U.S.	Detroit as Percentage of U.S.	Metropolitan Detroit	Metropolitan U.S.	Detroit as Percentage of U.S.
Median Annual Earnings for Persons Twenty-Five to Sixty-Four Who Reported Earnings						
1940	$17,284	$14,164	122%	$9,280	$8,190	113%
1950	22,445	20,435	110	13,072	11,055	118
1970	43,923	37,805	116	18,140	16,829	108
1980	46,631	38,062	123	19,993	17,774	112
1990	42,571	34,831	122	20,641	20,640	100
1997	40,000	32,000	125	21,000	20,000	105

Indicators of Earnings Inequality for Men Twenty-Five to Sixty-Four Who Reported Earnings

	Earnings at Designated Percentile for Detroit Men		Ratio of 80th Percentile to 20th Percentile	
Year	20th	80th	Metropolitan Detroit	Metropolitan U.S.
1940	$9,242	$24,372	2.64	3.18
1950	17,085	30,485	1.78	2.13
1970	31,245	61,399	1.97	2.15
1980	28,873	66,611	2.30	2.53
1990	21,931	64,501	2.94	3.14
1997	23,400	63,000	2.69	3.37

Sources: Ruggles and Sobek 1997; U.S. Department of Commerce 1996, 1997, 1998.
Note: Earnings data refer to wage and salary earnings and exclude self-employment earnings. Data pertain to persons who reported wage and salary earnings in the year prior to the census.

FIGURE 3.8   *Percentage Change in Number of Jobs in Metropolitan Detroit, by Pay Level, 1980 to 1990 (in 1989 Dollars)*

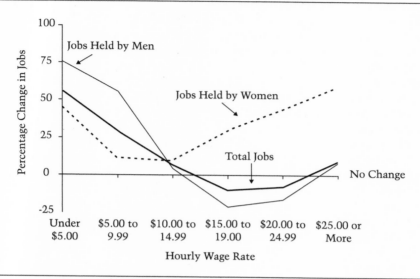

Source: U.S. Department of Commerce 1983.

going to them rose from 34 percent in the 1950s to 44 percent in the 1990s. Similar trends led to greater inequality for Detroit's families: prosperous families got a larger share of total family income income, while those at the bottom got less.

In the last couple of decades, Detroit's labor market—similar to the national labor market—created many jobs that pay well and many jobs that pay little, but few jobs in the middle, leading to greater economic polarization. Figure 3.8 classifies Detroit workers in 1990 and in 1980 by how much they earned per hour, with information shown separately for men and women. There is much discouraging news in this figure, especially for men. The number of jobs paying less than $5 per hour grew by 75 percent in the decade; those paying $5 to $10 per hour by 55 percent; but middle-income jobs paying between $15 and $25—in the $30,000 to $50,000 per year range—fell by 20 percent. For men in metropolitan Detroit, there was a large increase in the number of low-wage jobs, a tiny increase in jobs paying more than $25 per hour, but a substantial drop in middle-income jobs.

Trends among women were very different and more optimistic. Among young people now entering the labor force, women have educational attainments exceeding those of men. And, after completing their schooling, young women in the 1980s and 1990s typically entered the industrial sectors where employment was growing rapidly: financial services and insurance, the medical and legal fields, and lower- and middle-managerial position in many industries (Bianchi 1995). The pattern in Detroit was similar to the national one. There was a substantial growth of low-wage jobs for women, but a healthy increase—about 34 percent—in the number of jobs paying $15 to $25 per hour, and an even more rapid rise in the number of jobs paying more than $25, reflecting the current trends of many more young women entering the professions.

What about earnings differences by age and gender? Overall earnings increased rapidly during World War II and in the postwar boom, but slowly, if at all, after 1970. And there is only a little evidence that black men were catching up with white men in their earnings, but black women have reached earnings parity with white women.

It is a challenge to summarize the earnings of a group. Should you focus on full-time workers or include part-timers? Should you consider annual, weekly, or hourly earnings? This makes a big difference, especially in Detroit, where the cyclic nature of vehicle production means layoffs one year but overtime at high-wage rates the next. Should you use the mean or the median to summarize an earnings distribution? This is important since, in a time of growing earnings inequality, mean earnings go up while median earnings stagnate or fall.

Figure 3.9 reports two indicators, with information restricted to adults who reported wage and salary earnings in the year before the census or survey. The top figure describes *median annual earnings* and illustrates the beneficial effects of the economic changes between 1940 and 1970. In that span, median earnings for white men rose by a factor of 3, but the median went up even more for black men—so there was racial convergence, at least in relative terms. Median annual earnings for black men was 52 percent that of white men at the end of the Depression, but 74 percent as much in 1970. That was the high-water mark for male earnings. Those of both races declined at roughly the same pace so, among men who held jobs, African Americans have not fallen behind but neither have they gained on whites.

The earnings of black women have steadily risen and at a higher rate than those of white women. With regard to median annual earnings, African American women reached parity with white women in the mid-1970s.

The bottom figure takes labor supply into account. It reports *mean hourly earnings* as calculated from census questions about usual hours of work, weeks of work in the year, and annual wage and salary earnings. Hourly earnings rose among men from 1940 to 1970, with the rate of increase higher for African Americans. The typical black man earned

FIGURE 3.9 *Median Annual Earnings and Mean Hourly Wages for Black and White Men and Women Aged Twenty-Five to Sixty-Four, Metropolitan Detroit, 1940 to 1990*

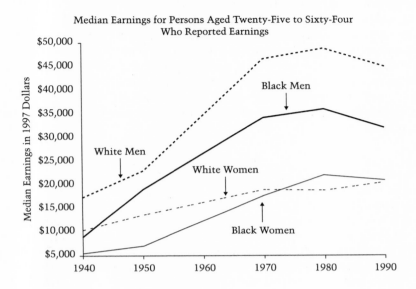

Median Earnings for Persons Aged Twenty-Five to Sixty-Four Who Reported Earnings

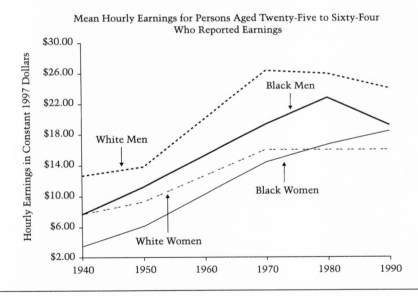

Mean Hourly Earnings for Persons Aged Twenty-Five to Sixty-Four Who Reported Earnings

Source: Ruggles and Sobek 1997.
Note: These data refer to the wage and salary earnings of persons who reported such earnings in the year prior to the census of survey. Self-employment earnings are excluded. Amounts are shown in 1997 dollars.

about $8 per hour in 1940, but $19 in 1970. The hourly earnings of black men held up a bit better than those of white men in the era of employment restructuring, so there is some evidence of a narrowing racial gap. On an hourly basis, black men in Detroit earned 60 percent as much as white men in 1940, 73 percent as much in 1970, but 80 percent as much in 1990. Recall, however, that a substantial fraction of black men withdrew from the labor market. Among women, hourly earnings went up more rapidly for African Americans than whites throughout this period, and, by 1990, black women earned about 15 percent more than white women per hour.

Are There Net Racial Differences in Earnings?

Educational differences and differences in age may explain some or all of the black-white gaps in earnings. Once again we use the procedure described with regard to hours of employment and occupational prestige scores by asking how large the racial difference in hourly earnings would be if Detroit blacks were similar to whites in educational attainment, age, and marital status. Estimates of the net effects of race are shown in table 3.12 for the 1940 to 1990 span.[9] We control for racial differences in labor supply by focusing on the percentage difference in hourly earnings attributable to race.

In 1940, a black man who had the demographic characteristics of the typical white man could expect to earn 35 percent less for each hour spent at work. For black women, the cost was equal to 54 percent of the earnings of whites. Blacks who worked typically held different and lower-paid jobs than whites and, undoubtedly, some employers paid them less than whites who performed similar tasks. By 1990, the situa-

TABLE 3.12   *Estimates of the Net Effects of Race on Hourly Earnings for Employed Persons Aged Twenty-Five to Sixty-Four, Metropolitan Detroit, 1940 to 1990*

Year	Men	Women
1940	−35%	−54%
1950	−12	−48
1970	−21	−10
1980	−10	+3[a]
1990	−10	+6

Source: Ruggles and Sobek 1997.
[a]This net racial difference is not statistically significant.

tion had improved. To be sure, there appeared to be a net cost associated with being black for men in Detroit's labor market, but it equaled only 10 percent of white wages. And black women, net of demographic characteristics, earned about 6 percent more per hour than white women. The net effect of race on earnings has declined over time, and similarly qualified blacks and whites are much more likely to be earning similar wages than they were a quarter century ago.

A few additional comments are called for here. The net effects of race were surprisingly small among men in 1950. The occupational distribution helps to account for this, since 53 percent of employed black men compared with 44 percent of whites worked in durable goods manufacturing. These were overwhelmingly blue-collar jobs in the auto industry, where black men earned as much as their white peers. The net effect of race on male earnings got larger after 1950 as occupational shifts occurred. Since the 1970s, norms—and strong federal policies—insist on equal pay for African Americans and whites and they appear to have had beneficial effects for employed African Americans in metropolitan Detroit.

Do Detroit employers prefer black women and pay them a little more than white women with similar skills? That is improbable, although some employers who have goals for hiring both minorities and women undoubtedly appreciate the benefits of hiring black women. Several factors not considered in this model may account for the advantage black women enjoyed in 1990. Black and white women probably differ in terms of their job seniority, and black women may be rewarded for their greater seniority with higher wages. Black and white women also differ in their employers, and it is possible that black women seek out occupations and industries where they will be paid the most since, more often than white women, they are the sole breadwinners in their families. For example, in 1990, 24 percent of Detroit's black women worked for local, state, or federal agencies, compared with 11 percent of white women.

Racial Differences in Educational Attainment: Persistent Gaps

Even though racial differences in poverty and employment remain large in metropolitan Detroit, we might have a brighter outlook if we knew that young African Americans and whites have similar educational attainments and that school enrollment rates no longer differ by race. Unfortunately, black-white differences in attainment have been large in the past and remain great, so there is no reason to expect a racial convergence in the foreseeable future.

Detroit's Top Earners: Who's Who?

Economic polarization leaves the bottom of the earnings distribution further behind the top, but it has the beneficial consequence of increasing the number of people with great earnings. With regard to race, an important change has occurred. Prior to the Civil Rights revolution, very few African Americans earned large amounts of money. White firms did not advance blacks to top-paying jobs, and even in sports and entertainment, blacks did not make it into the ranks of the top earners. There were a few rich blacks, but many of them owned their own firms serving black clients or they were self-employed professionals. With Title VII of the Civil Rights Act came a gradual change in white attitudes and, later, an emphasis on employment diversity. Largely white firms that only hired blacks for blue-collar jobs in the 1960s now hire and promote African Americans into management. The demand for highly educated blacks increased and, for the first time, a substantial black economic elite emerged (Freeman 1976). Indeed, the escalation of salaries in professional sports means that in many metropolises, the highest paid wage and salary employee is an athlete—often an African American.

Economic polarization occurred among both races. In 1970, the man at the 80th percentile of the white earnings distribution in Detroit earned twice as much as the man at the 20th percentile point, a difference that increased to 2.6 times as much in 1990. Among black men, even more polarization occurred and the shift was from the man at the 80th percentile point earning twice as much in 1970 to four times as much twenty years later.

Table 3.13 provides information about Detroit's top earners—those who earned more than $60,000 (in 1997 dollars). The census of 1950 turned up no Detroit African Americans earning the equivalent of $60,000 but opportunities expanded, discrimination in pay and promotions decreased, and, by 1990, about 1 black earner in 14 reported that amount. This analysis includes both genders, as well as persons reporting self-employment earnings.

The census of 1990 reveals that black and white high earners were similar with regard to some labor market characteristics. About one-fifth of both races worked at professional occupations, and roughly a similar proportion held advanced degrees. Detroit's labor market still permits blue-collar workers to enter the top ranks of earnings distributions. With the auto boom of the 1990s, many men in the auto plants are undoubtedly earning in excess of $100,000 each year because of their many hours of overtime. This is one way the African American economic elite differs from the white: they are more dependent on those high-paying blue-collar jobs in manufacturing, as illustrated in table 3.13. They are also more dependent on governmental employment. Nevertheless, government jobs are certainly not the backbone of the black middle or upper class. Five-sixths of high-wage African Americans in 1990 worked for themselves or for a

---

Continued

---

profit-making firm. Finally, there is a huge geographic difference that clearly distinguishes the races: a tiny fraction of high-earning whites live within the central city, but two-thirds of blacks do. (For a description of social class distinctions among Detroit's black community, see Graham 1999, chap. 13.)

There is evidence of educational progress, however, and the overwhelming majority of young people now complete high school or obtain a GED certificate, as shown in figure 3.10. Black and white men and women were classified by their year of birth. These data, gathered in the census of 1990, begin with the oldest population—those born before World War I—and end with those born recently, aged twenty-five to twenty-nine in 1990.

Although much higher proportions complete secondary school, whites still hold an advantage. Among both men and women, African

TABLE 3.13   *Detroit's High Earners*

Percentage of Earners Aged Twenty-Five to Sixty-Four Who Reported Earnings in Excess of $60,000 (in Constant 1997 Dollars)		
	White Earners	Black Earners
1950	2.80	0.00
1970	16.2	2.4
1980	17.3	5.9
1990	17.6	7.1
	Characteristics of Earners with Earnings in Excess of $60,000 in Census of 1990	
	Whites	Blacks
Number of high earners	220,368	20,473
Professionals by occupation	24%	20%
Post–B.A. degree holders	22	19
Employed in blue-collar jobs in manufacturing	18	33
Employed by governmental agencies	6	17
Percent who are women	10	23
Percent who live in city of Detroit	2	65
Mean earnings in 1989	$94,432	$80,333
Median earnings in 1989	$68,371	$77,400

Source: Ruggles and Sobek 1997.

FIGURE 3.10 *Percentage of Men and Women with Completed High School or College (Four-Year) Educations, by Birth Cohort, Metropolitan Detroit, 1990*

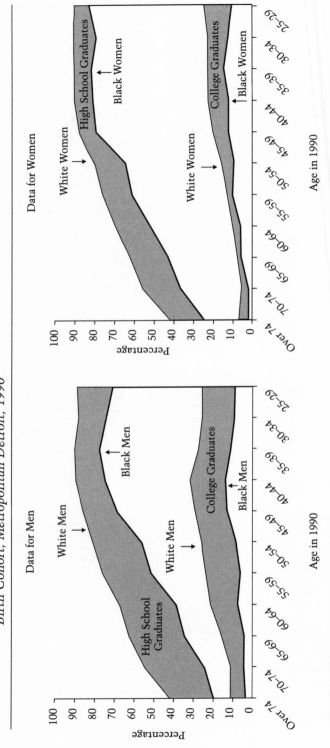

Source: U.S. Department of Commerce 1993.

Americans and whites born after 1940 have educational attainments more similar to each other than to those born earlier, but, among the most recent generations, a persistent gap remains. Among those in their late twenties or early thirties today, about 80 percent of black women and 90 percent of white women were high school graduates, while among men, the racial difference was even larger.

Detroit blacks fall far behind whites in obtaining four-year college degrees—the trend lines are shown toward the bottom in each panel of the figure—and there is no evidence of convergence. Among men born throughout the twentieth century, the proportion with a college degree has been twice as great for whites as for African Americans. Because conscription for the war in Vietnam increased college enrollment rates among men, especially white men, the proportion of young men graduating from college reached a peak for those born between 1945 and 1949. Later birth cohorts of men had lower rates of college completion, and the racial gap persisted. Selective migration into and away from Detroit helps to account for the unusually large black-white discrepancy. In 1990, racial gaps in attainment and enrollment were larger in Detroit than anywhere else in the country.

This figure presents a bleak picture, but it refers to the outcome of a long educational process. Perhaps, if we examine current college enrollments, we will find smaller racial differences. We should keep in mind that in Detroit, as across the nation, there is a substantial black-white difference in obtaining high school diplomas by the end of the teen years among men, but almost no difference among women. The numbers given in table 3.12 for 1990 show the proportion of white and black eighteen- and nineteen-year-olds who had a high school diploma or GED and reports parity among women.

Figure 3.11 shows the percent of high school graduates who were enrolled in college, but had not received either a two-year or a four-year degree. Once again a large racial difference is evident: the college enrollment rates of African Americans lagged behind those of whites, with the difference again being much larger among men than women. Black

TABLE 3.12　*Percentage of Eighteen- and Nineteen-Year-Olds with High School Diploma or GED, Metropolitan Detroit, 1990*

Gender	Blacks	Whites	Relative Odds of High School Diploma
Men	53%	65%	1.62
Women	68%	68%	1.00

Source: U.S. Department of Commerce 1993.

FIGURE 3.11   *Percentage of High School Graduates Lacking a College Degree Who Were Enrolled in College, Metropolitan Detroit, 1990*

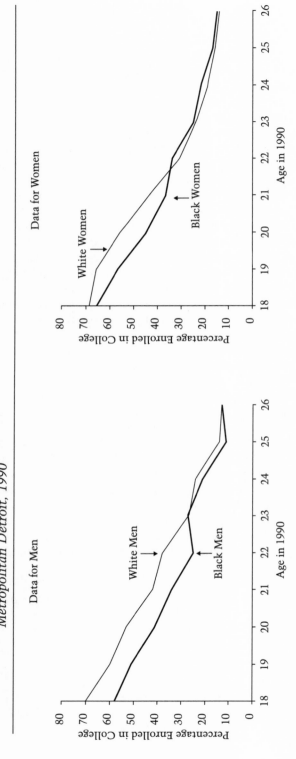

Source: U.S. Department of Commerce 1993.

women who graduated from high school were a bit less likely than white women to enroll in college. The favorable news is that two-thirds of the female high school graduates were enrolled in advanced education. Black men, however, were at a double disadvantage: both less likely than white males to have completed high school and, among those who did, less likely than whites to be enrolled in college. As the educational attainment of the Detroit population continues to increase, the racial gap is not narrowing.

When Detroit's labor market boomed, from the early 1940s to the early 1970s, many young men left high school and took jobs in the manufacturing industry, so few young men were idle. One of the dramatic indicators of how the job market has changed is the increased idleness of young black (but not young white) men in the Detroit area.

Figure 3.12 reports the percent of African American and white men who were neither enrolled in school nor participating in the labor market—that is, they neither had a job nor searched for one. Back in 1940, about 2 percent of young white men and 4 percent of black men were idle, as defined by this measure used by Sara McLanahan and Gary Sandefur (1994). This changed only a little over time for whites, but has steadily gone up for blacks, reaching a high of 18 percent in 1980. That figure reflects the growing disadvantages they face at the beginning of their work lives, which negatively affect their future economic attainment.

Conclusion

During World War II and for several decades thereafter, Detroit's labor market offered good jobs to blue-collar workers and excellent ones for those with advanced training. An informative way to describe that situation and changes over time is to examine the percent of adults whose earnings in a year would lift a family of four above the poverty line. This is shown in figure 3.13. In 1940, fewer than one-half of white and just 15 percent of black men earned such an amount. However, three decades later, nine out of ten white and three out of four black men earned enough to support a family of four above the poverty line. Those decades of prosperity had favorable consequences. After 1970, the labor market soured.[10]

In our view, Detroit is slowly recovering economically. Although real earnings began to decline in the 1970s, the transformation of Detroit's labor market began after the Korean War economic boom ended. To boost productivity, unskilled jobs were cut, marginal automakers went bankrupt, and new factories in the outlying suburbs and in the South and West replaced the aging ones near downtown Detroit. The

FIGURE 3.12   *Percentage of Men Eighteen to Twenty-Four Neither*
Enrolled in School Nor in the Labor Force,
Metropolitan Detroit, 1940 to 1998

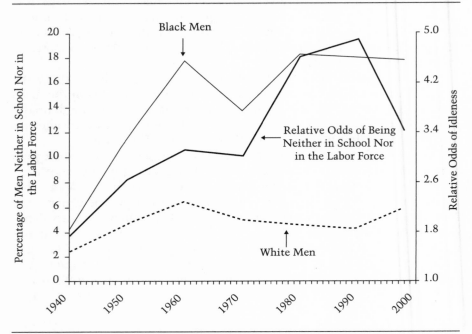

Source: Ruggles and Sobek 1997.

transformation accelerated with the energy crisis of the 1970s and continues. As figure 3.13 reports, only one-half of the African American
men in Detroit in the late 1990s earned enough to lift a family of four
above the poverty line. Changes in the labor market were generally beneficial to women, and particularly to African American women, since
there was a great expansion of employment in the central city of the
types of jobs black women filled, especially in the medical sector. As a
result, a growing share of women now earn enough to support a family
of four and, among women, the racial difference in this indicator is small.

Thomas Sugrue (1996, 4), the historian, overstates these labor market changes when he describes Detroit as being transformed from a magnet of opportunity to a reservation for the poor. Unfortunately that continues to be the popular perception.

What about the future of Detroit's labor market? The automotive
industry has been healthy in the 1990s, but the restructuring of employment will continue. Detroit may strengthen its position as the design,

FIGURE 3.13   *Percentage of Total Men and Women Aged*
                Twenty-Five to Sixty-Four Who Reported Earnings
                Greater than the Poverty Line for a Family of Four,
                1940 to 1997

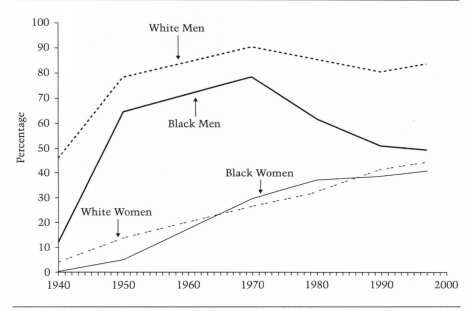

Source: Ruggles and Sobek 1997; U.S. Department of Commerce 1996, 1997, 1998.
Note: The poverty cutoff for a family or household of four in 1997 was $16,400. These estimates of earnings include self-employment earnings insofar as they were enumerated in censuses.

engineering, and administrative center for the worldwide automobile industry even as vehicle production continues to shift away from Michigan and toward places where labor costs are lower.

Figure 3.14 shows the total number of vehicles produced in the country since 1957 and the share made in Michigan. Overall production has been rising for a decade, but the percent built in the state fell from about 35 percent in the early 1980s to 25 percent in the late 1990s. Michigan's high wage and strong unions lead auto firms to build their new plants elsewhere.

What about racial differences in the labor market? Will they decline or persist? Will an economic boom eventually draw into the work force the large share of African American men who do not work and simultaneously reduce the black-white difference in unemployment? Blacks

FIGURE 3.14   *Total Vehicles Produced in the United States and the Percentage of Production in the State of Michigan*

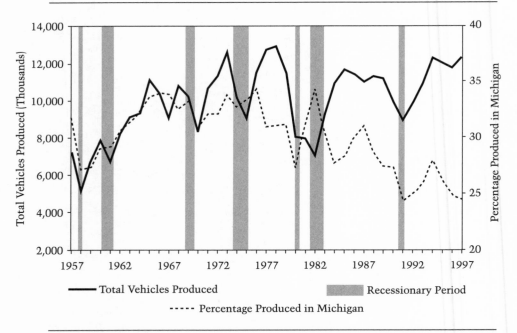

Source: Michigan Employment Security Commission 1997, table xiv-2.

continue to be handicapped by racial discrimination in labor and housing markets. While there is some evidence in this chapter of decreasing
labor market discrimination, the persistent upgrading of skill demands
on the part of employers present challenges for workers with no more
than a high school degree. Presumably, racial gaps in employment, occupational achievement and earnings would be lessened if blacks who enter Detroit's labor market in the future have higher educational attainment.

4

The Detroit Labor Market:
The Employers' Perspective

A NUMBER of major developments in Detroit's labor market adversely affected the employment and earnings of blacks, especially black men. The percentage of total employment accounted for by jobs in manufacturing—especially the automobile industry—and in blue-collar occupations has declined dramatically, while employment in the services and in white-collar occupations has grown rapidly. The percentage of total employment located in the city has also dropped off steeply in recent decades, even though most African Americans continue to live there.

These findings point to important changes taking place on the *demand* side of the labor market—that is, in the locations, characteristics, and behaviors of employers and jobs in metropolitan Detroit. To some extent, these changes are occurring everywhere in the United States, and have diminished the employment and earnings of less-educated workers, especially males, in all areas. But the decline in manufacturing jobs and in central-city employment appears to be far more dramatic in Detroit than in most other metropolises.[1]

These findings raise questions about the *current* demand for labor in the Detroit area. How do skills, race, and space interact on the demand side of the market? Have employers and jobs left the city and relocated to the suburbs even more rapidly than the population, thereby diminishing job opportunities for those who remain? If so, is this truer of some types of jobs than others? What kinds of jobs, and how many, are currently being filled that are available to less-skilled workers in either location? Do the differences in where whites and African Americans live affect the kinds of employers they apply to and where they are hired? How do these factors affect the ability of employers in various locations to find workers whose skills they demand?

This chapter presents data on the demand side of the Detroit labor market in the mid-1990s. First, we review the literature on recent changes in labor demand, and how they have affected the employment prospects of African Americans and other less-educated workers nationally. Next, we describe a survey recently administered to 800 employers in metropolitan Detroit.

Findings are presented on the current characteristics of jobs and employers in Detroit, focusing on comparisons between firms and jobs located in the central city and those in the suburbs. We analyze overall job availability, the kinds of jobs in each location, and the skill needs of employers. We also consider the extent to which employers in each location receive applications from black job seekers and the extent to which they hire them.

We document major imbalances on the demand side of the Detroit labor market, in terms of job location and availability by skill level. Given the patterns of where whites and blacks live and the attitudes that each group holds about the other (as laid out in chapter 8), as well as the generally lower levels of education and skill among black workers, the imbalances in labor demand imply major barriers in access to employment for black workers. These barriers contribute to the declining employment opportunities and low earnings of young and less-educated blacks.

Findings from Previous Studies of Labor Demand

What do we know about recent changes in labor demand, and how have they affected the employment and earnings of less-educated workers and blacks?[2] Which changes are especially relevant for understanding the declining employment outcomes described in the last chapter?

Among the major factors are the following:

Deindustrialization The employment of African American men in Detroit was heavily concentrated in the manufacturing sector. In 1970, 140,000 African American men were employed in metropolitan Detroit: 52 percent of them worked in durable goods manufacturing, and 94 percent of those men had blue-collar jobs. This concentration was typical in many other metropolitan areas of the Midwest. Durable manufacturing is also a sector in which blacks have traditionally been paid relatively well, as have been other less-educated workers (Krueger and Summers 1987). In the 1970s, black men in manufacturing earned 16 percent more in annual earnings than black men employed in other sectors, so these were among the best jobs available to African Americans at that time.

As employment in these sectors began to decline in the 1970s—a decline that accelerated in the 1980s and continues, though less drastically, today—blacks found it difficult to find employment in other sectors, especially at comparable wages (Wilson 1987; Kasarda 1989; Bound and Holzer 1993). The loss of manufacturing jobs appears to account for the fact that the relative earnings and employment losses experienced by blacks during the 1980s were more severe in the Midwest than in other regions (Bound and Freeman 1992).

Skill Mismatch   For a variety of reasons—international competition and technological changes among the most important—labor demand shifted away from industrial sectors in which few skills are needed and toward those where more skills are required (Katz and Murphy 1992; Levy and Murnane 1996; Berman, Bound, and Griliches 1994). Because the supply of skills in the workforce has not increased as rapidly as has the demand for them, a "mismatch" has resulted in which employment and earnings of less-educated workers deteriorated. Furthermore, as black workers are more concentrated among the less-educated than are whites, they have been particularly hurt by the declining demand for less-educated labor (Bound and Freeman 1992; Juhn, Murphy, and Pierce 1993; Neal and Johnson 1996).[3]

Spatial Mismatch   Another shift in demand away from black workers is due to the movement of employers out of inner-city areas and toward the suburbs. Because residential segregation and housing market discrimination made it difficult for African Americans to follow employers to the suburbs, and because inner-city blacks have limited access to the transportation or contacts needed for obtaining these jobs, a "mismatch" results between the locations of employers and those of central-city blacks.[4]

Racial Discrimination   Racial discrimination in employment declined quite dramatically in the late 1960s and early 1970s, following passage by the Johnson administration of the Civil Rights Act and the institution of affirmative action requirements for federal contractors (Freeman 1973; Heckman and Payner 1989; Leonard 1990).

But the recent "audit" studies conducted by researchers at the Urban Institute and elsewhere (for example, Fix and Struyk 1994)—in which pairs of African American and white job applicants with comparable credentials applied for jobs—suggest that racial discrimination remains a major employment barrier for blacks. In a Chicago test involving 197 matched pairs, 86 percent of the time *both* white and African American applicants were offered the job or both were turned down, but a white was offered a job and the black applicant was rejected twice as often as the black was hired and the white rejected. In a Washington,

D.C., case involving 241 tests, the white was offered the job and the African American was turned down about three times as often as the reverse (Heckman and Siegelman 1992, table 5.1). Although most tests suggested no racial discrimination, whites were favored when only one of the two testers received a job offer.

It is possible that racial discrimination against some groups of black men has worsened in recent years. This might be because of declining federal enforcement of antidiscrimination laws and affirmative action since the 1980s (Leonard 1990), or because of a growing perception among employers of deficiencies in the skill levels of black men and their attitudes toward work (Kirschenman and Neckerman 1991). The growing fear of crime and the increasing percentage of African American males with criminal records may also contribute to employer decisions to avoid hiring them (Freeman 1992). Whatever the reason, when employers hold such negative perceptions and attitudes, the relative employment and earnings of blacks are likely to suffer.

A Survey of Employers

To understand the effects of demand-side changes in the labor market, we need to understand the characteristics of jobs and employers: where they are located, what skills they seek, and whom they hire. But there is little information available about employers' unfilled jobs and hiring decisions.[5] To overcome this limitation, Harry Holzer developed and administered a unique survey to over 800 employers in the Detroit area between June 1992 and March 1993 as part of the Multi-City Study of Urban Inequality. The survey asked employers about their hiring needs and employment practices, including gross and net hiring behavior—that is hiring to cover turnover as well as to fill new jobs—the numbers and characteristics of currently vacant jobs; the characteristics of recently hired workers and the jobs they had been hired to fill; and general characteristics and demographics about the company. (See the appendix to this chapter for more information about the sample of firms drawn and response rates.)

Job Availability and Characteristics:
The Central City Versus the Suburbs

As we have seen, both people and jobs have left the city of Detroit in large numbers since 1950. How does the percentage of total metropolitan employment that remains in the central city compare with the percentage of metropolitan population that remains there?

In a recession, as during 1991 to 1992, there will not be enough jobs for all who seek work. Even in recovery, there might be a shortage of

TABLE 4.1   *Percentage of Metropolitan Employment and Population in the City of Detroit, 1960 to 1990*

Year	Percentage of Employment in Detroit	Percentage of Population in Detroit	Percentage Point Difference
1960	54	44	−10
1970	39	36	−3
1980	29	29	0
1990	21	26	5

Sources: U.S. Department of Commerce 1963, 1973, 1983, 1993.

employers and jobs in central-city Detroit relative to the population there, caused by the shift of firms to the suburbs and by large employment declines in the industries concentrated in the city. The "spatial mismatch" hypothesis would suggest that the lack of jobs in the city will lower overall employment levels.

Table 4.1 reports the percentages of both employment and population in the city, and the percentage point difference. In 1960, the city included 54 percent of employment and 44 percent of population, suggesting a large flow of commuters into the city. But the city did not hold on to its share of jobs: the fraction of employment located in the city declined more rapidly than did the population residing there between 1960 and 1990. And the fraction of the population located in the city today is higher than the fraction of overall employment located there. In most other large metropolitan areas, the opposite is true.[6] In metropolitan Detroit, there is much more reverse commuting from city to suburbs for employment than in most other metropolitan areas. So those without cars will have difficulty getting to suburban jobs, because there is no efficient public transportation system. Furthermore, if there were an excess supply of labor for the metropolitan area as a whole, the lack of job availability for central-city residents would be even more pronounced than these number suggest.

Table 4.2 presents information about the characteristics of the last job filled in each of the 800 firms surveyed. Given the size-weighting of the employer sample, the data provide an accurate representation of jobs available to current job seekers in the Detroit labor market.[7] The characteristics of jobs that we examine include their educational requirements, the occupations and industries in which they are located, and the starting pay rate.

Newly filled jobs in the central city are somewhat more concentrated at both the top and the bottom of the skill and earnings distributions, while those in the suburbs are more concentrated in the middle of those distributions. Thus, a slightly higher fraction of recently filled

TABLE 4.2   *Characteristics of Firms, Jobs, and Workers, by Location (in 1997 Dollars)*

	Central City	Suburbs
Percentage of most recently filled jobs requiring a college degree	22	20
Distribution of most recently filled jobs by occupation		
Professional, managerial, technical	25%	22%
Clerical	25	27
Sales	9	14
Craft	8	9
Operative	9	10
Laborer	5	4
Service	20	14
Distribution of most recently filled jobs by industry		
Construction	1%	3%
Transportation, communication, utilities	3	6
Wholesale Trade	6	7
Retail Trade	13	22
Finance, insurance, real estate	12	9
Services	53	33
Public	3	3
Manufacturing	9	18
Weekly wage (in 1997 dollars)	$405	$374
(Standard deviation)	(252)	(230)

Source: Author's tabulation of the Multi-City Study of Urban Inequality Employer Survey.
Note: Sample sizes for Central City and Suburbs are 168 and 599, respectively. "Central City" refers only to the city of Detroit; "Suburbs" covers the three-county metropolis.

jobs in the central city require a college degree (22 versus 20 percent); and larger fractions of city jobs are the unskilled service occupations (20 versus 14 percent) and in service industries (53 versus 33 percent) than in the suburbs. In contrast, blue-collar occupations and jobs in manufacturing (9 versus 18 percent) constitute larger fractions of jobs in the suburbs. Average weekly starting wages were about 8 percent higher for city jobs than for those in the ring: $405 versus $375.[8]

Manufacturing and retail trade establishments in the central city are also generally smaller than those in the suburbs, while service-sector establishments are much larger in the city. The median number of employees per manufacturing establishment was 90 in the suburbs and only 40 in the city; comparable numbers for the service establishments were 45 and 190, respectively. Thus, employment in the city is highly concentrated in large service establishments. Of the 108,000 persons working in service-sector industries in the city in 1990, 44 percent drew paychecks from hospitals or medical offices, 30 percent from schools or universities; and 7 percent from legal offices (U.S. Department of Commerce 1993).

Because the manufacturing sector has traditionally generated well-paying jobs for blacks and for less-educated workers, its relative disappearance from the city is noteworthy, and consistent with the shift away from such employment among younger black men that we documented with census data. This shrinkage of manufacturing jobs has contributed to lower employment among inner-city young African Americans, as well as to their lower earnings (Kasarda 1989; Bound and Holzer 1993).

In table 4.3 we consider various measures of skill requirements, such as tasks performed and criteria used in hiring the last worker for central-city and suburban firms. Many other studies of "skills mismatch" rely on educational attainment, since most data sets—including the census—do not report on specific skills of workers or requirements of firms. In contrast, our survey asked employers whether workers they hired recently perform each of a set of tasks on a daily basis. We inquired about simple cognitive and social tasks such as dealing with customers face to face or over the phone, reading or writing paragraphs, doing arithmetic, and using computers.

We also asked employers whether each of a set of hiring requirements is "absolutely necessary," "strongly preferred," "mildly preferred," or "not important." The requirements include having a high school diploma, previous experience in the specific line of work, references, and previous training or vocational education. We count these as "required" if employers claimed that they were either "absolutely necessary" or "strongly preferred."

This analysis is restricted to those jobs that do not require college degrees, in order to focus on the tasks demanded of workers who are most at risk of employment difficulties due to the restructuring of labor demand. We also look separately at the characteristics of blue-collar jobs, as these have traditionally been the jobs in which African Americans and less-educated males have been concentrated.

Table 4.3 reports modest differences in skill requirements between central-city and suburban jobs, with those in the city tending to be somewhat higher. But the key finding is that task requirements in each location are substantial. Employers have high expectations for their new workers. Dealing with customers in person is required in about 60 percent of suburban jobs and 70 percent of city jobs; reading paragraphs daily is required for about half of each; writing paragraphs daily is required for a quarter of suburban and a third of city jobs; and about two-thirds of all jobs require arithmetic on a daily basis. Furthermore, about

TABLE 4.3   *Task Performance and Hiring Criteria of Last Hired Worker in Jobs Without College Requirement*

	Central City	Suburbs
All jobs		
Percentage of workers who must daily		
Deal with customers face to face	72	62
Deal with customers over the phone	52	52
Read paragraphs	55	50
Write paragraphs	35	26
Do arithmetic	65	65
Use computers	39	46
None of the above	5	5
Percentage of employers who require		
High school diploma	74	70
Specific experience	69	53
References	61	64
Previous training or vocational education	40	29
None of the above	10	10
Neither tasks nor requirements	3	1
Blue-collar jobs		
Percentage of workers who must daily		
Deal with customers face to face	38	39
Deal with customers over the phone	21	22
Read paragraphs	42	47
Write paragraphs	19	15
Do arithmetic	55	61
Use computers	11	24
None of the above	14	10
Percentage of employers who require		
High school diploma	63	55
Specific experience	53	53
References	44	56
Previous training or vocational education	26	35
None of the above	16	14
Neither tasks nor requirements	9	1

Source: Author's tabulations of the Multi-City Study of Urban Inequality Employers Survey.
Note: Required characteristics are listed for firms where they are "absolutely necessary" or "strongly preferred."

40 percent of newly filled positions for non–college graduates require daily use of a computer. In all, only about 5 percent of all jobs involve *none* of these tasks on a daily basis.

Specific hiring requirements are also high. A high school diploma is required in almost three-fourths of these jobs; specific experience and references are each required in about 60 to 70 percent of the city jobs

and 50 to 60 percent of suburban jobs; and previous training or vocational education is required in 40 percent of city jobs and 30 percent of
suburban ones. Only about 10 percent of these jobs require none of these
credentials, and just 1 to 3 percent require neither the credentials nor
the tasks listed here.

When we focus only on blue-collar jobs, the daily performance of
tasks and use of hiring requirements are somewhat lower, as would be
expected. Nevertheless, employers are still quite demanding. The reading of paragraph-length material is required in over 40 percent of newly
filled blue-collar jobs, and arithmetic is used daily in 55 to 60 percent.
Specific experience is required in over half. Of all newly filled blue-collar jobs, only about 1 in 8 required none of the tasks listed and only 1 in
10 required none of the credentials at the time of hiring.

Among young black men—aged twenty to twenty-nine—living in
Detroit in 1990, 42 percent of those lacking a high school diploma reported no employment at all in the previous year. Among those with a
high school diploma (but no further education), 27 percent did not work
in 1989. The expectations of employers help explain these high numbers. A young person lacking numerical skills, having difficulty reading,
and having no specific job training or history of employment will not
easily find even a blue-collar job in the city.

The blue-collar jobs in the suburbs require even higher skills on
average than those in the central city. In addition, these jobs are farther
away from the areas where most African American workers live. This
contributes to an inability of many blacks to obtain them.

Employer attitudes about hiring, such as a strong reluctance to hire
anyone whom they suspect of having a criminal record, no doubt reduce
the availability of jobs to less-educated black males as well. Only about
one-third of employers hiring for blue-collar or service jobs would be
willing to put someone with a criminal record on the payroll (Holzer
1996). Because most employers do not actually check criminal backgrounds of workers, the mere suspicion of such activity may be sufficient to keep someone who is qualified for a job from being offered it.[9]
The data in Table 4.3 are consistent with the hypothesis that employers
have been increasing skill requirements and reducing their demand for
less-skilled workers, even in jobs that do not require a college degree.[10]
They also suggest limited job availability for those who lack basic skills,
such as high school dropouts or welfare recipients.

To further investigate this issue, we ran simulations in which we
matched job seekers from the household survey data into jobs from our
employer survey data on the basis of their educational credentials, occupational experience, and past performance of tasks, as well as their place
of residence, access to an automobile, and race. The result was that a

significant fraction of job seekers in Detroit (9 to 20 percent) would have difficulty being matched to any job, and these fractions are particularly high among African Americans, welfare recipients, and high school dropouts.[11] The availability of any kind of work seems quite limited for the most disadvantaged residents of Detroit (Holzer and Danziger 2000).

Other data in the employer survey indicate that blacks are less likely to be hired for jobs that require greater numbers of either tasks or credentials. Specifically, African Americans were much less likely than whites to be hired for jobs requiring significant reading or writing, arithmetic, or specific experience at the time of hiring (Holzer 1996). We will address this issue more fully in the next chapter. Here we consider the implications of these employer requirements for their ability to hire and retain qualified workers.

Job Vacancies and Durations

An important way to assess job availability is to estimate the vacancy rate among jobs in each location, and the characteristics of vacant jobs. Job vacancy rates are almost always lower than unemployment rates at both the aggregate and local levels (Abraham 1983; Holzer 1989), indicating that unemployed workers must vie for available jobs. A sample of vacant jobs at any point is also more likely to contain an oversampling of hard-to-fill jobs than is a sample of recently filled positions, and thus might exaggerate the skill demands or durations of current job openings.[12]

Nevertheless, a comparison of vacancy rates and vacant job characteristics across metropolitan locations, along with comparisons to the respective unemployment rates in each, sheds lights on questions of job availability and on mismatches between the supply and demand sides of the labor market. In particular, if relatively high unemployment and low vacancy rates are found in the same locations, this implies that a shortage of jobs relative to people is the primary cause of the unemployment. If relatively high vacancy rates accompany high unemployment rates, this suggests a major role for structural imbalances or mismatches between the characteristics of available jobs and people.

Table 4.4 presents data on job vacancies in the city of Detroit and its suburban ring. We present the overall vacancy rate and the rates for three major industrial groupings: manufacturing, retail trade, and services. We also consider the durations of hiring for recently filled jobs in the same locations and industries, which indicates the extent to which employers had difficulty filling available jobs.

The table shows that the overall job vacancy rate in central-city Detroit is 3 percent, while that in the suburbs is 4 percent. Both rates are substantially lower than the 1992 unemployment rates of 8.9 per-

TABLE 4.4   *Job Vacancies by Location*

	Central City	Suburbs
Vacancy rate[a]		
Total	3%	4%
Manufacturing	0	3
Retail trade	6	5
Services	3	3
Duration of hiring (weeks)[b]		
Total	3.93	1.80
Manufacturing	4.07	1.65
Retail trade	1.47	2.39
Services	5.29	1.56

Source: Author's tabulations of the Multi-City Study of Urban Inequality Employers Survey.
[a]Vacancy rate is defined out of total number of jobs (vacant or filled, including temps and contract jobs in the latter).
[b]Durations are measured in weeks.

cent for the metro area and 17.8 percent for the city. In other words, the number of unfilled jobs was much smaller than the number of men and women seeking work. These vacancy rates are consistent with those observed in earlier studies (for example, Abraham 1983; Holzer 1989). It is noteworthy that the job vacancy rates in the city are not substantially lower than in the ring, despite the much higher numbers of unemployed people in the city and the decline of overall employment there.

By industry, we find relatively low vacancy rates in manufacturing firms in both places, somewhat lower in the central city than in the suburbs. Vacancy rates in the service, and especially retail trade, sectors are higher in the central city. The higher vacancy rates reflect higher turnover rates (and low wages) in these sectors, as well as higher net employment growth.

We also find much longer durations of hiring in the central city than in the suburbs, especially in the service sector. It takes almost four weeks to fill a central-city vacancy, compared to less than two weeks for a service-sector job in the ring. Within the service-sector industries, the longer hiring durations in the city are particularly striking. That is, service-sector jobs in the city typically remain vacant for more than five weeks, reflecting, undoubtedly, the high skill levels now required in this industrial sector. This city-suburban difference in hiring durations suggests that central-city employers have greater difficulty filling vacant jobs than do their suburban counterparts.

Even when the jobs do not require a high level of education or skills, employers in Detroit have difficulty finding workers who are acceptable to them. Of course, the extent to which this difficulty reflects their own discriminatory judgments—as opposed to real deficiencies in the characteristics, attitudes, and work experience of applicants—remains unclear, though it is likely that both factors are at work.[13]

Even though city and suburban vacancy rates are roughly comparable, hiring durations for central-city jobs are higher than for suburban jobs, despite the greater number of available workers in the city. This suggests a mismatch in the city between the needs of employers and the characteristics and skills of available workers.

Job Applicant Versus Hire Rate

Differences in terms of the kinds of jobs attained and the earnings of African Americans and whites by location raise important questions about whether our results are determined primarily by the differential choices of black workers about where and what kinds of work to look for. Or do employers determine them when they make hiring decisions? The residential distribution of blacks in metropolitan Detroit has been strongly influenced by housing market discrimination. That discrimination, we will show, also influences the geographic areas in which African Americans and whites seek employment.

Now we consider how job applicant rates from black males, black females, and whites vary across firms and geographic locations.

The data in table 4.5 give us excellent measures of the supply of and demand for black labor. The fractions of applicants who are black males and black females give us measures of the relative supply of labor from each group; the ratio of hires to applicants provides an index of relative demand for each group, conditional on the skills and characteristics of the applicants.[14]

Overall, black applicants constitute about 53 percent of total applicants in the central city (about 27 percent and 26 percent from males and females, respectively) and 27 percent of applicants in the suburbs (15 + 12 percent). An employment-weighted average of these numbers suggests that blacks constitute a larger share of job applicants in metropolitan Detroit than their population figures would suggest, especially in the suburbs. Thus, an unwillingness of blacks to seek and apply for work can be ruled out as a major source of their employment difficulties. Of course, the applicant rates among blacks are likely to be higher than their share of the population at least partly because of unemployment rates that are more than twice those of whites.

The relative demand for blacks, as represented by the ratio of hires to applicants, presents the following striking findings:

TABLE 4.5   *Application and New Hire Rates of Black Males and Females, as Reported by Employers, by Location*

	Central City	Suburbs
Percentage of applicants who are		
Black males	27	15
Black females	26	12
Whites	47	73
Percentage of new hires who are		
Black males	22	9
Black females	32	11
Whites	46	80
Ratio of new hires to applicants		
Black males	.81	.60
Black females	1.23	.92
Whites	.98	1.10

Source: Author's tabulations of the Multi-City Study for Urban Inquality Employers Survey.

(1) blacks are hired with less frequency than they apply in both city and the suburbs;

(2) this is true for black females but even more so for black males in both locations;

(3) it is truer for both genders in the suburbs than in the city.[15]

For males, the ratio is .81 in the city and only .60 in the suburbs; for females, 1.23 and .92, respectively. Ratios for whites are roughly 1 or higher in both places.[16] (Because we are describing group data, ratios may exceed 1. For example, if black women made up one-quarter of a firm's applicants but 31 percent of their new hires, the ratio for this group would be 1.23.)

There is a pervasive pattern of lower relative demand for black labor—especially black males—than for white labor, and lower relative demand for black males in the suburbs than in the city. Whether these relative preferences for white employees are due to discrimination, as opposed to legitimate business decisions based on skill differences by race and gender, cannot be determined with these data. However, there is no evidence of higher skill needs overall among suburban employers relative to central-city ones, as shown in table 4.3. This implies greater discriminatory barriers facing blacks with regard to employment in the suburbs.[17] The relatively greater employer demand in both locations for black females relative to black males is consistent either with greater skill deficits or attitudinal problems among the latter. Because black women and black men attend the same schools, it is unlikely that em-

TABLE 4.6   *Applicants and New Hire Rates of Black Males and Black Females and Whites, by Location and Industry*

	Manufacturing	Retail Trade	Services
Central city			
Percentage of applicants who are			
Black males	36	44	21
Black females	30	54	22
Whites	34	2	57
Ratio of new hires to applicants			
Black males	1.58	.57	.90
Black females	.60	1.39	1.36
Whites	.74	0	.89
Suburbs			
Percentage of applicants who are			
Black males	15	17	10
Black females	12	12	12
Whites	73	71	78
Ratio of new hires to applicants			
Black males	.47	.65	.80
Black females	.50	1.08	1.08
Whites	1.19	1.07	1.01

Source: Author's tabulations of the Multi-City Study of Urban Inequality Employers Survey.

ployers are basing their decisions to hire black women and not black men on skills learned in the classroom. More likely, employers are more fearful of hiring black men than black women or believe that customers and co-workers will be more upset by the presence of black male employees than black women (Kirschenman 1991; Newman 1999, chap. 8).

Table 4.5 presents information about rates of application and new hiring for blacks in the city and suburbs. Based on the different skill and gender mix in employment by industry, we expect variation in both applicant and hiring rates for African Americans across different types of jobs. We therefore analyze these rates by industry, as well as by city or suburban location, in table 4.6; and by more detailed geographic locations, using Detroit and nine specific suburban municipalities in which firms are located, in table 4.7. This table also reports characteristics of each municipality, such as its distance from downtown Detroit and the fraction of its population that is white, as well as the estimated percent of firms' customers who are black.[18]

Results in table 4.6 show substantial variation in black application and hire rates across industries and locations. In the central city, blacks constitute virtually all applicants to retail trade establishments, revealing that neither central-city nor suburban whites apply for those few retail trade jobs in the city. Blacks also constitute a large majority of applicants to manufacturing establishments (66 percent) in the city and almost half of all applicants to service establishments (43 percent). This latter figure indicates that whites apply more frequently to service establishments in the central city (for example, hospitals and law firms) that are likely to offer many highly paid professional/technical or clerical jobs. Black males apply more frequently than females for jobs in manufacturing, while the opposite is more common in retail trade. In contrast, blacks account for just about one-quarter of applicants in the suburbs in every industrial sector.

As for hire rates relative to the pools of African American applicants, they are well below 1 for black males in all industries except manufacturing in the city, and lower in the suburbs than in the city in most areas. For females, the ratios are more frequently at or above 1. Employers are more likely to hire black male applicants than black females for those manufacturing jobs that remain in the city, while they are much more likely to hire black female applicants in retail trade and the services. Holding industry constant, suburban employers are less likely to hire black applicants than are city employers. Even in manufacturing, the ratio of black hires to applicants in suburban establishments is low.[19]

Some of the differences in hiring patterns across industries and location might reflect various demand-side differences—for example, in tasks performed, specific experience needed, and relative wages—as well as discrimination. For instance, the lower ratio of black hires to applicants of suburban manufacturing firms relative to their city counterparts might reflect the relatively higher skill demands on suburban blue-collar jobs (see table 4.3, bottom panel). On the other hand, the much lower ratio of hires to applicants for black males relative to females in suburban retail trade and service establishments might result from employers believing that African American men generally lack the soft skills required in today's labor market.

We now consider more detailed geographic differences in black application and hiring rates. Table 4.7 presents information about ten specific areas within metropolitan Detroit and reports substantial variation in the tendency of blacks to apply for jobs. African Americans sought employment very frequently in the Oak Park/Ferndale area and in Southfield, and to some extent in Royal Oak, Dearborn, and Livonia. In contrast, their application rates in places like Warren, Farmington Hills, Troy, and the Downriver area were quite low.

To some extent, application rates tend to decline with distances from the city of Detroit. Farmington Hills and Troy are relatively far away, and employers there seldom see black job applicants. Application rates from blacks tend to be higher in those suburbs, like Southfield,

TABLE 4.7   Application and Employment Rates of Black Males, Black Females, and Whites for Selected Locations

	Detroit	Southfield	Warren	Troy	Down-river	Royal Oak	Oak Park/ Ferndale	Farmington Hills	Livonia	Dearborn
Percentage of applicants who are										
Black males	32	28	10	13	12	19	35	11	16	26
Black females	33	22	6	8	9	19	27	4	22	17
Whites	35	50	84	79	79	62	38	85	62	56
Percentage of new hires who are										
Black males	22	12	9	3	7	10	13	3	4	11
Black females	31	14	7	5	5	7	18	5	13	10
Whites	47	74	84	92	88	83	69	92	83	79
Ratio of new hires to applicants										
Black males	.68	.42	.92	.25	.57	.55	.36	.28	.25	.43
Black females	.94	.64	1.20	.66	.55	.34	.61	1.14	.59	.59
Whites	1.34	1.49	1.00	1.16	1.11	1.34	1.83	1.09	1.34	1.39
Distance from downtown Detroit	—	13.75	10.63	12.50	14.58	11.25	9.31	20.00	17.50	9.11
Percentage of residents who are white		22	70	99	99	92	80	98	100	99
Percentage of customers who are black	42	42	23	13	14	9	40	19	29	20

Source: Author's tabulation of the Multi-City Study of Urban Inequality Employers Survey.

where more blacks live locally. For example, even though Warren is no farther from downtown Detroit than is Southfield or Oak Park, it receives dramatically fewer applications from blacks.

When the fraction of customers who are African American in an area is higher, black application rates tend to be higher as well. A higher black customer base might signal perceived friendliness to or comfort among blacks in an area, or perhaps more information about the jobs there.[20] If employers perceive that their customers prefer employees of the same race as themselves, they may hire these applicants more frequently as well. This appears to be the case in jobs with a high degree of contact with customers, such as the sales occupations (Holzer and Ihlanfeldt 1998).

Somewhat surprisingly, the likelihood that black applicants are hired is relatively high among Warren's employers. This may reflect the fact that only very highly qualified blacks or those with connections apply for jobs in Warren. It may also be because many employers in Warren are in the vehicle industry, so they are particularly aware of the importance of Title VII and possible lawsuits about employment discrimination. In any event, these data suggest that there may be some scope for raising black employment rates in parts of the metro area by raising the rates at which they apply for jobs there.

Conclusion

The four hypotheses described at the start of this chapter regarding characteristics and trends on the demand side of the labor market—deindustrialization, skills mismatch, spatial mismatch, and racial discrimination—all contribute to the poor employment and earnings of less-educated blacks in Detroit. Other factors, such as the involvement of young African American males in illegal activities, along with a strong employer aversion to hiring anyone whom they suspect of such participation, may contribute as well to the difficulties young blacks have in obtaining work.

Our survey findings imply that African Americans face a real quandary in terms of where to seek employment. There appear to be substantial imbalances within the central-city labor market, in terms of job versus availability of people, or workers' skills versus employers' needs. In other words, there appears to be both a relative lack of jobs in the city and a major mismatch between the jobs that are available and the skills or behaviors of city workers who can fill them.

In contrast, the suburban labor market may hold more potential for black workers from the inner city—in terms of greater availability of jobs, especially those in manufacturing that require more limited skills but pay relatively well. But the barriers in the suburbs to African Americans are more likely to be "space" and "race" as well as skills. Evidence of discriminatory employer behavior is stronger at the hiring stage in the suburbs, and factors such as distance or perceptions of friendliness toward blacks seem to limit the tendency of blacks to apply to many occupations or locations within the suburban market.

Policy implications will be discussed in the final chapter. It seems safe to conclude, however, that overall job availability, as well as the skills and behaviors of black workers in the inner city, should be a major focus of concern, as should their access to suburban employers and the hiring behaviors of these employers once they receive applications from blacks.

Appendix: Sampling Issues in the Employer Survey

Detroit area employers were selected from samples that were drawn from two sources: a listing based on telephone directories, compiled and updated by Survey Sampling Incorporated (SSI); and a listing compiled from the households surveyed in the 1992 Detroit Area Survey (DAS). While the latter have the advantage of being matched to household respondents, they would not alone have generated a sample of sufficient size to conduct our analysis.[21]

The establishments from the SSI listing represent a stratified random sample based on employment size categories that were drawn to approximate the actual distribution of employees across establishment sizes in the labor force. This was done to ensure that we had enough medium and large firms, which are few in actual number but account for large fractions of overall employment. In contrast, the firms drawn from the household sample represent a sampling of firms that is already weighted by employment among the DAS respondents.[22]

The SSI establishments were also limited to those who had hired non–college graduate workers in the past several years, while the DAS firms included those that have hired in the relevant occupational group—that is, the occupation of the respondent in the DAS. Sampling weights have been computed to correct only for the nonrandomness of respondents in the DAS and for the omission of employers of college graduates in the SSI.[23]

Overall response rates were roughly 65 percent for firms that had made it through our initial screening process. Successful screenings consisted of establishments with which a contact had been made and that had hired in the relevant occupational category in the recent past. Checks for biases in response rates among screened firms were made by testing differences in these rates across variables such as industry, firm size, and location that were available for both respondents and nonrespondents in the SSI listings. Few statistically significant differences in response rates were observed across these categories, and most of those observed were not large (Holzer 1996, app.). The distributions of occupations and industries in the sample are also consistent with those observed in census data for metropolitan Detroit. Therefore, the establishments in this survey constitute a representative sample of establishments for these areas.

5

The Detroit Labor Market:
The Workers' Perspective

THIS CHAPTER focuses on the extent to which the continuing concentration of the African American population in Detroit, while
jobs relocate to the suburbs, contributes to the deteriorating
employment outcomes of black residents in the city. How does the
location of one's residence influence the location of one's job search?
Do blacks who seek and find suburban jobs have relatively better employment outcomes than those working in the city? If so, why don't
African Americans search more frequently or more intensely for suburban work? Answers to these questions help explain why a spatial mismatch between black central-city residents and suburban jobs may persist over time, despite strong economic incentives that should induce
African Americans to seek and find suburban jobs, even if they do not
live there.

We also investigate several other issues related to searching for employment. For instance, Lawrence Mead (1992) contends that low black
employment rates are largely due to a lack of commitment to work. In
his view, unemployment and nonparticipation in the labor force may be
high among African Americans because

- their expectations regarding acceptable wages are higher than the
  wage offers they obtain (Holzer 1986);
- relatively high incomes and status can be gained from their participation in criminal activity; and
- African Americans may be "discouraged" or "defeated" because they
  do not expect a job search to yield job offers (Mead 1992).

The Detroit Area Survey contains extensive data on the locations of
both jobs and residences for whites and blacks, and also data on the
search patterns of prospective workers, which provide important and innovative information about these issues.

TABLE 5.1   *Locations of Residence and Workplace of Detroit-Area Workers, 1990*

Percentage of Employed Persons Who Work in	White Residents			Black Residents		
	City	Suburbs	Total	City	Suburbs	Total
City of Detroit	47	12	14	59	22	52
Three-county suburban ring	51	88	86	39	73	46
Outside three-county metropolis	2	< 1	< 1	2	5	2
Total	100	100	100	100	100	100
Number of employed persons (thousands)	82	1,303	1,384	234	61	295

Source: U.S. Department of Commerce 1993.

Residential and Workplace
Locations of Detroit Residents

We begin by comparing the tendencies of whites and blacks to live in the city of Detroit with their tendencies to work there, and how these two factors interact. Then we compare the characteristics of jobs and workers in each location, and how they differ by race and gender.

Table 5.1 shows place of residence by place of work for whites and blacks in 1990.[1] Residential and work patterns are highly correlated for each racial group—in other words, city residents are much more likely to work in the city than are suburban residents and vice versa. Among whites living in the city, about half held a job in the city and one-half in the ring, but among whites who lived in the ring, only one in eight worked in Detroit.

The overwhelming majority of whites and nearly half of African Americans worked in the ring, reflecting the long-term trend toward the suburbanization of employment. Differences in residential location account for a substantial part of the greater tendency of blacks to work in the city. However, within each residential area, blacks are more likely than whites to work in the city. For example, among city residents, 47 percent of whites but 59 percent of blacks held city jobs. These results are consistent with evidence presented earlier that fewer African Americans work in the suburbs, partly because employers there receive fewer applications from them, and partly because these firms hire a smaller percentage of black applicants.

About half of the central-city residents engage in reverse commuting to suburban jobs. But relatively small fractions of suburbanites commute to the city: 12 percent of employed whites and 22 percent of blacks. These data confirm not only the declining fraction of metropolitan jobs located in city but also the much greater dependence of blacks than whites on this dwindling pool of jobs.

Table 5.2 presents information for employed adults and for each racial group separately, about the characteristics of workers and their jobs, classified by job location. We consider weekly and hourly earnings, the educational attainment of workers, their occupational and industrial distributions, and two characteristics of commuting: the percent who use their cars and vans to get to work and the mean commuting time.

These data confirm several findings regarding characteristics of city and suburban jobs noted in the previous chapter. For instance, weekly and hourly wages were higher in the city. Educational attainment among employees is generally higher for those who work in the city, especially when we consider those who have graduate degrees; and the fraction of workers in professional or managerial occupations is considerably higher as well.

Clerical and sales jobs made up a larger share of the suburban than the city workforce (32 versus 16 percent), whereas the concentration of blue-collar jobs there is a bit higher as well. Finally, the share of total jobs in manufacturing was also higher in the suburbs than in the city (29 versus 16 percent), while those in the services are concentrated in the city (51 versus 33 percent). Among service occupations and service industries, the story is very different. The *service occupations* tend to have few educational requirements and generally pay little, since they include jobs such as waiter, counter help, cook, bartender, and building cleaner. *Service industries*, on the other hand, often demand a highly trained workforce, since this sector includes hospitals, clinics, law offices, educational institutions, and consulting firms.

City-suburban differences in worker characteristics vary dramatically by race. Earnings are typically higher for African Americans employed in the suburbs than for those working in the city. For instance, blacks working in suburban jobs earned $855 per week, whereas those working in the city earned only $723 per week (in 1997 dollars). Similar results can be found with respect to educational attainment of black workers and the occupations in which they are employed; that is, those working in the suburbs have higher levels of education and are more likely to work in professional or managerial occupations than are central-city workers.

The opposite, however, is true for whites: central-city workers typ-

TABLE 5.2 *Characteristics of Employed Persons Aged Twenty-Five to Sixty-Four in 1990, by Race and Workplace Location*

Characteristics of Jobs	Employed in City of Detroit			Employed in Suburban Ring		
	Total	Whites	Blacks	Total	Whites	Blacks
Mean wages in 1997 dollars						
Hourly	$19.31	$20.97	$16.85	$19.44	$19.65	$17.22
Weekly	$826.00	$919.00	$682.00	$844.00	$855.00	$723.00
Educational attainment						
High school dropout	12%	11%	14%	11%	9%	19%
High school diploma	51	47	57	55	56	58
Associate's degree	8	8	9	9	9	9
Bachelor's degree	16	20	11	16	17	10
Graduate degree	13	14	9	9	9	4
Total	100%	100%	100%	100%	100%	100%
Occupational distribution						
Professional, managerial and technical	37%	42%	29%	34%	35%	22%
Clerical	17	16	23	16	16	19
Sales	8	8	4	12	12	7
Crafts	11	13	7	13	14	9
Operatives	12	11	13	12	11	24
Laborers	3	2	3	3	2	4
Service occupations	13	8	20	10	9	15
Total	100%	100%	100%	100%	100%	100%
Industrial distribution						
Construction	4%	5%	3%	5%	5%	2
Manufacturing, durable goods	15	18	11	25	24	32
Manufacturing, nondurable goods	5	6	3	4	4	3
Transportation, communication	9	9	10	6	6	9
Wholesale trade	4	5	2	5	5	4
Retail trade	8	9	7	14	15	12
Finance, insurance, and real estate	7	7	7	6	6	7
Service industries	39	34	44	30	31	26
Public-sector employment	9	6	13	3	3	4
Total	100%	100%	100%	100%	100%	100%
Journey to work						
Uses own car or van	89%	94%	83%	96%	96%	93%
Mean one-way commute time (minutes)	28	31	24	25	24	26

Source: U.S. Department of Commerce 1993.

ically have higher earnings, educational levels, and occupational status than whites who work in the suburbs. Thus, gaps in earnings between whites and blacks employed in the city were quite high, while the earnings of blacks working in the ring are more nearly comparable to those of whites employed there. For example, black/white weekly earnings ratio is .74 in the city and .85 in the suburbs.

The pattern of higher earnings for whites working in the city, but higher earnings for African Americans working in the suburbs, has been documented previously.[2] Data on relative educational attainment, occupations, and industries of employment in table 5.2 suggest four possible causal forces at work:

(1)   Because most African Americans live in the city and most whites live in the suburbs, each group must be compensated for time spent commuting to the more distant location. Thus, white suburban residents earn a premium for working in the city and black central-city residents earn one for working in the suburbs;

(2)   Because African Americans are "crowded" into the city by discriminatory suburban housing and labor market barriers, there is an excess supply of central-city black labor relative to available jobs, which depresses wages. In contrast, an excess demand for whites relative to available jobs for them in the city raises their wages (Hirsch and MacPherson 1994);

(3)   The quality of black workers who either live in or commute to work in the suburbs is higher than that of those who stay and work in the central city, whereas the opposite is true for whites;

(4)   The quality of *jobs* to which blacks have access in the suburbs exceeds the quality of those available to them in the city.

There is evidence in our data supporting each hypothesis. For instance, earnings rise with commute times for whites but not for blacks.[3] For each additional ten minutes of commuting time (in each direction), wages for whites increased by 5 percent per hour, whereas for blacks they remained essentially unchanged.[4] Indeed, the average commute time of central-city black workers was only seven minutes shorter than that of whites who worked there, even though the earnings of the former are much lower than those of the latter.

The concentration of African Americans in central-city workplaces certainly suggests "crowding" there, thus contributing to lower wages. The fact that automobile transportation is highly correlated with the likelihood of blacks being employed in the suburbs suggests that this crowding is linked to differential access to suburban jobs. The simultaneous effects of housing segregation and labor market discrimination are thus reinforced by transportation factors.[5]

The relatively high educational levels of black suburban workers reflect two factors:

- the higher education levels of black suburban residents relative to central-city residents; and

- the fact that, among central-city residents, higher-skilled blacks are more likely to obtain jobs in the suburbs either because they "self-select" into such jobs or because suburban employers are more likely to hire them.

Our data support both interpretations. Census data report that central-city whites had less educational attainment than white suburbanites did.[6] The higher education attainment of whites who work in the city is driven entirely by the higher attainments of those commuting from the suburbs relative to those working there.

Finally, differences in the characteristics of city and suburban jobs appear to contribute to the observed outcomes in table 5.2 as well. As noted, manufacturing and/or blue-collar jobs are more concentrated in the suburbs than in the city, as are clerical and sales jobs; whereas jobs requiring at least a college diploma are more concentrated in the city, as are low-wage jobs in the service occupations.

Whites capture the vast majority of jobs at the top end of the educational and occupational distributions in the city. And among whites who work in the city, more than four in ten have managerial, professional, or technical jobs. Similar percentages of black and white suburban workers are employed in mid-level white-collar and blue-collar jobs and in manufacturing jobs. But a greater percentage of metro-area whites than blacks work in the suburbs, thus allowing them to capture more of these types of jobs as well. In contrast, African Americans are overrepresented among the lower-wage blue-collar and service occupations—jobs that remain in the city.

All four of these factors contribute to the geographic pattern of racial earnings differentials observed for blacks and whites in table 5.2, and this finding is supported by regression analyses. The characteristics of workers and jobs account for some, but not all, of these geographic earnings differentials by race. In regression equations that have weekly earnings as the dependent variable, the inclusion of controls for worker education, occupation and industry reduces the positive coefficient on central-city workplace location for whites, but it does not totally disappear. Net of other characteristics determining wages, whites working in the city earn more than whites working in the ring. The same is true for the negative coefficient on city workplace location for African Americans.[7]

The higher education and skill levels of suburban whites enable them to obtain most of the high-paying jobs in the city, even though few live there. Highly educated people are generally well informed about employment opportunities throughout the entire metropolis and have little difficulty commuting to good jobs. In 1990, 94 percent of white suburban households reported ownership of at least one car or van, while two-thirds owned two or more. Whites can choose both where to live and where to work in ways that maximize their overall incomes and their personal preferences with regard to housing amenities.

In contrast, less-educated black city residents have difficulty gaining access to the better-paying jobs requiring less education, which are more heavily concentrated in the suburbs, than do less-educated whites who live in those suburbs. This differential access appears to be due to "space"—that is, the transportation and informational problems associated with their residential concentration in the central city. In 1990, 35 percent of the city's black households reported no car or van. It is also due to "race"—that is, apparent discrimination in both the housing and labor markets.[8]

Even the skills and employability of central-city African Americans are limited by residential segregation, which reduces the quality of their schooling and increases their "social isolation."[9] Thus, the housing patterns and racial attitudes of Detroit area residents limit the labor market opportunities of less-educated blacks in many ways.[10]

Given the relative paucity of good central-city jobs for less-educated workers, and the costs and barriers they face in gaining suburban employment, it is important to analyze how frequently African Americans look for work in the suburban labor market. Table 5.3 presents information about whether whites and blacks have ever searched for work in each of five local areas within the metropolis. Job search questions were asked of all respondents who had searched at any time in the ten years prior to the 1992 Detroit Area Study. Results are presented for all white and black job seekers, as well as for subgroups of each—younger (below age thirty-five) versus older workers, those living in Detroit versus those living elsewhere, those living in each of the particular cities being considered, and those with and without access to cars during their search.

The key finding is that African Americans are much more likely than whites to search in the city of Detroit, and are more likely to search in the city than anywhere else. About three-quarters of blacks but only 40 percent of whites had searched in Detroit. The differences hold within all subgroups of whites and blacks as well, and are even more pronounced among the young. Only among the small fraction of

TABLE 5.3 Percentage of Workers Who Have Searched in Each Area During Previous Ten Years

Access	Total	Young	Old	Living in Detroit	Living in Suburbs	Living in Specific Location	Not Living in Specific Location	Has Access to Car	No Access to Car
Whites									
Detroit	42	39	45	72	39	72	39	44	53
Southfield	40	38	42	48	39	100	39	43	30
Troy	43	48	38	35	44	84	41	47	22
Warren	34	32	35	40	33	94	31	37	30
Downriver suburbs	24	26	23	30	24	84	20	27	17
Sample size	398	186	212	46	352	—	—	299	8
Blacks									
Detroit	73	83	62	77	59	77	59	74	75
Southfield	56	66	46	54	67	75	55	65	43
Troy	31	34	27	31	33	—	31	39	13
Warren	30	35	24	28	36	—	30	38	15
Downriver suburbs	29	25	34	26	40	—	29	33	22
Sample Size	377	190	185	339	36	—	—	223	92

Source: University of Michigan, Detroit Area Study 1992.
Note: These data refer to the residents of the three-county metropolis and to persons who searched for a job within the last decade.

whites who actually live in Detroit was the tendency to search there about the same as for blacks. City of residence clearly influences where people look for work.

African Americans were somewhat more likely than whites to have searched in Southfield and the Downriver suburbs, but somewhat less likely to have searched in Warren and especially Troy. Over half of blacks searched in Southfield, whereas less than a third ever searched in the other three suburban locations. Among younger blacks, the tendency to search in the Downriver area, where there are manufacturing plants, was somewhat lower than it was for older blacks, whereas their tendency to search in Southfield, Troy, and Warren was greater.

For those living in the suburban ring, residence also affected job search. Thus, for both blacks and whites, residents in each specific location were far more likely to search where they live than are those living elsewhere. All of the entries in column 6 are above 80 percent for whites, except for Detroit, at 72 percent. About three-fourths of blacks living in Detroit or Southfield have searched where they live. White residents of the city of Detroit differed from African Americans who lived there in an important way: they were more likely to have looked for work in the outer suburbs.

Finally, access to cars during the search period raised the tendency of African Americans to seek employment in the suburbs. However, there is a puzzling finding: even blacks with access to cars had search probabilities under 40 percent in Troy, Warren, and the Downriver area.[11]

Why job seekers search in some areas but not others may involve factors beyond access to cars and place of residence. Respondents who reported not having searched in a particular location were asked why not, and their responses were coded into several categories.

The predominant reason (46 percent) given for not searching in any area was travel distance or transportation problems. This is consistent with our demonstration that city of residence strongly predicts where people search. About 14 percent of respondents stated that they just did not bother to search in an area, which suggests to us some combination of a lack of information and distance. Ten percent of the answers stated that the jobs in an area or the employers there were not appropriate for the skills of the respondent. About 9 percent of the reasons indicated that the respondent believed no jobs were available there. Four percent of the answers stated that no search was carried out because of "crime in the area" or because the person would not feel safe there. These were primarily suburban whites who refused to look for a job in the city. That is, 16 percent of the whites who did not look for work in Detroit gave a fear of crime as their reason.

The tendency to mention travel and distance as the predominant reasons for not searching does not explain why much larger fractions of blacks sought work in Southfield than in Warren or the Downriver suburbs. The latter are geographically close to black neighborhoods of Detroit. More African Americans live in Southfield than in the other areas, but it is a small fraction of all metropolitan blacks—only 2.4 percent—who live there. Residential differences thus cannot fully explain the geographic search differential among blacks. Personal networks and contacts between African Americans living in Southfield and those living in Detroit probably account for some of the tendency of blacks to seek employment in Southfield.

It is also probable that African Americans feel more welcome in some areas than in others, perhaps due to the great reputations of these areas, as well as their own experiences there. People are likely to be more comfortable searching for work in areas that are perceived as being friendlier, and may seek jobs in areas viewed as hostile only if they have an extremely promising lead.

Table 5.4 shows how white and black respondents in the household survey thought white residents in five specific suburbs would react if blacks moved there. Because the question refers to residence rather than employment, it is not a perfect measure of attitudes toward the latter. Presumably, whites will be much less hostile to blacks who work in their area and live elsewhere than to blacks who move into their neighborhoods. In any case, it is African American perceptions that affect their job search, and they may be less likely to distinguish between attitudes toward residence or employment. The areas about which the questions were asked overlap somewhat with those from the search questions, though Dearborn and Taylor are included in these attitude questions rather than Detroit and Downriver.

African Americans—and whites—perceive Southfield as being much more welcoming toward blacks than are the other areas. For example, about 70 percent of blacks thought of Southfield as a place where they would be welcome, whereas only about one-third perceived Troy or Taylor as such a place. African Americans saw Warren—renowned as the home of "Reagan Democrats" (Greenberg 1995; chap. 2)—and Dearborn—with its legendary Mayor Orville Hubbard (Good 1989)—as hostile areas. Whites think that blacks would generally receive a warmer welcome in these places but, when looking at all five suburbs, we find that both races pretty much share the same cognitive map about where black movers would be welcomed or would face hostility.

Data in the lower panel of Table 5.4 classify the search efforts of blacks by how they perceive three suburbs. They indicate that African Americans are more likely to search in particular areas if they personally perceive the areas as being friendly to blacks.[12] Thinking that the

TABLE 5.4   *Perceptions of Friendliness to Blacks and Tendencies for Blacks to Search in Area*

Perception of Whether Current Residents Would Welcome or
Not Welcome Blacks Moving into Their Area

	White Respondents' Perception			Black Respondents' Perception		
	Welcome	Not Welcome	Indifferent	Welcome	Not Welcome	Indifferent
Southfield	59%	26%	8%	69%	16%	12%
Troy	27	60	7	32	51	7
Warren	34	48	9	16	73	3
Dearborn	29	58	8	9	86	2
Taylor	42	36	10	38	40	13

Percentage of Blacks Who Have Ever Searched in the Area by
Their Perceptions of Friendliness of Whites There

	How Blacks Perceive Their Reception		
	Welcome	Not Welcome	Indifferent
Southfield	61%	48%	47%
Troy	39	33	28
Warren	32	31	25

Source: University of Michigan, Detroit Area Study 1992.
Note: Sample sizes for respondents in the upper panel are 539 and 496 for whites and blacks, respectively. Sample size for the lower panel is 360. The percentages in the upper panel do not sum to 100% because some respondents said they did not know what kind of reception blacks would receive.

whites who live in a suburb are hostile to African Americans discourages them from looking for work there. But there are other factors. Blacks are more likely to search in Southfield than in Troy or Warren, even when they perceive similar friendliness among whites in these suburbs. The greater concentrations of black residences and social contacts in Southfield probably account for this. Nevertheless, the differences in perceived friendliness contribute to these differing search patterns, perhaps in ways that are understated by these data.[13]

Thus, the subjective impressions that African Americans have about friendliness or hostility toward them in Detroit suburbs may influence where they seek employment, and therefore whether they obtain jobs. The lower tendency of black applicants to be hired in the suburbs, despite the apparently higher relative skills of those who search there, also suggests that these perceptions might be based on actual experiences of the respondents or their friends and family when seeking employment.

The racial attitudes of whites and African Americans, the high degree of racial residential segregation, and the absence of good public transit clearly affect where white and black people search for work. These results are strongly consistent with the spatial mismatch hypothesis, and give us more insight into why these effects tend to persist over time.[14]

Other Characteristics of the Job Search

The geographic dimension of job search is one of many along which whites and blacks might differ. It is possible, for instance, that blacks are choosier than whites with regard to the jobs that are available to them; or that blacks do not search as thoroughly as do whites; or that they use search methods that are not as productive; or that they have less accurate perceptions about employers' hiring requirements and preferences than whites.

These hypotheses have been stated forcefully by Lawrence Mead (1992), and his arguments have been frequently repeated as a major explanation for why blacks fare poorly in urban labor markets. He contends that blacks with modest educations often do not seek or accept available jobs, albeit they might be jobs with low wages. He attributes this to "defeatism" or discouragement.[15]

Data from the household Detroit Area Study allow us to test his ideas, since they provide information about "reservation wages," defined as the minimum wage a job seeker requires for accepting employment. This household survey also inquired about search effort, search methods, tendencies to contact employers and receive offers, and general perceptions of labor market characteristics and employer behavior.

We analyze these data by race and sometimes by age as well, as these questions frequently center around the behavior and motivation, or lack of motivation, of younger blacks. We also emphasize search behavior among the nonemployed, as their current or most recent behaviors and attitudes are most relevant to their current employment status.

Information about the job search efforts and search outcomes of whites and blacks is presented in table 5.5. Only nonemployed persons who had searched for work in the last thirty days are included. This table shows the fraction of nonemployed persons who looked for work, the techniques they used, the average number of methods used, hours per week spent searching, access to cars during the period of search, number of employers contacted, and whether an offer had been received.[16]

Several findings emerge. First, nonemployed African Americans were much more likely than nonemployed whites to be searching for

TABLE 5.5   *Characteristics of Job Search for Nonemployed Persons in Detroit Area Study Who Searched for Employment in the Thirty Days Prior to Their Interview*

	Whites	Blacks
Percentage of non–currently employed persons who searched in last thirty days	13	22
Sample size	592	532
Among those who have searched, percentage who used specific means of search:		
Talked to relatives and friends	74	79
Read newspaper ads	96	84
Checked with labor unions	11	5
State employment agency	17	42
School placement officers	13	20
Looked for "help wanted" signs	29	53
Mean number of search methods used	2.86	3.04
Hours spent searching per week	8.17	9.81
Had access to car during search	98%	69%
Employers contacted per week		
Mean	2.01	1.53
Median	0.83	0.50
Job offers received per week	0.09	0.06
Sample size	77	115

Source: University of Michigan, Detroit Area Study 1992.

work (22 versus 13 percent). This is true even when we limit the samples to the young. Both races reported similar methods, although blacks were more likely than whites to have looked for Help Wanted signs and to have had recent contact with the Michigan State Employment Service Commission. African American searchers spent more time and used more methods of search than did white searchers. These results strongly imply that the longer durations of search and nonemployment that have been observed among blacks *cannot* be attributed to lack of effort. They also cast considerable doubt on the notion that African Americans lack motivation or display a "defeatist" attitude toward work, as Mead suggests.[17]

These data also show that almost all white searchers have access to automobiles, where almost one-third of African Americans do not. This may be why white searchers contact many more employers (means of 2.01 versus 1.53 per week, respectively) and receive more offers (means of .09 versus .06 per week, respectively) than do black searchers. Job offers received per hour of search are almost twice as high for white job seekers as for blacks (.011 versus .006). On average, it took a white job seeker 91 hours of search time to generate an offer; it took an African American 167 hours. Thus, the rates at which *employers* make job offers to white and black job seekers have large effects on the search and nonemployment durations of each group.

To what extent are the difficulties of black job seekers caused by their greater unwillingness to accept available low-wage jobs? The ratio of reservation wages among any group of workers to the wage offers they receive would be the most informative measure of that group's willingness to accept jobs that are available to them. But since we cannot observe potential wage offers from employers, we go by the previously received wages of workers in the group.[18]

Data on reservation wages and received wages among all nonemployed white and black searchers and among the young (under age thirty-five) appear in table 5.6. Several summary measures of the reservation and received wage distributions—the means and medians of each distribution—are shown, as well as percentage of the relevant sample willing to accept a job with a wage below certain low-income benchmarks: $4, $5, or $6 per hour.

There is modest support for the notion of relatively high reservation wages among young blacks. In particular, we find that mean and median reservation wages for nonemployed African Americans are somewhat higher, relative to their received wages, than are the comparable numbers for whites, especially among the young. The ratio of mean reservation to received wages is comparable for all nonemployed blacks and whites (.81), but is higher among young blacks than whites (.95 versus .87). Ratios of median reservation to median received wages are higher among blacks than whites in both groups (.79 versus .67 among all the nonemployed, and 1.06 versus .75 among the young). Reservation wages are higher for young whites than blacks in absolute terms, whereas the received wages of whites exceed those of blacks by considerable amounts (with respective medians of $8.00 versus $5.64 among the young). These findings are consistent with Harry J. Holzer (1986) and Stephen Mark Petterson (1997), who also find relatively high reservation wages among young black males using a nationwide survey of data from the 1980s.[19]

On the other hand, the magnitudes of these differences in relative reservation wages—that is, reservation wages relative to received wages—are generally on the order of 10 to 30 percent. These differences are not sufficient to account for large parts of the black-white differences in labor force participation and unemployment described in chapter 3.[20] Furthermore, considerably higher fractions of young black males than whites are willing to accept very low wage employment. Forty-two

TABLE 5.6   *Received Wages and Reservation Wages of Young*
            Nonemployed Workers, by Race and Age (in 1992
            Dollars)

	Whites	Blacks
All nonemployed workers		
Previously received wages		
Mean	$10.32	$8.47
Median	$8.98	$6.33
% ≤ 4.00	4	17
% ≤ 5.00	18	43
% ≤ 6.00	26	50
Reservation wages		
Mean	$8.44	$6.87
Median	$6.00	$5.00
% ≤ 4.00	17	29
% ≤ 5.00	34	53
% ≤ 6.00	52	68
Sample Size	60	134
Young nonemployed workers		
Previously received wages		
Mean	$9.23	$8.04
Median	$8.00	$5.64
% ≤ 4.00	8	18
% ≤ 5.00	26	46
% ≤ 6.00	33	55
Reservation wages		
Mean	$8.01	$7.65
Median	$6.00	$6.00
% ≤ 4.00	19	20
% ≤ 5.00	27	42
% ≤ 6.00	52	63
Sample Size	31	65

Source: Author's tabulations of the Multi-City Study of Urban Inequality Employer Survey.
Note: A "young" worker is defined in this chapter as being under the age of thirty-five.

percent of Detroit's young nonemployed African Americans were willing to work for less than $5.00 per hour (in 1992 dollars), in contrast to only 27 percent of similar whites.

An important caveat is in order. It seems probable that the DAS household survey underrepresents those men who have very high reservation wages relative to received wages, including those who have or anticipate high earnings from illegal activity. Presumably it is difficult to include such respondents in a survey.[21] On the other hand, the racial differences in employment outcomes among those who were interviewed are very large, and differences in their reported reservation wages cannot account for much, if any, of the large observed differences in employment. Thus, we find, at best, limited support for the hypothesis that young African Americans are relatively less likely than whites to accept low-wage employment available to them.[22]

In table 5.7 we consider additional measures of job search perceptions among those under age thirty-five in the upper panel, and among those young persons who were not employed at the time of the survey in the lower panel. These data present the fractions of each group who perceive that particular characteristics are very or somewhat important to employers in deciding whom to hire.

Young African Americans consider "hard" skills to be important in the job search process, at least as important as do young whites. On the other hand, young nonemployed blacks differed from whites in judging the emphasis that employers place on "soft" skills. With regard to how someone looks and dresses, 44 percent of young nonemployed whites, but only 28 percent of African Americans, said this was important to employers. With regard to being a team player, it was 56 percent for whites, 37 percent for blacks. There was also a racial difference, although small, with regard to how employers rate the demographic characteristics of applicants: African Americans, more so than whites, thought employers took these characteristics into consideration when deciding whom to put on the payroll.

While young blacks realize the importance of education, experience, and a good command of English, they may underestimate the importance to employers of soft skills, such as attitudes and communication. This has been stressed by Philip Moss and Chris Tilly (1995), who find that employers claiming to put the most emphasis on soft skills in the hiring process are less likely to employ African Americans than employers who chiefly emphasize hard skills. However, it is unclear from their data to what extent this reflects real racial differences in soft skills, as opposed to discriminatory employer perceptions.[23]

Conclusion

Why do African Americans, especially men, fare so poorly in Detroit's labor market? In these chapters we tested the most frequent explanations, and we can now draw unambiguous conclusions:

• We reject the idea that African Americans underestimate the importance of skills such as educational credentials and work experience. They emphasize them more than whites.

TABLE 5.7   *Perceptions of What Employers Emphasize When Hiring, Persons in Metropolitan Detroit Under Age Thirty-Five*

	White Respondents	Black Respondents	Racial Difference (Black Minus White)
Total young sample			
"Hard" skills			
Specific experience in your line of work	54%	53%	−1
Formal education	39	50	11
References	26	31	5
Ability to speak English well	51	53	2
"Soft" skills			
How someone looks and dresses	33	34	1
Being a team player	62	51	−11
Demographic characteristics of job candidate			
Where someone lives	2	13	11
Age	2	8	6
Race	3	4	1
Gender	5	6	1
Sample size	184	190	
Currently nonemployed young sample			
"Hard" skills			
Specific experience in your line of work	49%	61%	12
Formal education	24	53	29
References	28	26	−2
Ability to speak English well	63	63	0
"Soft" skills			
How someone looks and dresses	44	28	−16
Being a team player	56	37	−19
Demographic characteristics of job candidate			
Where someone lives	4	10	6

TABLE 5.7   *Continued*

	White Respondents	Black Respondents	Racial Difference (Black Minus White)
Age	3	11	8
Race	3	8	5
Gender	3	4	1
Sample size	33	65	

Source: University of Michigan, Detroit Area Study 1992.

- We reject the idea that African American do not search much for jobs or that they consistently use the least effective search methods. Black job seekers spend more time looking than whites.

- The evidence casts some doubt on the idea that high unemployment among African Americans is due to unrealistically high estimates of what they are worth in the labor market. Indeed, more nonemployed blacks than whites say they will work for the minimum wage or less.

- There is some evidence that blacks may underestimate the importance of soft skills in the job search process.

- There is some evidence that blacks may not search frequently in the outlying suburbs where jobs may be available.

- There is strong evidence of a skills mismatch. Inner-city employers— and it is in the inner city where blacks concentrate their job search— report many openings, and the long duration of these vacancies suggests that applicants do not meet their standards.

- There is evidence of a reluctance of suburban employers to hire African American applicants. Although black applicants for suburban jobs seem somewhat more qualified than black applicants for city jobs, they are turned down more frequently, strongly suggesting an employer preference for white workers.

- The simultaneous effects of housing market and labor market discrimination seem considerable. Blacks remain in the city while the jobs for which they are most qualified—manufacturing-sector jobs— suburbanized. The city retained employment in the industrial sectors where the skills deficits of African Americans make it difficult for most of them to be employed—the professional services sector. Given that both black and white job seekers concentrate their search fairly close to home, blacks are at a disadvantage. And whites are advantaged, since they retain a great share of the best jobs in the city and dominate jobs in all occupational ranks in the suburbs.

6

The Evolution of Racial Segregation

A FTER graduation from Wilberforce College, Dr. Ossian Sweet earned his medical degree at Howard University, then went to Europe for postgraduate training. He studied in Vienna and later at Madame Curie's Institute in Paris, learning to use radium to halt cancer. In 1921, he moved to Detroit and established a practice that thrived, since the post–World War I boom was attracting southern blacks to the Motor City. After a while, Dr. Sweet wanted to move away from the crowded Black Bottom neighborhood where most Detroit blacks were forced to live, so he and his wife used their savings to buy a home at 2905 Garland Avenue, in the city's northeast corner. His decision led to the nation's foremost civil rights trial of the 1920s, one that would test the rights of blacks to live where they wished.

White residents hastily organized a "neighborhood improvement" association to keep the Sweets out. Realizing that he and his home were at great risk, Dr. Sweet sought protection from the Detroit police, but did not expect much help. So he asked ten of his relatives to spend the first few nights in his new home with him. They were armed. He had been raised in Florida and had witnessed a lynching as a child, so he knew about white violence and the need for self-defense. On the Sweets' second night of occupancy—September 9, 1925—with seventeen Detroit police officers on duty outside, a mob of whites surrounded his home and, after nightfall, pelted it with rocks and bottles. The situation deteriorated, but the police did not halt the violence. As the crowd grew meaner, the Sweets feared for their lives. Shots rang out from the home. One white person in the crowd, Leon Breiner, lay dead and another, Erick Houghberg, was critically wounded. The police then arrested Dr. Sweet and all the present members of his family, charging them with premeditated murder. Bail was denied, and the city's police chief himself led the questioning of the Sweets (Conot 1973, 300–303; Levine 1976, 163–65).

The National Association for the Advancement of Colored People (NAACP) recognized the importance of this trial. It was, black leaders knew, fundamentally about the rights of the growing African American middle class to live outside the ghettos to which they were confined. It was also about whether a black man had the right to protect himself and his family when threatened by violence akin to that of the lynch mob. In the early 1920s, about fifty southern blacks died each year at the end of a lynchman's rope (U.S. Bureau of the Census 1975, 122), so the NAACP realistically feared that similar violence would be used by northern whites to deal with blacks who transgressed racial codes. The NAACP recruited the most famous trial lawyer of that era, Clarence Darrow, who had just finished defending schoolteacher John Scopes in the Tennessee "monkey trial." Detroit prosecutors sought to convict Dr. Sweet of murder, stressing that he brought arms with him when he moved to his home, but the defense contended that the prosecution could not identify who actually fired the fatal shot. After days of acrimonious deliberations, the jury of twelve white men remained deadlocked. Recorder's Court Judge—and subsequently Supreme Court justice—Frank Murphy declared a mistrial (Fine 1975, chap. 7).

The retrial introduced new legal precedents. Dr. Sweet's brother, Henry admitted that he fired the shot, so only he was tried. But in an innovative legal argument, Darrow focused on the civil and property rights of blacks, their inability to exercise those rights, the discrimination against them in Detroit's housing market, and the unwillingness of the city's police to protect blacks when whites threatened to burn them out of their homes. This persuaded the second jury and, in May 1926, Henry Sweet was acquitted (Conot 1973, 300–303; Capeci 1984, 6–7; Shapiro 1988, 186–95).

The Sweets symbolized black resistance to white violence, as well as the strong desire of middle-class African Americans to live in housing commensurate with their status. But the message this event sent to prosperous blacks of the 1920s was that moving into white neighborhoods had disastrous consequences. (For a description of similar incidents in Cleveland, see Kusmer 1976, 167–69; in Chicago, Chicago Commission on Race Relations 1922, chap. 5.)

The Development and Enforcement of Residential Segregation in Detroit

The Ossian Sweet trial was one important incident in the larger struggle to establish racial residential segregation in American cities. Before World War I, there were few, if any, exclusively African American neighborhoods. In many cities, a small handful of prosperous blacks lived with white neighbors, while larger numbers of low-income blacks lived alongside immigrants arriving from eastern and southern Europe. Before the great migration from the South, there were at least six neighborhoods in Detroit with clusters of black residents but, as Olivier Zunz (1982, 353) has demonstrated, blacks were numerically dominant in none of them, so they would be classified as integrated areas by today's standards.

As soon as blacks migrated in substantial numbers, whites sought to keep them out of their neighborhoods. Originally, the strategy was to legislate who could live where, a practice begun in Baltimore in 1910. Blacks there sought to buy homes in the all-white Druid Hills neighborhood. City council hastily enacted an ordinance specifying that blacks could only move into certain neighborhoods, while whites could only move into others. A dozen or more southern cities passed a variety of segregation ordinances, such as those stating that no one could move into a city block unless his or her race was in the majority there (Rice 1968). Such ordinances (including Baltimore's) were generally thrown out by courts for infringing on the rights of property owners. In a definitive ruling, and an important early victory for the NAACP, the Supreme Court (*Buchanan v. Warley* 1917) ruled that residential segregation laws violated property owners' rights, and were therefore unconstitutional (Johnson 1943, 174; Rice 1968).

When World War I cut off the flow of European immigrants, northern employers turned to an underutilized labor force: blacks from the rural south. But when blacks moved to the cities, they found that the only places to rent were in or near the neighborhoods that already had some African American residents: the near east side in Cleveland, the south side in Chicago, and Detroit's emerging east side ghetto. Many of the first blacks to arrive were single men who needed simple lodging, not apartments or homes for a family. Real estate brokers found they could subdivide their properties into small units and then rent each of them to several African American men at high prices. Given the tremendous demand for housing, the ignorance and poverty of the newcomers, and the inability of blacks to secure any housing in white neighborhoods, real estate owners had strong incentives to "pile up" blacks, thereby creating the first racial ghettos. Langston Hughes lived on Cleveland's east side at this time and described a housing market process that undoubtedly characterized Detroit:

> Rents were very high for the colored people in Cleveland, and the Negro district was extremely crowded because of the great migration. It was difficult to find a place to live. We always lived, during my high school years, either in an attic or a basement and paid quite a lot for such inconvenient

quarters. White people on the east side of the city were moving out of their frame homes and renting them to Negroes at double and triple the rents they could receive from others. An eight-room house with one bath would be cut up into apartments and five or six families crowded into it, each two-room kitchenette apartment renting for what the whole house had rented for before.

But Negroes were coming in a great dark tide from the South, and they had to have some place to live. Sheds and garages and storefronts were turned into living quarters. As always, the white neighborhoods resented Negroes moving closer and closer—but when the whites did give way, they gave way at very profitable rentals. [1940, 27]

With the tremendous demand for housing and the increasing incomes of a growing black middle class, it is not surprising that some tried to move out of the emerging northern ghettos. Many violent incidents are documented. The Chicago Commission on Race Relations (1922, 123–139) cited fifty-eight bombings of homes or apartments owned or occupied by African Americans in that city between the summer of 1917 and the spring of 1921. One of the first such incidents in Detroit occurred in the summer of 1917, when a white owner converted an apartment building at 202 Harper Avenue and rented it to blacks. Shortly after their arrival, neighborhood whites invaded the building and threw out the possessions of the new tenants. The black renters appealed for help from a nearby police officer, but he encouraged them to leave the area for their own safety (Levine 1976, 46–47; Zunz 1982, 374). By the mid-1920s, a black middle class developed in Detroit and they sought better housing. Their attempts to do so led up to violent incidents involving Dr. Sweet and many others.

Describing this era in Detroit, Zunz (1982, 373) concluded:

> Blacks became the victims of many forms of terrorism designed to keep them in place, and the ghettos sprang up, in part, as a reaction to the xenophobic violence which no other group of migrants to the city had ever experienced. In many ways, the violent pressures of the white community upon black newcomers worked as they were meant to . . .

The year after Dr. Sweet's trial, one of his attorneys, Julian Perry, bought a home close to the city's border with Grosse Pointe Park. When the neighbors learned of his race, they fire-bombed his home and he quickly did what prosperous blacks of that era had to do—flee back to the safety of the ghetto (Levine 1976, 204).

Violence was a troubling, costly, and unacceptable way to preserve neighborhood purity. The search for a more gentle and perhaps more effective strategy was successful in the 1920s and 1930s. Restrictive covenants—statements specifying that a property cannot be owned or rented by a member of a designated minority group, sometimes specifying forever, other times for several decades or a century—helped establish the segregation found in Detroit and other metropolises today. They originated in California in the 1890s, when whites sought to prevent Asians from buying land or living in white neighborhoods. They spread to the east, where Jews and blacks were targeted for exclusion. But restrictive covenants had a rocky road, since courts in California and Virginia declared them illegal. They were, however, upheld in Louisiana. After World War I, developers began including restrictive covenants in deeds, a practice that became common in Michigan. When restrictive covenants made their first appearance in Detroit in 1910 (Sugrue 1996, 44), African American leaders contested them. Twelve years later, the state Supreme Court upheld their validity in a case involving a Pontiac black who sought to buy property (Levine 1976, 132).

But the matter awaited an authoritative ruling from the nation's highest court. The definitive case arose from a neighborhood in northwest Washington, D.C. White property owners there feared a Negro invasion and agreed to write restrictive covenants into their deeds, but soon afterward one of the owners sold to a black man. The trial court in Washington upheld the restrictive covenants and overturned the sale, but the white seller appealed to the Supreme Court. That court, in 1926, heard the case and then voted, 9 to 0, to approve restrictive covenants. Justice Sanford argued that the issue of denying blacks the right to live in white neighborhoods was so insubstantial as to be without color of merit and frivolous. He argued that the Thirteenth Amendment did not protect the rights of individual Negroes and that the due process clauses of the Fifth and Fourteenth amendments prohibited states, but not individuals, from discriminating on the basis of race.

Restrictive covenants were apparently written into the deeds of most developments built after World War I. By the late 1940s, approximately 80 percent of residential properties in the city of Detroit located beyond Grand Boulevard were covered by restrictive covenants. In the five years following World War II, the vacant outlying parts of the central city were filled in with the building of some 43,000 homes and apartments, virtually every one of them restricted to white occupancy (Sugrue 1996, 44).

Apart from restrictive covenants, two additional developments further confined the housing options of African Americans. By the mid-1920s, the real estate industry successfully popularized the idea that brokers were violating a norm and breaking their code of ethics if they introduced blacks, Jews, or other racial minorities to formerly white neighborhoods (Helper 1969, 227; McEntire 1960, 245). Today, when the principle of equal opportunity is almost universally endorsed, it is easy to overlook the deliberate development of the moral principle that white property owners and those who sold housing had a moral obligation to preserve the quality of neighborhoods by excluding ethnic and racial groups deemed undesirable.

President Roosevelt, in 1933, created the Home Owners Loan Corporation (HOLC), designed to provide low-cost loans to owners facing eviction during the Depression. About 40 percent of the nation's homeowners got help from this innovative program (Jackson 1985, 196). Shortly thereafter, this agency developed the modern mortgage system with its small down payment and modest monthly costs. Being a national agency, it sought a national standard with regard to property assessment in order to monitor the creditworthiness of borrowers. Assessors were encouraged to prepare color-coded maps for their cities: green designating the best properties, where appreciation was highly likely; blue for the next best; yellow for neighborhoods where property values would be likely to decline; and red for neighborhoods where property values were already dropping. Their rules specifically stated that neighborhoods with a Jewish population could not be placed in the green category, regardless of property values. Black neighborhoods, and neighborhoods seen as at risk of having black residents, were marked in red, since there was consensus that property values would fall if African Americans lived there or might live there. This redlining procedure would continue for three decades (Jackson 1985, 208). Every Detroit neighborhood with black residents was colored red on the HOLC maps, thereby denying blacks access to federally backed housing loans (Sugrue 1996, 44).

An incident in Detroit illustrates the pervasive influence of these federal policies. A small enclave of blacks had lived in poor quality housing close to Eight Mile Road since World War I. A builder wished to put up homes for whites in a nearby area in 1941, but knew that his buyers would never get a federally approved loan because of the proximity of blacks. Being an enterprising developer, he surrounded his property with a concrete wall six feet high and one-half mile long and removed the onus of redlining (Levine 1976, 204).

The Struggle over Detroit
Neighborhoods After World War II

Thomas Sugrue argues that housing was the most divisive racial issue in Detroit after World War II (1995, chap. 9). Between 1950 and 1980, the white population of the city fell from 1.5 million to 414,000, while the

The Sojourner Truth Housing Controversy

When thousands of blacks moved into Detroit in the early 1940s to build tanks, airplanes, and jeeps, they found they had to live within the already overcrowded black neighborhoods. Civic leaders and the NAACP understood the housing crisis when blacks migrated into Detroit during World War II, and called for the construction of new homes. Federal dollars were readily available to build housing for defense workers, and the Detroit Housing Commission wished to construct a project for blacks. But there was a problem. Whites would not tolerate homes for blacks in their neighborhoods, but African Americans were so densely packed in their own neighborhoods that there was no room for new construction there. After much deliberation, the city commission selected a white neighborhood for defense housing for whites and then chose a block at Dequindre and Modern for the black housing—a neighborhood with a substantial African American population already. But federal housing officials in Washington decided instead to build the black project in a sparsely populated neighborhood at the corner of Nevada and Fenelon. They named it after the Michigan woman who became the nation's preeminent African American poet of the nineteenth century: Sojourner Truth. It was completed in December 1941.

White residents of the area, led by Congressman Rudolph Tenerowicz, the Reverend Constantine Dzink, pastor of St. Louis the King Church, and Joseph Bulla, head of the Seven Mile Neighborhood Improvement Association insisted that the federal government change the race of residents. They successfully pressured the Federal Housing Authority not to approve loans in the surrounding area if blacks moved to the Sojourner Truth homes (Meier and Rudwick 1979, 178). In January, federal officials gave in and agreed that whites would get the homes. Detroit's blacks, along with some city officials, including Mayor Jefferies, appealed to Washington. Officials there went back to the original plan for black occupancy.

On February 28, 1942, a few African American families tried to move into the units they had been paying rent on since the first of the year. Local residents and white militants surrounded the homes and began pelting the blacks as they approached. Despite the presence of 200 police officers, the violence increased. Shots were fired and scores of people were injured, but there were no deaths. By day's end, Detroit's police separated blacks and whites and arrested 106 blacks and 3 whites (Sugrue 1996, 74). National newspapers the next day carried reports and pictures of the nation's first racial riot of World War II.

For the next two months, Detroit officials feared that a racial riot might break out as local residents continued to march around the homes to symbolize their dedication to keeping their neighborhood white. President Roosevelt's Attorney General sent lawyers to Detroit to see if leaders of the neighborhood association should be prosecuted for conspiracy and federal intelligence officers infiltrated neighborhood organizations. Finally, at the end of April, 1,100 city and state police officers and 1,600 members of the Michigan National Guard were mustered to guard the 168 black families who moved into the Sojourner Truth homes. That show of force broke the back of white resistance and there were no further incidents (Thomas 1992, 143–48; Jenkins 1991, 408–17).

black population grew from 300,000 to 750,000, so the majority of the city's neighborhoods went from white to black. This was not a peaceful transition. Throughout the city, whites feared that the increasingly prosperous black population would move into their neighborhoods in great numbers, so they used a variety of techniques to keep them out. In 1946, City Councilman William Rogell—best known for playing on the Tigers' championship teams in 1934 and 1935—collaborated with City Councilman Gus Dorias (then head coach of the Detroit Lions) to propose the establishment of an exclusively Negro section of the city. Whites residing there would be paid to leave. Needless to say, nothing came of this proposal (Shogan and Craig 1964, 126).

Neighborhoods differed in what techniques they used and how fast demographic change took hold, but in many areas there was organized resistance to blacks. Sugrue describes a defensive strategy in which active block groups spread information and rumors about the possible arrival of African Americans and what should be done to maintain racial purity, with an emphasis on building strong neighborhood associations. Defenders of white neighborhoods drew on a readily available labor reserve: women at home raising their children. They could be easily mobilized to picket the homes of whites who were considering selling to blacks and the offices of real estate brokers deemed to be soft on the race issue.

While the daytime protests were staffed by women, those occurring after dark were carried out by men, who emphasized that keeping blacks out would not only maintain property values but protect their wives and children from black criminals. Sugrue reports that teenage boys—who were unlikely to be arrested—were enlisted to toss garbage on the lawns of blacks, shatter their windows, rip down their fences, and burn their garages. Against such attacks, the NAACP and other liberal organizations stressed the rights of blacks to live where they wished and, given their prosperity and need for better housing, some moved into formerly white areas (Thomas 1997, chap. 4).

In the late 1950s, black leaders regularly criticized Detroit's police for seldom breaking up mobs of whites that stoned or firebombed the

Ending Restrictive Covenants

Orsel McGhee was a maintenance supervisor at the Detroit Free Press. His wife, Minnie, held a job that is still common among African American women: she worked in the post office. The McGhees saved their money with hopes of buying a substantial home. They found one on Tireman Avenue—the street that separated the neighborhoods where blacks could buy or rent from those they could not enter—and moved in during the middle of a summer night in 1944. They knew a restrictive covenant was in force.

The local neighborhood association was not known for extreme hostility to blacks. Indeed, a few blacks had rented there during the Depression, when owners sought anyone who could pay, but there was fear that middle-class blacks might seek homes there. The association prevailed upon Mr. McGhee's neighbor, Benjamin Sipes, to seek a court order evicting the black family. The NAACP joined the litigation and challenged the eviction order, but the local judge upheld the restrictive covenant and ordered the McGhees out. When the NAACP appealed, the Michigan Supreme Court ruled unanimously two years later that restrictive covenants had legal standing and could be used to keep neighborhoods "Caucasian."

A similar case from St. Louis was making its way through the federal courts. Robert Bishop, a black broker in that city, catered to prosperous African Americans, but he faced a great challenge: there were almost no suitable homes for his clients. He found a sympathetic white woman, Geraldine Fitzgerald, who purchased a house in a white neighborhood and then promptly sold it to an African American client of Mr. Bishop, the Shelley family. When the whites learned of the ruse, they sued for enforcement of the restrictive covenant. The municipal court ruled in favor of the Shelleys but, on appeal, the Missouri Supreme Court decided in 1946 that restrictive covenants were legal (Irons 1999, 373–76).

The NAACP took both of these cases to the Supreme Court in Washington. President Truman's attorney general, Tom Clark, personally argued the case, contending that restrictive covenants violated the constitutional rights of Jews, Asians, blacks, and other groups (Klueger 1975, 253). In the summer of 1948, the Supreme Court ruled unanimously that restrictive covenants violated both the Fourteenth Amendment and the Civil Rights Act of 1866. This decision not only allowed the Shelleys and the McGhees to keep their homes, but freed a California man who was serving time for violating a restrictive covenant (Vose 1967, 211). The Supreme Court ruling did not prohibit placing restrictive covenants in deeds, so many developers continued to include them, presumably to reassure their white customers and discourage black ones. The ruling prohibited courts from enforcing them.

homes of blacks. A particularly high number of attacks on black new-comers occurred in the late 1950s, when a downturn in auto production slowed the suburban movement of whites (Sugrue 1996, 223). George Edwards, Mayor Cavanagh's police chief, tried to stop such harassment, but learned that it would not be easy. In November 1961 a black family, the Griffins, moved into a home on Riverview. They soon moved out when a suspicious fire damaged their home. The Griffins returned three months later. Almost immediately, someone poured gasoline on their home and set it ablaze. After this, Commissioner Edwards ordered a patrol car to guard the home. The Griffins returned in a few weeks and, despite the police surveillance, their home was fired upon. A police offi-cer who lived next door gave a party for his friends soon after that. The celebrants ended up stoning the Griffins' house. Eventually, a judge is-sued contempt citations for the neighbors, including the police officer's wife, and the harassment came to an end. Commissioner Edwards con-cluded that there was not a white police officer or sergeant in the pre-cinct who would arrest a white man for destroying the property of a black (Stolberg 1998, 180–84). Detroit's Commission on Community Relations found the number of such incidents to range from a low of 7 in 1953 to a high of 63 in 1963 (Sugrue 1996, 233).

If lenders and brokers would not allow African Americans to enter white areas, how did so much racial change occur so rapidly in Detroit neighborhoods? Albert Mayer (1960) described the Russell Woods neigh-borhood, an area of attractive homes built in 1919. In the 1950s, some white residents wanted to sell, either because they found better homes in the booming suburbs or because of job shifts. Although most strongly preferred to sell to other whites they were not always successful, and some sold to prosperous blacks. A few African Americans were able to pay cash, while some turned to lenders other than the established banks. In Detroit, a common means for purchasing a home was the land contract, an instrument that maximized the racial discrepancy in power. The white seller obtained 20 percent of the purchase price as a down payment from the buyer, and then required monthly payments for a dozen years. The owner retained title until the final payment was made, so he or she could use the property as collateral. If the buyer missed a single payment, the owner could repossess the property without cum-bersome foreclosure proceedings (Mayer 1960, 208). There was, of course, great profit to be made in neighborhoods undergoing racial tran-sition, so a "fringe" real estate industry developed in Detroit capitaliz-ing on the great black demand for better housing and the unwillingness of licensed brokers to violate their code of segregation. Racial change in some neighborhoods was helped along by "blockbusting," in which a broker or speculator would select a white area near a black one, and

153

then conspicuously "show" a vacant home to an African American family, or hire young black men to go through the neighborhood passing out handbills encouraging whites to sell their homes "before it is too late." The broker would then purchase from whites at fire-sale prices and, because of racial constraints in Detroit's housing market, turn around and sell the homes to blacks at great profit.

Homeowners' organizations and civil rights groups frequently sought legislation to outlaw blockbusting. By the early 1960s, city ordinances prohibited brokers from making racial appeals and put limits on the posting of "For Sale" signs (Sugrue 1996, 197). In the early 1960s, civil rights organizations proposed ordinances in many cities to outlaw racial discrimination in the sale or rental of housing—forerunners of the Open Housing Law of 1968. In 1963, Mayor Cavanagh proposed an equal housing opportunity ordinance for Detroit, but it was rejected by the city council. This galvanized the powerful white neighborhood groups, and they put a measure on the ballot in 1964 specifically protecting the right of a property owner to sell or rent to whomever he or she wished. It passed in racially divided Detroit, winning 2 to 1 in white neighborhoods, but losing 4 to 1 in black. It never went on the books since Wayne County courts ruled it unconstitutional.

Between the end of World War II and the late 1960s, block-by-block skirmishes took place throughout Detroit as blacks sought better housing. The lure of attractive homes in all-white suburbs, available at moderate cost because of federal housing policies, led most whites to switch rather than fight, and so the city's white population was reduced by two-thirds.

The Creation and Maintenance of Suburban Segregation

The suburban story is different in some ways, but similar in others. During World War I, two developers recognized that blacks needed housing and had very few options within the city. One of them, Henry Stevens, owned land just north of Eight Mile Road and decided to sell lots to blacks. Unfortunately, there were no water or sewage systems, but blacks moved there anyway, since it was one of the few places they were welcome, and put up tents or temporary structures until they could build their own homes. By 1926, about 4,000 lived in this location—a squatter settlement, since municipal authorities provided few services to the area (Dancy 1966, 57–59; Levine 1976, 129). Another developer realized that many blacks working for Ford in Dearborn needed housing. In 1921, he purchased a twenty-acre tract in Inkster, a suburb west of Dearborn, and began constructing small cottages

The Catholic Church and Residential Integration in Detroit

A Catholic church and school were prominent in many of Detroit's neighborhoods where resistance to residential integration was strong. There was a tradition of considerable racial segregation in Detroit's Catholic church. As early as the 1860s, one chapel and one school were designated for "colored" Catholics. More formally, the church established four racial parishes for blacks in the city between 1911 and 1943, and then another in Inkster in 1945. Apparently this was done to discourage Inkster's black Catholics from attending church in Dearborn (Tentler 1990, chap. 15).

By the 1950s the attitudes and policies of church leaders changed to strong support for equal racial opportunities—including the rights of blacks to live where they wished, even if that meant in largely white Catholic neighborhoods.

John Dearden was appointed archbishop in Detroit in 1959 and promptly took a stand in favor of equal housing opportunities. He urged priests and parishioners to welcome African Americans who came to their neighborhoods, and organized a team of experts to go from parish to parish holding seminars encouraging equal treatment for black newcomers. Later he held meetings with his priests and mandated that they preach against racism. Following the riots of 1967, he appropriated one million dollars of church funds for black organizations and community development projects, with the monies controlled by a board of inner-city residents. (McGreevy 1996, 209–14).

Those who organized Cardinal Dearden's civil rights seminars and activities reported much indifference and some hostility. Similar to the UAW and the Michigan Democratic party, the leaders of Detroit's Catholic Church in the 1960s took a strong liberal stand on rights for African Americans but it was not endorsed by the white rank-and-file.

that he sold to blacks at low cost. By 1930, about 2,000 blacks lived in this suburb. Inkster got an unusual boost in the early 1930s. Henry Ford introduced the first V-8 and announced he was hiring after several years of layoffs. He recruited blacks from Inkster and while he believed they could work in his plants, he felt they needed much guidance. In particular, he thought that Jewish merchants would get blacks into debt and then take all of their wages. So Mr. Ford paid his new black workers only one-quarter of their salaries in cash using the remainder to developing community institutions in Inkster, so Henry Ford became known as the Patriarch of Inkster (Conot 1973, chap. 60). This place continues as one of the few suburban pockets of African Americans. About 19,000 lived there in 1990.

These were the exceptions. In Detroit's suburban building boom—

both in the 1920s and after World War II—officials in the suburbs joined with real estate brokers to convey the message that black residents were unwelcome. Dearborn, surrounded by the city of Detroit on three sides, became a nationally known symbol of suburban hostility to blacks. It was—and remains—home of the Ford Motor Company. By 1940, it had a population of 64,000—only 35 of them black (U.S. Department of Commerce 1943, table 28). Its factories, however, employed many blacks. In 1970, 12,000 of the 77,000 holding jobs in Dearborn were African Americans, but only 12 blacks were among the 104,000 residents (U.S. Department of Commerce 1973a, table 2; 1973b, table 24).

The Sojourner Truth controversy convinced federal housing officials that it would be impossible to build any housing for black defense workers in the city of Detroit. So they turned to vacant lands in the suburbs. The Federal Public Housing Authority purchased 170 acres in Dearborn and planned to build 1,400 temporary homes. Fearing that federal officials might permit some Dearborn black workers to live there, Mayor Orville Hubbard of Dearborn led a spirited fight to block such construction. For a while, federal officials stressed the key role black workers played in the war effort and refused to back down. Dearborn officials turned to the courts, got injunctions, and succeeded in delaying the project until V-J Day when housing for defense workers became a moot issue (Good 1989, 141–43; Sugrue 1996, 76–77).

In 1948, the John Hancock Insurance Company revealed plans for a $25 million development in Dearborn. It would be built on land owned by Ford Foundation and Ford Motor and would provide upper-middle-class housing for 45,000 residents. Many Dearborn residents endorsed the proposal, thinking it would strengthen the suburb and increase its already hefty tax base. Mayor Hubbard objected, apparently fearing an influx of prosperous residents who would object to his dictatorial style of running the municipality. To thwart the development, he insisted upon an advisory vote. He had one and only one theme. He argued that over the years, with considerable help from his police, he had kept black residents out, but that the liberal developers of the Hancock project would allow African Americans to live there. On election day in 1948, Hubbard ordered that city employees distribute a leaflet that proclaimed:

> Keep Negroes Out of Dearborn
> Protect your Home and Mine!
> Vote No on the Advisory Vote

The city's residents followed their mayor's advice.

During the bus boycott in 1956, the *Montgomery Advertiser* sent reporters North seeking Jim Crow practices similar to those prevalent in Alabama's capital. In an interview with Mayor Hubbard entitled, "Why No Negroes Live in Dearborn," the reporter asked how Dearborn kept blacks out, and the mayor replied:

> They can't get in here. We watch it. Every time we hear of a Negro moving in—for instance, we had one last year—we respond quicker than you do to a fire. That's generally known. It's known among our own people and it's known among the Negroes here.

The incredulous reporter reminded Mayor Hubbard that federal laws and Supreme Court decisions gave blacks the right to live where they wished, but the mayor insisted that as far as he was concerned, it was against the law for Negroes to live in his suburb and that none would live there while he remained in office (Good 1989, 264). During his thirty-five-year reign, Dearborn's police cars carried a large logo "Keep Dearborn Clean," which was widely interpreted as the mayor's promise to "Keep Dearborn White."

With generous tax revenues from Ford's huge offices and factories, Dearborn was—and continues to be—a well-financed suburb. Indeed, one of Mayor Hubbard's challenges was finding ways to spend revenues. After World War II, he developed an extensive system of attractive parks within the suburb, and also purchased a 240-acre recreational area named Camp Dearborn, 35 miles away. Over the years, the complex tripled in size. Finally, opposition surfaced to such unusual spending. In the 1961 election, Mayor Hubbard boosted Camp Dearborn by distributing leaflets to voters succinctly stating: "37 hours to Africa, 37 minutes to Belle Isle [Frederick Law Olmsted's beautiful park in the city of Detroit] but who wants to go to either place?" The message was clear: Mayor Hubbard could provide his citizens with a Jim Crow park.

Mayor Hubbard was finally charged with violating civil rights laws, but for most unusual reasons. Giuseppe Stanzione migrated to Dearborn from Italy in 1958 and established a contracting business. His neighbors detested him for his loud parties and the cement mixers parked on a vacant lot near his house. When confronted by angry neighbors, Stanzione lost his temper and told them that he would sell his home to "niggers" and move to California.

In the summer of 1963, Stanzione rented out an upstairs apartment in his home on Kendall Street. On Labor Day, three blacks arrived. A mob immediately surrounded the home and began pelting it with rocks. Dearborn police showed up, but did not disperse the crowd, which continued to circle the home for twenty-nine hours before drifting away. What the white mob did not know was that the apartment had never been rented to African Americans. The blacks were delivering furniture to new white tenants.

Stanzione claimed that Mayor Hubbard and the Dearborn police failed to provide him with protection and encouraged attacks on his house. Mayor Hubbard was indicted for violating Michigan's Riot Act. Later the federal Department of Justice indicted the mayor, police chief, and director of public safety for violating a Reconstruction Era law prohibiting conspiracy to deny civil rights. So one of the nation's most outspoken segregationists faced charges for violating the rights of a white man who threatened to sell his home to blacks (Good 1989, chap. 36). Mayor Hubbard was acquitted in a trial presided over by Judge Wade McCree who subsequently was appointed by President Johnson as the nation's first African American Solicitor General (Darden et al. 1987, 119–25).

Certainly, Mayor Hubbard's views did not represent the racial attitudes of all Dearborn residents. Ministers quite often condemned his racism and, in 1963, while the open housing marches led by Dr. King in Chicago suburbs turned violent, peaceful ones took place in Dearborn. But Hubbard, who ruled from 1942 through 1977, symbolized white suburban hostility to blacks.

No other Detroit suburb has a history of racial exclusion as thoroughly documented as that of Dearborn, but very few African Americans moved to the suburban ring during or after World War II. Those who sold real estate cooperated with the officials of suburban governments and school systems to convey the message that Detroit's suburbs did not welcome black homeowners or renters.

Before the civil rights era, a different approach was used to keep "undesirables" out of the Grosse Pointes—five of the nation's most attractive suburbs built along the Detroit River after World War I. Property owners' associations worked with brokers to develop a formal point system for scoring those seeking to buy or build in these suburbs. Points were awarded on the basis of the applicant's swarthiness of appearance, religious affiliation, club memberships, absence of accent in spoken English, neatness, and whether the way of life seemed "typically American." Negroes, Orientals, and Mexicans were categorically excluded. Northern Europeans needed a score of only 50 points to qualify, but for southern Europeans it was 65, and for Jews, 85. Indeed, a Jewish doctor reminded the scorers that he could trace his genealogy back to a signer of the Declaration of Independence, but that wasn't good enough; he was turned down (Conot 1973, 605; Sugrue 1996, 193). When the Grosse Pointe system of discrimination was publicly revealed in 1962, it provoked the formation of an Open Occupancy Conference by Catholic,

Protestant, and Jewish leaders—one of many in the continuing series of efforts to create equal opportunities in Detroit's housing market.

Blacks were not the only group targeted for discrimination. The census has never asked a question about religion, so it was impossible to measure the residential segregation of Jews. After World War II, discriminatory policies—less explicit than those mandated by the Grosse Pointes, but motivated by the same anti-Semitism—restricted Jews in the housing market. Jewish brokers, for example, were denied membership in the city's association of real estate agents. Conot (1973, 604) estimates that at the end of World War II, more than one-half of Detroit's real estate brokers refused to do business with known Jews. But in the mid to late 1950s, Southfield and Oak Park developed reputations for being "open" to Jews leaving the city of Detroit. The prosperity and success of those suburbs, despite their Jewish composition, helped break down those practices that once denied housing to Jews. And, undoubtedly, the Supreme Court's restrictive covenant decision greatly increased the ability of Jews to move into "Caucasian" neighborhoods.

The strategies used in the suburban ring were highly effective in containing blacks in the city. The Census of 1970 revealed that most of Detroit's suburbs had minuscule numbers of black residents. Table 6.1 lists the 27 suburbs that had populations exceeding 35,000 in that year. The three biggest—Warren, Livonia, and Dearborn—were home to almost 400,000 residents. Only *186* of them were African Americans.

There have been many attempts to break down the barriers that kept blacks out of Detroit suburbs, including an innovative one in the early 1970s when national attention was given to policies that might "open up the suburbs" (Downs, 1973). After his election, President Nixon appointed George Romney to head the Department of Housing and Urban Development (HUD). His experience as governor of Michigan during the 1967 riots made him aware of the housing problems of urban blacks and the terrible consequences of concentrating African Americans in deteriorated inner-city ghettos. Once in his Washington office, he announced his dedication to enforce the Fair Housing Act of 1968 and to greatly expand housing opportunities for the poor and minorities. He favored the construction of scattered site public housing, including clusters in the suburbs (Keating 1994, 41–42). Influenced by the gloomy predictions of the Kerner Commission, the Federal Civil Rights Commission held hearings in 1970 and implicated HUD in the creation and perpetuation of suburban segregation. Title VI of the Civil Rights Act of 1964 said there could be no racial discrimination in any program supported by federal funds. Many white suburbs received federal dollars for an array of housing and urban renewal programs. Secretary Romney de-

TABLE 6.1   *Representation of Blacks in Suburbs of Detroit That Had Populations of 35,000 or More in 1970 and 1990*

Suburb	Population in 1970			Population in 1990		
	Total	Black	Percentage Black	Total	Black	Percentage Black
Warren[a]	179,260	132	< 0.1	144,864	1,067	0.7
Livonia	110,199	41	< 0.1	100,850	265	0.3
Dearborn[a]	104,199	13	< 0.1	89,286	494	0.6
St. Clair Shores	88,093	167	0.2	68,107	141	0.2
Westland	86,749	2,234	2.6	84,724	2,829	3.3
Royal Oak	85,499	26	< 0.1	65,410	332	0.5
Dearborn Heights[a]	80,069	12	< 0.1	60,838	277	0.5
Redford Township[a]	71,901	17	< 0.1	54,387	379	0.7
Taylor	70,020	20	< 0.1	70,811	2,980	4.2
Southfield[a]	69,285	102	0.1	75,728	22,053	29.1
Sterling Heights	61,385	38	0.1	117,810	475	0.4
Roseville	60,529	606	1.0	51,412	513	1.0
The 5 Grosse Points[a]	58,708	96	0.2	49,310	182	0.3
Waterford Township	59,123	33	< 0.1	66,692	701	1.1
Lincoln Park	52,984	5	< 0.1	41,832	385	0.9
Farmington Hills	48,933	83	0.2	74,652	1,429	1.9
Clinton Township	48,865	1,296	2.7	85,866	2,586	3.0
East Detroit[a]	45,920	13	< 0.1	35,286	87	0.2
Bloomfield Township	42,788	213	0.5	42,137	1,011	2.4
Garden City	41,864	10	< 0.1	31,846	76	0.2
Wyandotte	41,061	18	< 0.1	30,928	73	0.2
Allen Park	40,747	29	0.1	31,092	144	0.5
Troy	39,419	1	< 0.1	72,884	983	1.3
Madison Heights	38,599	15	< 0.1	32,196	292	1.0
Inkster	38,595	17,189	44.5	30,772	19,199	62.4
Oak Park[a]	36,762	72	0.2	30,462	10,449	34.3
Highland Park[a]	35,444	19,889	56.1	20,121	18,673	92.8

Sources: U.S. Department of Commerce 1973b, 1991.
Note: African Americans as a percentage of metropolitan population: 1970, 18 percent; 1990, 24 percent. The city of Pontiac is not shown, since it was defined as a central city on the basis of data from the censuses of 1950 and 1990.
[a]Shares a common border with the city of Detroit

cided that the flow of federal dollars should be contingent upon these suburbs demonstrating that they had equal housing opportunities programs in place. The test case, in the summer of 1970, concerned the Detroit suburb of Warren. That year's census counted just 132 African American residents among the 178,415 inhabitants, although thousands of blacks worked in its auto plants. Warren officials assumed their request for $2.8 million in HUD funding would be automatically approved as earlier requests had, but Secretary Romney ordered a hold on the funds. This set off a firestorm of protest. Suburban mayors and suburban congressmen demanded that Secretary Romney revert to the traditional policy. They quickly developed an effective national campaign stressing the rights of local suburban government to be free of federal interference. Detroit suburbs filed lawsuits, and Warren residents went to the ballot box to vote out federally funded housing programs.

Secretary Romney's idealism was not popular. As the mid-term elections approached, the administration realized that efforts to open the suburbs could cost them an immense number of votes. In September of 1970, the Nixon Administration announced that programs promoting integration would be put on hold until a thorough study was completed. The following year President Nixon announced an end to HUD's pro-integration strategies and, two years later, a moratorium on all construction of public housing. (Darden et al. 1987, 145; Quadagno 1994, 110).

Metropolitan Detroit: Segregation in the 1990s

The residential practices described in this chapter produced a metropolis that is exceptionally segregated—by 1990, Detroit was more residentially segregated than any other U.S. metropolis. The most common measure of segregation is the "index of dissimilarity," which assesses the evenness with which blacks and whites are spread across the urban landscape. If a system of apartheid were so complete that all neighborhoods were either exclusively black or exclusively white, this index would take on its maximum value of 100. Were skin color to make absolutely no difference with regard to where people lived, the index would approach 0. The numerical value of the index reports the percent of either blacks or whites who would have to move from one neighborhood to another to eliminate residential segregation. These indexes of dissimilarity are based on data about people who identified themselves as either black or white by race.

To measure neighborhood segregation, we used census data showing the number of blacks and whites living in each block group. These are units composed of contiguous blocks created by the Census Bureau for enumeration purposes, and include an average of 150 homes or apartments. In 1990, the black-white segregation index for metropolitan Detroit was 89—not far from the index of 100 that would result with complete apartheid. Almost 90 percent of either whites or blacks would have to move to end segregation.

Table 6.2 compares this index to those of the nation's other large

TABLE 6.2   *Indicators of Racial Residential Segregation for Fifteen Largest Metropolises in 1990*

Metropolis	Population in 1990 (Thousands)	Index of Black-White Residential Segregation[a]	Change in Segregation Index, 1980 to 1990	Residential Isolation Indexes[b]	
				Percentage Black for Blacks	Percentage White for Whites
Los Angeles	8,863	75	−9	45	65
New York	8,547	72	−1	64	77
Chicago	6,070	88	−4	83	84
Philadelphia	4,857	79	−1	73	91
Detroit	**4,382**	**89**	**0**	**83**	**92**
Washington	3,924	68	−4	64	78
Boston	3,784	71	−6	46	91
Houston	3,302	71	−9	58	74
Atlanta	2,834	73	−6	69	86
Long Island	2,609	66	−1	52	90
San Bernardino-Riverside	2,589	52	−9	17	71
Dallas	2,553	64	−15	55	80
San Diego	2,498	62	−4	21	75
Minneapolis-St. Paul	2,464	66	−5	27	94
St. Louis	2,444	81	−4	74	92

Source: Farley and Frey 1994.
Note: Block groups have an average population of 504.
Metropolises are Primary Metropolitan Statistical Areas or New England County Metropolitan Areas, as defined for the Census of 1990.
[a]This is the index of dissimilarity, computed from block group data measuring the segregation of non-Hispanic blacks from non-Hispanic whites.
[b]These indices show the average percentage of blacks in the block group of residence of non-Hispanic blacks and the average percentage of whites in the block group of residence of non-Hispanic whites.

metropolises. Detroit and Chicago were most segregated, with scores of 89 and 88, respectively, but in other areas the segregation was somewhat lower: 75 in metropolitan Los Angeles; 73 for Atlanta; 71 for Boston. In rapidly growing metropolises of the South and West, blacks and whites were much less segregated: 62 in San Diego, and 52 for San Bernardino–Riverside.

Did segregation increase or decline during the 1980s? Across the country, there is evidence that federal laws designed to provide equal housing opportunities—the Open Housing Law of 1968, the Community Reinvestment Act of 1974, and the Home Mortgage Disclosure Act of 1975—had a modest effect, since there was an extensive pattern of small declines in black-white segregation (Farley and Frey 1994). Column 3 of table 6.2 shows that the index fell by 9 points in both Los Angeles and Houston, and by 15 in Dallas. At the other extreme were New York City, Philadelphia, and the metropolis that includes Long Island—where the segregation score dropped just 1 point. Detroit was the *only* large metropolis where black-white residential segregation was just as extensive in 1990 as it had been ten years earlier.

When blacks and whites look around their neighborhoods, when they send their children to local schools or shop in local stores, do they find other members of their own race or do they see a mix representing the diversity of the metropolitan population? "Residential isolation indexes" measure this dimension of segregation and are shown in the last two columns of the table. Some blacks in metropolitan Detroit lived in block groups where all the residents were African Americans, but a few lived in block groups where almost all the other inhabitants were white. The typical black, however, lived in a neighborhood where 83 percent of the other residents were black. Blacks made up 22 percent of the metropolitan population, so this finding reflects a high degree of racial isolation.

The residential isolation index for whites in Detroit in 1990 was 92, meaning that the typical white lived in a neighborhood where 92 percent of the other residents were white. These isolation indexes report that both whites and blacks can go about their daily lives seldom meeting someone from the other race. Thomas Sugrue observed that in 1940 a visitor to Detroit "could have walked or driven miles in large sections of the city and seen only white faces" (1996, 24). When gathering data in our 1992 survey, one of the authors drove for miles in Oakland and Macomb counties with the same result.

How does Detroit compare to other metropolises with regard to the racial isolation of its black and white residents? Among the 15 largest metropolises, Detroit tied Chicago for having the most racially isolated black population. Detroit, Boston, Philadelphia, St. Louis, and Minneapolis were at the top of the list for the racial isolation of whites. The isolation index, unlike the index of dissimilarity, is strongly influenced by the relative size of the racial groups, so the very high degree of racial isolation for whites in Minneapolis reflects not only the segregation of the races into distinct neighborhoods but the relatively few African Americans there.

The isolation indexes in table 6.2 show substantial variations in the living arrangements of the races. In Boston, blacks lived in neighborhoods where only 46 percent of the residents were black; the majority of their neighbors were whites, Asians, or Latinos. In Los Angeles, the isolation index for African Americans was 45, also implying much interracial contact at the local level. And in San Bernardino and San Diego, blacks lived in predominantly white neighborhoods. Blacks in Detroit live in neighborhoods different from those of African Americans in other metropolises: their neighborhoods have a much higher density of blacks.

Residential Segregation in Detroit: Skin Color, Class, or Ethnic?

Blacks and whites in Detroit differ greatly in both their economic status and their neighborhoods. In fact, differences in income, occupational achievement, and educational attainment account for only a small fraction of residential segregation in Detroit or elsewhere. Census data provide us with information about the incomes of all households living in a block group and the incomes of all blacks and whites throughout metropolitan Detroit. We used a computer simulation to assign households to block groups on the basis of their income and the incomes of households enumerated there in 1990. That is, in this model everyone was assigned to a neighborhood on the basis of household income, not on the basis of skin color. The result are as shown in table 6.3.

TABLE 6.3   *Actual and Expected Indexes of Residential Segregation of Blacks from Whites, Metropolitan Detroit, 1990 (Block Group Data)*

	Index of Dissimilarity
Householders classified by income	
Actual black-white segregation index of householders	88
Segregation index expected solely on the basis of household's income	15
Employed householders classified by occupation	
Actual black-white segregation index of householders	88
Segregation index expected solely on the basis of householder's occupation	5
Adults age twenty-five and over classified by educational attainment	
Actual black-white segregation index of persons aged twenty-five and over	88
Segregation index expected solely on the basis of adults' educational attainment	6

Source: U.S. Department of Commerce 1992a.

164

Residential segregation is a matter of skin color, not income, occupation, or education. If household income alone determined where people lived, the index of dissimilarity would be 15 instead of 88. Some segregation results from the large difference in income, but if residents were assigned to their neighborhoods on the basis of income, metropolitan Detroit would be thoroughly integrated.

People with high-status jobs may wish to live near others with good jobs, while those working at the least prestigious jobs may have few residential options, so they live near others of their occupational class. But if whites and blacks were assigned to neighborhoods on the basis of their occupational achievement, the residential segregation score would only be 5 instead of 88.

Educational attainment is an often used indicator of social class and is a solid predictor of earnings over the lifetime. Blacks and whites still differ in their years of schooling. In Detroit, in 1999, 31 percent of whites aged twenty-five and over had a two- or four-year college degree, compared with only 20 percent of blacks. Yet, if people were assigned to neighborhoods on the basis of how many years they spent in classrooms, the black-white residential segregation score would be only 6.

Racial attitudes have changed greatly in recent decades and, fortunately, the era when white residents violently intimidate a new black neighbor has ended. But the segregation pattern of that earlier era persists. Rich blacks do not live in the same neighborhoods as rich whites, nor do poor blacks live alongside poor whites. Figure 6.1 presents indexes of dissimilarity in 1990, controlling for household income (top panel) and for the educational attainment of the household head (bottom panel). The segregation score comparing the residences of blacks and whites households with income of under $5,000 (in 1989 dollars) was 80. As incomes went up, so did the residential segregation of blacks from whites, at least until the $100,000 threshold was reached. Similarly, the residential segregation scores for those with less than a high school education were only a little greater than those comparing the residential distributions of blacks and whites who had college degrees. In Detroit, income, education, and occupation did not explain why blacks and whites were so highly segregated.

The segregation of blacks from whites in metropolitan Detroit is extremely high, but is it unique? If we look at other ethnic or racial groups, will we find similarly high levels of segregation? As immigrants came to American cities, they clustered in specific neighborhoods and, in Detroit, ethnic terms are still used: Corktown for the neighborhood southwest of the central business district and Poletown for neighborhoods near Hamtramck.

Metropolitan Detroit has attracted only a few of the new immi-

FIGURE 6.1 *Residential Segregation of Blacks from Whites,*
Controlling for Income and Educational Attainment,
Detroit Metropolitan Area, 1990

Residential Segregation, Controlling for Income[a]

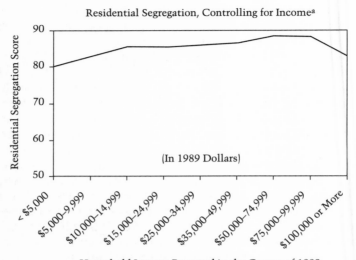

Household Income Reported in the Census of 1990

Residential Segregation, Controlling for Education[b]

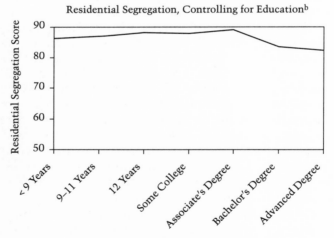

Educational Attainment of Householder

Source: U. S. Department of Commerce 1992a.
Note: Indexes of dissimilarity were computed from block group data and refer to Macomb, Oakland, and Wayne counties including the city of Detroit.
[a]Households were classified by reported income in 1989 and by race of household head.
[b]Indexes are based upon the population aged twenty-five and over, classified by race and educational attainment.

TABLE 6.4   *Residential Segregation of Racial Groups, Metropolitan Detroit 1990*

	Index of Dissimilarity Measuring Residential Segregation From	
Racial or Ethnic Group	Non-Latino Whites	Non-Latino Blacks
Latinos	44	83
Non-Latino Native Americans	47	79
Non-Latino Asians	51	86
Non-Latino blacks	89	—

Source: U.S. Department of Commerce 1992a.

grants from the streams now coming in great numbers to New York, Los Angeles, Miami, and other ports of entry. In 1990, just 1.4 percent of metropolitan Detroit residents marked an Asian race on their census form, while 1.8 percent said they were Spanish in origin. However, these minorities, and the small Native-American population living in Detroit, were much less residentially segregated than were African Americans. Shown in table 6.4 are indexes of dissimilarity based on block group data from the Census of 1990, reporting on the segregation of these groups from non-Latino whites and from non-Latino African Americans.

While Latinos, Native Americans, and Asians are not highly segregated from whites, they, like whites, are highly segregated from blacks. This is a common finding in segregation research. New international immigrants are highly segregated from the black population, but their residential decisions leave them only moderately segregated from whites.

In addition to race and Spanish origin, the census asks about ancestry or ethnicity. People could write any phrase they wished, but most wrote well-known terms such as English, Irish, German, or African American. Again using block group data for the metropolis in 1990, we classified residents by the first ancestry they reported, then computed indexes of dissimilarity. Although the first European settlers in Detroit were French, the dominant group since the early 1800s has been the English. For that reason, we compared white ancestry groups—and African Americans—to those who said they were English by ancestry. These indexes are shown in table 6.5.

Ethnic groups are residentially segregated from those reporting English ancestry, but nowhere near as thoroughly as they are from blacks. Detroit residents whose ancestral group arrived in the United States before the Civil War frequently lived in the same neighborhoods as the descendants of the English, as shown by scores of 25 for the Irish and 23 for Germans. Descendants of groups arriving between 1880 and World War I are somewhat more residentially segregated from the "English,"

TABLE 6.5   *Indexes of Residential Segregation of Ancestry Groups and Blacks from Detroit's English Ancestry Population, 1990*

	Index of Dissimilarity Measuring Segregation from the English	Number (Thousands) in 1990
Groups arriving before the industrialization of Detroit (prior to 1880)		
Germans	23	638
Irish	25	285
Scottish	34	108
French	42	128
Groups arriving during the industrialization of Detroit (1880 to World War I)		
Polish	36	377
Italian	40	193
French-Canadian	42	51
Russian	67	35
Recent immigrants to Detroit (post–World War I)		
Arabs	67	51
Blacks	91	929

Source: U.S. Department of Commerce 1992a.

with scores of 36 for Poles and 42 for Detroiters claiming French-Canadian ancestry.

A substantial proportion of Americans who identify as Russian by ancestry are Jewish. Detroit continues to have one of the nation's largest Jewish populations, with a concentration, including a large number of orthodox Jews, in Southfield. Russians in 1990 were much more residentially segregated from the "English" population than any other European ethnic group. This may reflect the preference of some Jews for residing within walking distance of their synagogues, as well as the persisting consequences of real estate practices that once truncated housing market opportunities for Jews.

One major stream of international immigrants that has been arriving in Detroit recently are immigrants from the eastern Mediterranean. We do not know how these people identify themselves when asked the ancestry question; many are Christians, and some have mother tongues other than Arabic. Nevertheless, in 1990, about 1.4 percent of metropolitan Detroiters said their ancestry was Arabic. The suburb with the long history of opposition to black residents, Dearborn, is a center for this new immigration stream. Fourteen thousand Arabs were enumerated there—16 percent of the suburb's total residents. This newly arriving group is also rather highly segregated from the "English" population.

What about blacks? Their residential segregation from the "English" was the greatest: a score of 91.

A Glimpse of the Future: Will New Demographic Trends Promote Residential Integration?

In the 1980s, black-white residential segregation declined a bit in most metropolises. Two factors accounted for much of that reduction. First was the construction of many new homes and apartments in rapidly growing metropolises, especially places in the South and West. Those new neighborhoods were less segregated than older central-city areas or the immediate post–World War II suburbs, presumably because federal laws now prohibit discriminatory practices that created and enforced segregation. Second, a new demographic pattern emerged in the 1980s: the suburbanization of blacks (Frey 1994, 1995). Three decades after whites started moving from central cities to the suburbs in great numbers, African Americans began the same trek. Among the causes of this suburbanization are the growth of a black middle class, the aging of central-city housing and decreases in racial discrimination in the real estate industry. By 1990, the majority of blacks in metropolitan Atlanta, Los Angeles, and St. Louis lived in the suburbs and, in Washington, D.C., two-thirds lived in the ring rather than the central city. Detroit and Chicago stood out for the exceptionally high concentration of blacks in the central city—about 82 percent in both places.

In the 1980s, the suburban black population in Detroit grew noticeably. Looking back at that list of large suburbs in table 6.1, you will see information about their populations in 1990. Similar to the city of Detroit, most of them lost a large share of their inhabitants as the white baby-boom children who once filled suburban bedrooms grew up and moved away. But the barriers that kept blacks out were apparently lowered. Suburbs that had a tiny number of African Americans twenty years earlier had, in 1990, substantial black populations: Bloomfield Township, Farmington Hills, Taylor, and Southfield. In most of the other suburbs, the number of blacks increased and, in all but two places, the proportion of residents who are African American rose.

As Frey (1994, 1995) has shown, black suburbanization in the 1980s was highly selective of the middle class, just as white suburbanization had been several decades earlier. Is this process occurring in Detroit? Does it signal decreases in segregation?

In 1990, prosperous blacks were more likely to live in the ring than

FIGURE 6.2   *Percentage of Metropolitan-Area Blacks and Whites*
Living in the Suburban Ring, 1990

Households Classified by Income in 1989 (in 1989 Dollars)

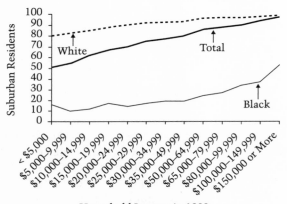

Household Income in 1989

Households Classified by Education in 1989

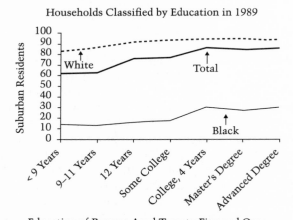

Education of Persons Aged Twenty-Five and Over

Source: U.S. Department of Commerce 1993.

were those with low incomes, as illustrated in figure 6.2. The upper
panel classifies black and white households by income; the lower panel
refers to the educational attainment of the household head.

Regardless of their poverty or prosperity, Detroit whites generally
lived in the suburbs and blacks in the central city. No more than 20

percent of whites with the least favorable socioeconomic characteristics had central-city addresses, but for similar African Americans it was 85 percent. More than 90 percent of whites with household incomes exceeding $100,000 or with postgraduate degrees resided in the suburbs. For similarly advantaged blacks, less than 50 percent lived in the ring. Nevertheless, as the economic status of Detroit blacks increased, so too did the proportion living in the suburbs.

As social and economic trends encourage growth of the black middle class, the suburbanization of African Americans will likely increase. Between 1990 and 1997, the Census Bureau estimates that the black population of outlying Oakland and Macomb counties rose by 16 percent, while the white population grew by only 6 percent. The Census of 2000 will reveal whether black suburbanization in Detroit means racial integration, or is primarily the emergence of largely African American neighborhoods in the ring.

The City-Suburban Exchange of Local Movers: Implications for the Future?

In metropolitan Detroit, as in most older locations where central-city boundaries were drawn before the Depression, those who moved from the city to the suburbs in the 1980s were more numerous and more prosperous than those who moved from the ring to the city. Thus, there is a selective out-migration from Detroit of the more economically successful among both races. A look at what happened just prior to the last census gives us an indication of current and future demographic shifts.

Table 6.6 presents information about persons aged twenty-five to sixty-four in 1990 who lived in the metropolis in both 1985 and 1990. These individuals were classified by their place of residence. Five characteristics of "movers" and "stayers" are shown.

Eighteen thousand adult blacks who lived in the city in 1985 were counted in the ring five years later, but only 4,000 moved in the opposite direction. For whites, the discrepancy was much larger, reflecting their continuing exodus. There were 21 white residents of the city moving to the suburbs for every white who moved from the ring to the city: 149,000 going in one direction, but only 7,000 in the other. Detroit's overall white population fell by more than 200,000 in the 1990s, but the suburban flow will undoubtedly be smaller in the 1990s, since there were only 222,000 whites in the city at the start of the decade.

With regard to socioeconomic indicators, those who lived in the suburbs at both dates were the most successful, while those who moved

TABLE 6.6 *Characteristics of Metropolitan Detroit Area Residents Aged Twenty-Five to Sixty-Four in 1990, by Place of Residence in 1985 and 1990*

	Central-City Residents in Both 1985 and 1990	Central City in 1985, Suburbs in 1990	Suburban Residents in Both 1985 and 1990	Suburbs in 1985, Central City in 1990
Blacks				
Number (thousands)	325	18	51	4
Characteristics in 1990				
Average age	41	39	42	36
Average household income	$33,100	$41,500	$44,300	$35,000
Percentage below poverty line	27	19	15	23
Percentage with some college degree	16	27	24	23
Percentage married-spouse-present	38	44	48	29
Whites				
Number (thousands)	88	149	1,055	7
Characteristics in 1990				
Average age	43	38	43	36
Average household income	$35,200	$52,000	$59,200	$34,800
Percentage below poverty line	18	6	4	21
Percentage with some college degree	18	31	30	28
Percentage married-spouse-present	52	66	74	37

Source: U.S. Department of Commerce 1993.
Note: College degree refers to Associate's Degree or higher. Amounts are shown in 1997 dollars.

from the city to the ring were more prosperous than those who remained in the city. Blacks who left the city for the ring reported average household incomes of $52,890 in 1989 (in 1997 dollars), but those staying in the city reported only $42,700. For both races, the percent with a college degree was at least 10 points higher for city-to-ring movers than it was for those remaining in the city: the typical pattern of selective movement to the suburbs found throughout the nation. Similarly, those leaving the city were more likely to be married and living with a spouse in 1990 than were those who stayed.

Changes in economic status or marital status are often linked to local migration in less than obvious ways, and these data are influenced by out-migration from the city of those young persons who earned degrees at Wayne State or Detroit–Mercy, as well as those who lived in the city while completing internships at the Henry Ford medical complex. Nevertheless, they provide discouraging information about the economic standing of city residents, since those who moved away were economically more successful than those who remained. In addition, the city, with its stock of older and inexpensive housing, may now be attracting a small stream of suburban whites and blacks who are not very successful. The poverty rates for blacks and whites moving from suburbs to the city of Detroit were similar to the elevated poverty rates for city residents and much higher than the poverty rates of those who remained in the suburbs.

During the 1990s, a number of middle- and upper-income housing developments were completed along the Detroit River. The Census of 2000 will tell us whether the city is now attracting a modest flow of prosperous suburbanites who seek the amenities offered by these additions to the housing stock.

New Migrants to Metropolitan Detroit: Where Do They Choose to Live?

The locational decisions of those who moved into metropolitan Detroit from around the country also give an indicator of future trends. While there was a substantial net out-migration from Detroit in the late 1980s, there were many who moved into the metropolis: about 115,000 whites and 18,000 blacks aged twenty-five and over moved from outside the state of Michigan to metropolitan Detroit. The small flow of immigrants from abroad is included. Figure 6.3 classified them by their educational attainment and the place they selected for their home within metropolitan Detroit.

Four destination locations were considered: the central city, the remainder of Wayne County, Macomb County, and Oakland County. Each panel shows a bar graph to the far right reporting the educational distribution of persons who lived in the metropolis from 1985 to 1990—the residential stayers. The heavy black in each bar shows the percent living in the city, while the shaded and white areas report the percent living in three suburban locales.

For both races, there was much destination selectivity, with those lacking a high school diploma most likely to opt for the city or for Wayne County, where quite a few older and industrial suburbs are found. In-migrants who had college diplomas, on the other hand, were most likely to move into rapidly growing and prosperous Oakland County. While black in-migrants at every educational level were much

FIGURE 6.3   *Distribution of In-Migrants to Metropolitan Detroit from Outstate and of Nonmovers, by Race and Education, Aged Twenty-Five and Over*

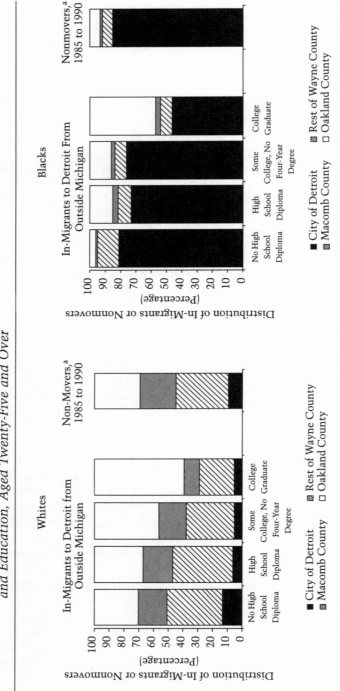

Source: U. S. Department of Commerce 1993.
[a]These data refer to people who resided in metropolitan Detroit in both 1985 and 1990.

more likely than whites to select the city, those with college degrees were about as likely to choose Oakland County as the city of Detroit—another indication of the new pattern of black suburbanization.

There is a slowly growing black middle class in Detroit, as in the remainder of the nation. Major employers undoubtedly recruit many highly educated African Americans from around the country to work in their clinics, labs, design studios, and offices. These economically secure black migrants seek, quite likely, the same housing amenities and pleasant communities that their white counterparts seek. Frequently, the neighborhoods they find most attractive are located in the outlying suburbs, especially in Oakland County.

Conclusion

Over the course of the last century, Detroit's African Americans have become increasingly isolated from whites. Using information about the distribution of blacks and whites across city wards for the early decades and across census tracts in the metropolis for recent census dates, we can assess the long-run trend in racial isolation (Cutler and Glaeser 1997). Figure 6.4 reports the average percentage of residents who were African American in the neighborhood of the typical Detroit black area. In 1890, blacks lived alongside the whites who numerically dominated the city. In that year, blacks lived in neighborhoods where only 11 percent of the residents were African Americans, so as they went around their neighborhoods they saw many whites. As blacks moved to Detroit in greater numbers, their isolation from whites rose. By 1940, the typical African American lived in a census tract in which 60 percent of the residents were black. Residential isolation continued to climb throughout the last half century, so that by 1990 the typical census tracts where blacks lived averaged 85 percent African American.

What are the consequences of this residential segregation and racial isolation? For purposes of political organization it may be desirable for minorities to be concentrated into a few neighborhoods, but there are also liabilities. If one group has been the target of discrimination for generations and if many members of a more prosperous and powerful group harbor negative sentiments about a minority, residential concentration may be harmful. As Gunnar Myrdal observed in his landmark study, "Residential segregation and segregation at places of work hinder whites from having personal acquaintance with Negroes and recognizing that Negroes are much like themselves." (1944, 391). He concluded that residential segregation denied blacks access to schools, parks, and opportunities available to whites, and it allowed local and state officials to provide African Americans with second-rate services (1944, 618–22).

FIGURE 6.4   *Percentage Black in the Residential Area of the Typical Black in Detroit: A Century-Long Trend*

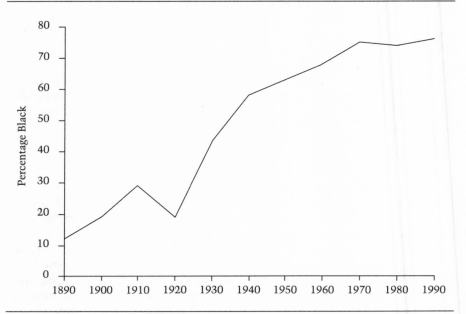

Source: Cutler and Glaeser 1997.
Note: These measures of residential isolation were calculated from ward data from 1890 through 1930, and census tract data for later years. Data pertain to the city of Detroit for 1890 through 1950 and to the metropolis for later years.

Segregation continues to have important consequences. In chapter 4, we report that suburban employers are less likely to hire central city applicants than suburban applicants, and in chapter 5, we describe how residence influences job search. Chapter 7 shows that African Americans who owned homes in the city of Detroit have lost more of their equity than did suburban white home owners—an effect of segregation and the limited demand for housing in the city.

After reviewing racial differences in social and economic status, John Yinger (1995, 248) concluded that housing discrimination and segregation played key roles in maintaining racial differences in employment, income, poverty and wealth holdings. Douglas Massey and Nancy Denton (1993, chap. 5) describe the process whereby residential segregation concentrates poverty, and in turn creates the urban underclass neighborhoods found in many cities.

Examining the nation's metropolises in 1990, David Cutler and Edward Glaeser analyzed the consequences of residential segregation for young African Americans making the school to work transition. They found that young blacks living in highly segregated places were significantly more likely to drop out of high school and were more likely to be idle—that is, neither working nor going to school—than those living in more integrated locations. And African American young women residing in highly segregated places were more likely to be single mothers. They concluded that if residential segregation were eliminated, "black-white differences in earnings, high school graduate rates and idleness would disappear as would two-thirds of the black-white difference in single motherhood" (Cutler and Glaeser 1997, 847).

Other studies have estimated the net impact of racial residential segregation upon the death rates of African Americans. Apart from other explanatory factors, black infants in highly segregated cities are more likely to die before their first birthday than those living in more integrated cities (LaViest 1989, 1993; Polednak 1991); the homicide rate of African Americans is higher in segregated metropolises (Peterson and Krivo 1993, 1999), as are the death rates of adult blacks (Hart et al. 1998; Polednak 1993; Collins and Williams 1999).

7

The Persistence of Residential Segregation

WHY DO blacks and whites continue to live in different places more than fifty years after the Supreme Court overturned restrictive covenants and thirty years after federal open housing legislation outlawed discrimination in the housing market? Four reasons are frequently cited for persistent segregation:

(1) Economic differences lead blacks and whites to seek differently priced housing; hence they do not live together.

(2) Blacks and whites may differ in their knowledge of the housing market. African Americans may overestimate the cost of suburban housing and fail to seek homes and apartments that they can afford. In addition, the races may differ in the type of housing and amenities they prefer.

(3) Blacks may desire to live in predominantly black neighborhoods, while whites may prefer white areas.

(4) Discriminatory practices in real estate and mortgage lending may steer blacks and whites to different neighborhoods.

The last chapter demonstrated that economic differences do not account for residential segregation. In this chapter, we primarily address the second and third explanations. Findings in this chapter come from household surveys carried out in the three-county metropolis, one in 1976 and the other in 1992. In both, census data (from 1970 or 1990) were used to select a sample of residential blocks. Housing units within those blocks were randomly sampled, and a random adult was selected in every occupied housing unit by the interviewer. The sample size in 1976 was 1,134 and in 1992 it was 1,543. In both years, if the census reported that blacks made up at least 70 percent of the residents in a block, the sampling ratio was increased. Thus, our sample included 400 African Americans in 1976 and 750 sixteen years later.

Racial Differences in the Knowledge of the Housing Market

When people decide where to seek a new home or apartment, they surely draw on their own knowledge of the local housing market. We all know about the desirability of living in some neighborhoods and that others are unattractive either because of the poor quality of housing or the people. We know where expensive housing is located, and where more reasonably priced homes and apartments may be found. A few people may do library research to investigate property values, tax rates, crime rates, and the test scores of children in the local schools but those individuals are rare exceptions. When a person contemplates moving or staying, he or she normally relies on information—and misinformation—provided by friends, relatives, co-workers, and neighbors. Over time we develop images of where we would like to live and where we would avoid living.

In these Detroit Area Surveys, we wished to determine whether blacks and whites shared these "cognitive maps." To do so, we considered three important dimensions of neighborhoods:

(1) whether both races share similar information about the cost of housing and whether that housing is within the financial reach of African Americans

(2) whether blacks and whites share similar values about which locations are desirable and which are unattractive

(3) whether blacks and whites share similar views about which areas would tolerate or welcome blacks should they move there and which areas would not.

Respondents were shown a map identifying Detroit and five suburbs. We selected locations largely because they were well known, but we wanted them to vary with regard to housing costs, distance from the city of Detroit, and reputations for hostility to African Americans. In some metropolises where there is a great deal of recent construction, much of the housing stock may be in places that are not well known and have not yet developed a clear reputation with regard to either economic class or racial issues. That is not the case in Detroit. Just 11 percent of the 1990 housing stock had been built in the previous ten years. (In Atlanta, the comparable figure was 37 percent; in Dallas, 34 percent; and in Los Angeles, 16 percent.) Map 7.1 shows the suburbs selected for this analysis and their locations.

MAP 7.1   *Map of the Detroit Metropolitan Area*

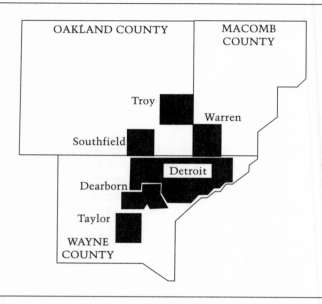

Southfield   Southfield, a suburb just across Eight Mile Road from the city of Detroit with a population of 75,000 in 1998, has had a favorable tax base for years because it includes several large office complexes, shopping centers, and auto-parts plants. Its tax revenues provide its residents with excellent public services and attractive schools. Indeed, it is known as a suburb with unusually good services. Southfield has had a Jewish population since the suburban boom started, presumably the largest concentration in the metropolis. Housing prices have been relatively high—a median estimated value of $85,100 in 1990, compared with a suburban ring median of $70,700 (in 1990 dollars). It has the distinction of being the only prosperous Detroit suburb with a large and growing black population: 29 percent in 1990.

Dearborn   Dearborn, an older suburb of 92,000 in 1998, also shares its borders with the city of Detroit. Housing costs in 1990 were about average for the metropolis, but the range of housing was great. Several neighborhoods (originally designed for Ford executives) include expensive homes adjoining lovely parks and a golf course, and are among the most attractive places in the suburban ring. Other neighborhoods, those closest to the city of Detroit, contain older and much less costly housing built after World War I for the families of factory workers. Dearborn has traditionally had a strong reputation for hostility to blacks.

Warren   Warren, a suburb of 142,000 in 1998, also shares a border with the city of Detroit and has had a solid economic base for years since many of the automobile plants built in the ring after World War II were located there. Warren and surrounding Macomb County became well known in the 1980s as the home of the Reagan Democrats. Political analysts regularly visited and described the traditionally Democratic blue-collar workers who felt threatened by the liberal policies of their party and so voted Republican, thereby playing a key role in the election of President Reagan (Greenberg 1996, chap. 2). Warren had a reputation in the past for considerable hostility toward blacks.

Taylor   Taylor, a suburb of 73,000, once had a reputation for inexpensive housing and was known for its large population of white migrants from Appalachia. It has never been seen as a desirable or prestigious location, since it is adjacent to Detroit's Metropolitan Airport and several industrial complexes. Unlike Dearborn and Warren, it does not have a reputation for hostility to blacks. In the 1990s, this suburb embarked upon a major effort to upgrade its image by tearing down public housing that dated from World War II, building more expensive housing, and attracting stores that catered to prosperous shoppers.

Troy   This booming suburb of 79,000 in Oakland County symbolizes suburban prosperity and prestige. It anchors the most rapidly growing section of metropolitan Detroit and is close to office, shopping, and entertainment complexes that are, arguably, the most attractive in the metropolis. Chrysler Corporation located its new headquarters there, not far from the impressive new arena built for the Detroit Pistons' National Basketball Association team (Garreau 1991, chap. 4). The residents of Troy in 1990 estimated that their homes were worth $128,900, far above the suburban ring median of $70,700 (see table 7.1). (In 1976 we did not ask about Troy, since it was a smaller and less well known suburb then.)

Housing Costs

Almost everyone searching for housing rules out some neighborhoods because they are too pricey, and others because the homes there are too shabby or too small. Do blacks and whites share identical information about housing costs in the five suburbs? Is their information accurate?

We asked respondents to estimate the average cost of homes in each area and then, much later in the interview, asked them whether they thought that "almost all," "many," "about half," "only a few," or "almost no" black families could afford to live there.

Both blacks and whites overestimated the cost of suburban housing. The actual value of homes in any location is determined by the housing market, but when people search for a home they make decisions on the basis of their belief about housing costs and seldom consult statistics that would tell them what homes are really selling for in some area or how assessors evaluated them.

The census asks the owners or renters of single-family residences to estimate their home's current market value. We compared the estimates obtained in the 1992 Detroit Area Survey to the estimates provided by residents in the area two years earlier, using the median estimated value. We did not adjust for inflation in the 1990 to 1992 interval (the national Consumer Price Index went up about 7 percent in that span) since there was no reason to think that homes in every area were appreciating at the national rate of inflation.

Blacks and whites thought that homes in Troy were the most costly and those in Taylor the least costly—a finding corroborated by census data. Indeed, both races ranked the suburbs' housing costs much the same, since they agreed that Dearborn and Southfield had more expensive homes than Warren. In addition, they hardly differed in the degree to which they overestimated housing costs, as shown by information in the right-hand columns of table 7.1. The estimates of both races for housing costs in Southfield were about 15 percent higher than the estimate of homeowners there. And blacks and whites were similar in overestimating prices in Taylor, the one lower-priced suburb we included. So, with regard to the price of housing, African American and whites shared similar information.[1]

Affordability

To further explore whether perceptions about costs contribute to segregation, we asked respondents what proportion of metropolitan black families they thought could afford to live in each location. We wanted to determine whether both races shared the view that the some suburbs were too costly for African Americans. Figure 7.1 shows the percent of black and white respondents who said that "about half," "many," or "almost all" blacks could afford to live in each locations. That is, the percent who thought the suburb was in the price range blacks could afford.

Both races shared similar views about blacks' financial capabilities. They recognized that most blacks could afford to live in Taylor; that is, in 1992 79 percent of whites and 66 percent of blacks told us they

TABLE 7.1   Information About Cost of Housing, Estimated by Survey Respondents and Residents (in 1990 Dollars)

	1990 Census Data		Median Value of Homes, Estimated by Owners	Median Value as Estimated by Respondents		Ratio of Respondents Estimate to Owners' Estimate	
	Population Size (Thousands)	Percentage Black		Black	White	Black	White
Southfield	76	29	$85,100	$99,700	$98,200	1.17	1.15
Warren	145	< 1	69,500	76,400	87,800	1.11	1.26
Dearborn	89	< 1	68,600	95,200	100,200	1.37	1.44
Taylor	71	4	48,400	69,700	75,500	1.44	1.56
Troy	73	1	128,900	128,600	145,000	1.00	1.12
City of Detroit	1,028	76	25,600	n.a.	n.a.	n.a.	n.a.
Entire Suburban Ring	2,887	5	79,700	n.a.	n.a.	n.a.	n.a.
Entire Metropolis	3,915	24	60,200	n.a.	n.a.	n.a.	n.a.

Source: University of Michigan, Detroit Area Survey 1992; U.S. Department of Commerce 1992b, tables 3 and 51.
Note: The census estimate was provided by the owners of single-family dwelling units, excluding those attached to commercial space.

FIGURE 7.1   *Percentage of Respondents Saying "About Half,"*
"Many," or "Almost All" Blacks Could Afford to Live
in Selected Locations, 1976 and 1992

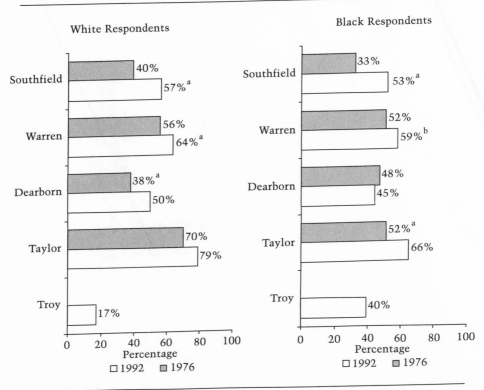

Source: University of Michigan, Detroit Area Study 1976, 1992. For additional information, see Farley et al. 1978, 1993.
[a]Change is statistically significant at .01 level.
[b]Change is statistically significant at .05 level.

thought half or more blacks could afford to live there. They also agreed
that many fewer blacks could afford Troy. Blacks and whites thought
that all the other locations were more affordable to blacks.

Between 1976 and 1992, both races thought that increasing proportions of African Americans could afford to live in the suburbs, with the
exception of a slight decline in blacks' views about Dearborn as an affordable place. Although they generally overestimated suburban housing
costs in 1992, we emphasize that both blacks and whites believed that

184

most African Americans could afford to live in Detroit suburbs—except for the most costly, Troy.

In the past, whites may have assumed that the lack of income and wealth holdings on the part of blacks was a major reason why so few lived in suburbs, but this has changed. By 1992, significantly more whites than in 1976 saw the suburbs as within the price range of most black families. And blacks, much more so in 1992 than in 1976, also viewed Detroit suburbs as within their budgets.

The Desirability of Suburbs

Do blacks and whites share the same "congitive map" when it comes to evaluating suburbs? Or if blacks evaluate a suburb as desirable, do whites almost inevitably see it as undesirable?

To find out, we asked the following question: First [name of location such as Southfield or Dearborn], Do you think [name of location] is a very desirable place to live, somewhat desirable, somewhat undesirable, or very undesirable? Responses are shown in figure 7.2.

In 1992, blacks viewed Southfield as the most desirable of the suburbs—88 percent called it very desirable or somewhat desirable. The expensive and distant suburb of Troy was next on the list, while Dearborn was at the bottom. These rankings were similar to those given by blacks in 1976.

There were significant black-white differences in the evaluation of Southfield in 1992, and for Dearborn in both years, strongly suggesting that race influences these ratings. In 1976, both races saw Southfield as a highly desirable location. Sixteen years later, whites had shifted their evaluations downward, while blacks gave it an even more positive ranking. Successful African Americans who wished to buy a high-quality modern home in a prosperous suburb with a sound tax base knew that one could be found in Southfield—along with quite a few black neighbors. This suburb's increasingly mixed racial composition undoubtedly led some whites to change their views. In 1976, 81 percent said it was a desirable place to live, but in 1992, only 54 percent did. Indeed, Warren, with its blue-collar population and homes worth about 20 percent less than those in Southfield, was more highly evaluated by whites. For whites, Dearborn was the most positively evaluated one in 1976, and second only to Troy in 1992.

Our aim in this chapter is to explain the persistence of segregation, so we sought information about one more key component of the cognitive maps people bring to the housing market. Do blacks and whites share the same views about which locations might welcome African

FIGURE 7.2   *Percentage of Black and White Respondents Rating Selected Suburbs as "Very Desirable" or "Somewhat Desirable" Places to Live, 1976 and 1992*

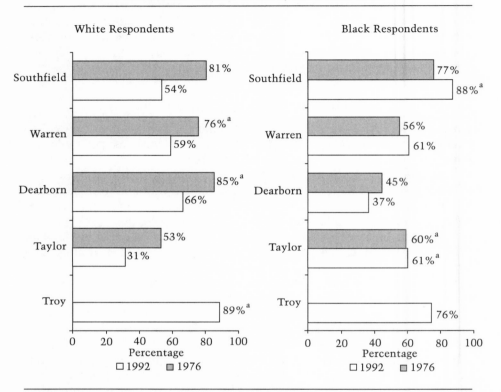

Source: University of Michigan, Detroit Area Study 1976, 1992. For additional information, see Farley et al. 1978, 1993.
[a]Change is statistically significant at .01 level. Racial difference is significant at .01 level.

Americans and which would treat them with hostility? When searching for housing, many blacks—but certainly not all—may rule out some neighborhoods because they think the whites living there would be upset by their arrival, would make them feel unwelcome, would scrutinize their behavior, and would taunt their children in school. Do whites share the views of blacks with regard to which suburbs are "open"?

We asked: "Now think about [name of location such as Southfield or Dearborn]; if a black family moved into that area, do you think they

FIGURE 7.3   *Percentage of Black and White Respondents Reporting that Area's White Residents Would React Negatively if a Black Moved in, 1976 and 1992*

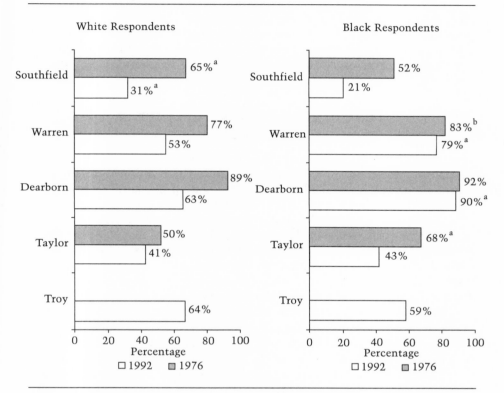

Source: University of Michigan, Detroit Area Study 1976, 1992. For additional information, see Farley et al. 1978, 1993.
[a]Change is statistically significant at .01 level.
[b]Change is statistically significant at .05 level.

would be welcome, or do you think the people living there would be upset?" We gave respondents a choice of only "would be upset" or "would be welcome."

Figure 7.3 presents the results. Blacks and whites share similar views about where blacks are and are not welcome. Most whites and blacks in 1992 thought that the residents of Southfield and Taylor—the two suburbs with more than a few black residents—would not be upset if a black family moved there. But most respondents thought the residents of Warren and Dearborn would be.

As for the changes between 1976 and 1992, whites perceived an overall improvement in race relations, since the percentage who thought the residents of the suburbs (that is, other whites) would be upset declined for all four suburbs. Blacks did not share that judgment. To be sure, the comparison of African Americans in 1976 and 1992 reveal that they saw Southfield and Taylor as increasingly "open" to blacks. But with regard to the two suburbs with the strongest reputations for racial hostility, Dearborn and Warren, blacks saw no decline in whites' opposition.

The Neighborhood Preferences of Whites

The cognitive maps of Detroit area blacks and whites overlap when it comes to knowledge of housing costs and which suburbs might welcome or be hostile to blacks. They also overlap, to some degree, with regard to the evaluation of places, since both races put an emphasis on race, albeit a different evaluation. Having established those findings, we moved on to test the idea that residential segregation persists because whites want to live with white neighbors and blacks with blacks. To measure the neighborhood preferences of both races, we presented every respondent with five cards, each representing a neighborhood of fifteen houses. Figure 7.4 diagrams the cards shown to whites.

We showed the first card, with its all-white neighborhood, and asked the white person to imagine that he or she lived in such a place (a realistic assumption for most). They were then shown the second card, which portrayed them living at the center, with one of their fourteen neighbors as African American. We asked whether they would be very comfortable, somewhat comfortable, somewhat uncomfortable, or very uncomfortable if their own neighborhood came to resemble that minimally integrated neighborhood.

If they said "somewhat" or "very" comfortable, they were then shown cards with increasingly higher proportions of blacks until a card elicited a response of "somewhat uncomfortable" or "very uncomfortable" or until they came to the fifth card, showing a majority black neighborhood (Farley et al., 1978).

How comfortable whites feel is strongly linked to the racial composition of the neighborhood, but there are clear indications that racial attitudes have evolved from the era when the arrival of one black family triggered an out-movement of whites. In 1992, 84 percent of the 736 whites said they would be comfortable if one black moved into their neighborhood and 70 percent said they would be comfortable if blacks

FIGURE 7.4   *Neighborhood Diagrams Used for White Respondents,*
1976 and 1992

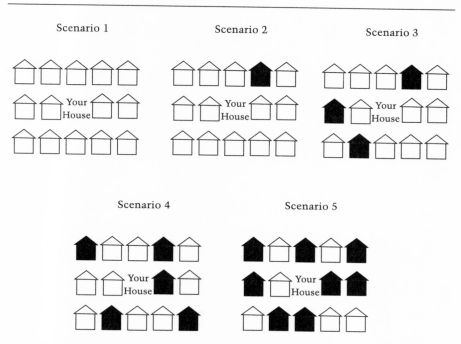

Source: University of Michigan, Detroit Area Study 1976, 1992. For additional information, see Farley et al. 1978, 1993.

were as highly represented in their own neighborhood as in the entire
metropolis; that is, if their neighborhood were made up of 3 blacks and
12 whites (Scenario 3 in figure 7.4). As the proportion of blacks increased, white comfort levels decreased. More than a majority said they
would be comfortable with Scenario 4, but only one-third said they
would be comfortable in the majority black area—the composition portrayed on the final card.

Figure 7.5 contrasts findings for 1976 and 1992, showing the shift
toward more acceptance of blacks in white neighborhoods. In every
comparison, higher proportions of whites in 1992 than in 1976 said they
would feel comfortable were their own neighborhood integrated.

But interracial neighborhoods will not last long if there is "white
flight" after blacks enter. We sought to determine whether whites

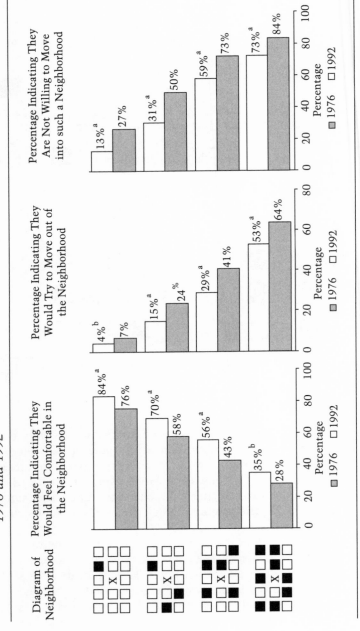

FIGURE 7.5   *Attractiveness of Neighborhoods of Varying Racial Compositions for White Respondents, 1976 and 1992*

Source: University of Michigan, Detroit Area Study 1976, 1992. For additional information, see Farley et al. 1978, 1993.
Note: The denominator for each percentage is the toal white population.
[a]Change is statistically significant at .01 level.
[b]Change is statistically significant at .05 level.

would leave when African Americans came to their neighborhoods—realizing, of course, that we were asking about hypothetical neighborhoods. We took the first racially mixed neighborhood that elicited a response of "uncomfortable" and asked the white if he or she would try to move away if their neighborhood came to have that racial composition. If the respondent said no, we presented the card with the next higher representation of blacks and repeated the question. Responses are shown in the middle panel of figure 7.5. We assumed that a white who would try to leave a 3-black/12-white neighborhood, would certainly try to leave an area with a higher density of blacks. We also assumed that the 35 percent of white sample that would be comfortable living in a majority African American neighborhood would not try to move out.

Few whites in 1992—only 4 percent—said they would try to move away if only one black entered their neighborhood, a drop from 7 percent in 1976. If whites were evenly distributed across the metropolitan landscape, neighborhoods would resemble the 3 black/12 white scenario. In 1992, only 15 percent of whites would try to leave such a location. Greater densities of African Americans, however, led more whites in both years to say they would move away. But, even in the majority black scenario, there was a significant increase over time in the proportion of whites who said they would stay.

Racially integrated neighborhoods will remain so only if some whites replace those who move away. To assess the willingness of whites to move into integrated neighborhoods, we gave every person the same set of five cards and asked which areas they would be willing to move into should they find an attractive home they could afford in each area. We directed their attention to the difference in racial composition and, to focus their attention on this task, we asked them to actually handle the five cards.

Are whites willing to move into neighborhoods that already have African American residents? The answer is yes if there are just a few blacks but no if there are many. In 1992, almost nine out of ten whites said they would move into the neighborhood with one black resident if they found an attractive home there (see the right-hand panel of figure 7.5). Considering the neighborhood with a racial composition similar to that of the metropolis, almost 70 percent of whites said they would consider moving in. But the racial tolerance of whites was limited, and in both 1976 and 1992 the majority of whites would not consider places with higher concentrations of black residents.

What Were Respondents Thinking When They Evaluated the Five Suburbs?

When blacks and whites rated a location as desirable or undesirable, did they primarily consider the quality of housing, the adequacy of city services, the economic status of the people who lived there, or the skin color of the residents? What judgments and opinions go into the cognitive maps people use when they think about their metropolis?

An hour-long face-to-face interview does not allow for lengthy discussions of what is good or bad about any specific place. But race is such a strong determinant of where one lives in metropolitan Detroit that we explored the thinking behind neighborhood evaluations by using open-ended questions. These questions about the desirability of Dearborn, Southfield, Taylor, Troy, and Warren were asked at the start of the interview—before any questions were asked about racial issues or how many African Americans could afford to live in a suburb.

If a respondent said that a specific suburb was "somewhat undesirable" or "very undesirable," he or she was asked, "Why do you say that (Name of Area) is an undesirable place to live?" In pre-tests, we found that we elicited more information by asking why a place was undesirable than by asking why it was desirable.

Many respondents replied with negative phrases or derogatory adjectives, such as the African American who said Taylor was undesirable because "Taylor is Hickstown, U.S.A. I wouldn't want to live there," or the white who, when asked about Southfield, replied: "Because of the Jewish and colored element. Or crime, whatever you choose." Others were more specific, including the white respondent who, when asked about Warren, said: "It has unstable land values. Detroit is moving in. Street people are moving in with drugs and shootings."

A coding scheme was created to capture as fully as possible the range of ideas respondents expressed when they explained why a suburb was undesirable. This is an excellent procedure for getting at what goes into the thinking of respondents when they tell us that they would not want to live in an area. Nine major themes were identified, such as the residential environment, crime in the suburb, or the deterioration of the suburb and its housing stock. These are listed in table 7.2. All responses were coded by two individuals after a training period in which they had to achieve an overall agreement rate of at least 70 percent (Krysan 1999a, 12 and app. A). A response could be classified into several categories. Indeed, many answers included a simultaneous mention of crime and the residential environment, or crime and race.

TABLE 7.2   *Respondents' Explanations for Why They Find Suburbs Undesirable*

	Dearborn	Southfield	Taylor	Troy	Warren
White respondents					
Number of respondents explaining why a suburb was undesirable	218	286	385		251
Reasons					
Residential environment	29%	36%	16%		31%
Crime	16	36	23		27
Deterioration of suburb and homes	17	16	18		20
Lack of or inadequate services	5	12	15		14
Lower-class population	0	1	16		8
Too expensive	1	6	.2		2
Too far away	14	3	13		6
Type of people who live there	4	5	12		9
Total racial reasons	27	14	4		7
Racial prejudice of its residents	11	1	3		4
Racial composition of its residents	18	14	2		4
Other	16	12	20		16
Black respondents					
Number of respondents explaining why a suburb was undesirable	403		184	131	241
Reasons					
Residential environment	2%		2%	0%	1%
Crime			9	5	8
Deterioration of suburb and homes	1		1	1	2
Lack of or inadequate services	9		7	5	7
Lower-class population	0		11	0	6
Too expensive	2		4	10	2
Too far away	4		14	21	7
Type of people who live there	18		10	9	12
Total racial reasons	83		41	46	70
Racial prejudice of its residents	78		32	36	59
Racial composition of its residents	10		11	12	18
Other	9		24	22	13

Note: These data are from the Detroit Area Study 1992, and pertain to those suburbs that at least 20 percent of whites or 20 percent of blacks found somewhat or very undesirable. The reasons do not sum to 100 percent because an explanation given by a respondent may have been coded into two or more categories.

Continued

White Respondents

The upper panel of table 7.2 reports that the proportion of whites rating these suburbs as undesirable went from a low of 11 percent for Troy to a high of 68 percent for Taylor. If at least 20 percent said that a suburb was undesirable, we show the reasons whites gave for their dislike of living there. Typical is the response of a white about Southfield: "Not gracious. Doesn't suit my taste. Doesn't have curvy streets, or architectural diversity. It's a suburban waste." Others put environment together with concerns about the social class of suburb's residents. For example, one white respondent clearly revealed his feeling about Taylor by explaining: "It's a redneck area. The environment isn't good. I visualize Taylor as a guy sitting on his porch in his T-shirt drinking beer. That's not desirable to me."

Three findings are apparent from the coding and classification of white responses. First, Taylor is distinguished from other locations in the frequency with which whites emphasized its lower-class population. Of the 736 whites in the survey, 81 commented about the class—not the race—of the people who lived there, often elaborating, such as the person who said: "It's on the lowest of the socioeconomic ladder. The folks that live there are on the low end of the pay scale. They are not asked to maintain property. This includes their vehicles, lawns or painting their houses. It's a redneck mentality." And another told us: "The knowledge I have of the area is that it's essentially a lower-income, blue-collar area. It has some stereotypical visions of cars parked on lawns which I don't prefer."

Second, even though the actual crime rates of Southfield and Dearborn are roughly comparable, whites perceived more crime in Southfield. In 1993, property crimes reported to the police were 7 per thousand in both suburbs, while violent crimes were .8 per 1,000 in Southfield and .6 per 1,000 in Dearborn. About 120 whites explained their evaluations of Southfield by mentioning crime, but only 40 cited crime as a reason for not wanting to live in Dearborn. Warren, Dearborn, and Southfield all share boundaries with the border of Detroit, but whites cited crime problems in Southfield much more frequently than in the other two places. In other words, crime came up relatively frequently when whites evaluated the one suburb with numerous black residents.

Third, whites gave racial reasons for the undesirability of Southfield and—surprisingly—also of Dearborn. We distinguished between those who gave a racial reason based on the people living there—such as the white who said about Southfield, "I worked in Southfield. Blacks are moving in. Blacks are taking over and it's going downhill"—from whites who said they did not want neighbors they perceived to be bigots or racists. For example, a white respondent told us that Dearborn was undesirable because: "It has a history of intolerance." Another said: "They are closed-minded toward blacks. Even though I am white, I notice it."

Continued

Although the proportion of whites giving racial reasons for the undesirability of Southfield was small, it is the one suburb that has a substantial black population, and their presence clearly disturbs some whites. One told us: "Rich Jewish people moved out, blacks moved in. Housing values have not risen at all since then." And another: "Too many blacks running down the city. Property values are going down."

The racial objections to Dearborn focus directly on the distaste some whites have for living with Arab neighbors. Forty of the white respondents offered explanations such as: "Personally, I do not like the Middle Eastern ethnic people that live there," or "Because of the nationality living there now—the camel jockeys. There are parts going downhill like Detroit."

It is important to remember that the majority of whites found all of these suburbs desirable with the exception of Taylor, and whites' objections to Taylor focused on its closeness to the airport, the unattractive homes thought to be there, and the lower economic status of its residents. But the explanations expressed in the open-ended questions imply that racial and ethnic factors are important for the cognitive maps used by a substantial minority of Detroit-area whites.

Black Respondents

It is much easier to summarize the explanations blacks gave for classifying suburbs as undesirable: it is a racial issue. To be sure, blacks agreed with whites about the economic composition of Taylor. As one Detroit black told us: "Why do I have to go way out there to live in some poor white community? We have plenty of poverty here." Another linked the social class of Taylor's whites to prejudice: "Poor whites live there and they don't want blacks to live near. They are prejudiced and jealous. Most of them are as poor as many blacks, so they don't like blacks."

With regard to the other four suburbs, blacks criticized their white residents, with Dearborn and Warren singled out for numerous comments, many of them long and specific. About 340 blacks—out of 750—mentioned racial reasons when explaining why Dearborn was undesirable, and almost 200 for Warren. A frequent response about Dearborn was, "They have an attitudinal problem toward blacks," or "They don't want blacks out there," or the polite statement that "They have a strong dislike for blacks living in their neighborhoods." That motivates some African Americans to action such as the respondent who told us: "They will tell you they don't want blacks out there. I will not go where I'm not wanted. The problem out there at the shopping mall—I'm not going to spend my money there." One respondent told us: "I worked in Dearborn for thirty years and when I finished work, I got out of there. The mayor of that city

---

Continued

also wanted to keep blacks out. I don't go to Dearborn. I don't shop at Fairlane or at any shops in that area."

Others related specific experiences, such as the black man who classified Warren as undesirable because "I had some bad incidents there. While out with a white girl, some white guys jumped on her car and called her a nigger lover." Another said about Warren: "Because of the prejudice. I go to a mixed church and we have mixed schools and we rent a school in Warren and they didn't want to lease it to us because it was a mixed group." Quite a few blacks mentioned being stopped by suburban police, including one woman who explained why she found Warren undesirable: "Because of a personal incident that occurred in Warren. Warren seems to be not as friendly from what I experienced when shopping in the area. My second husband had a lawsuit against Warren because of police brutality. We won the suit. But he had eighty stitches, a broken jawbone, just because they pulled him over for a faulty taillight. But really it was because he was a young black man who was in Warren after dark." Another Detroit black explained: "I had a dear friend move there and the people burned a cross on her lawn. Set fire to the home. They had a hard time out there."

These comments reflect the thinking, evaluations, and feelings of Detroit residents, but they may contain misinformation. And it is important to remember that, the majority of blacks reported that all suburbs except Dearborn were desirable. For African Americans, racial reasons overwhelm other explanations for why suburbs are undesirable. And the finding that so many blacks reported specific incidents and went on at length, especially about Dearborn and Warren, reveals that Detroit's blacks share a cognitive map of the suburban ring. It is one that sees most suburbs but Southfield as hostile to them.

How Widespread Were the Changes in Whites' Willingness to Live in Integrated Neighborhoods?

Whites are increasingly willing to remain in their neighborhoods when African Americans move in, and increasingly willing to think about moving into an area that is already integrated. To find out whether this shift was widespread or restricted to younger whites, or to those with college educations, we calculated scores indexing white attitudes concerning two dimensions of residential integration. First, we created an "index of discomfort with black neighbors" by assigning a maximum score of 100 to any white who said that he or she would be "very uncomfortable" when the first black moved into the neighborhood (4 percent of whites felt that way). At the other extreme, whites who said they would be "very comfortable" should their neighborhood come to have a composition of 8 black and 7 white families were assigned a score of 0 (18 percent of whites were that tolerant). High scores on this index mean strong opposition to integration; low scores mean acceptance.

Next we calculated an "index of unwillingness to move into mixed neighborhoods." A white who would not consider moving into an attractive, affordable home located in a neighborhood with a single black family received the maximum score of 100 (5 percent of whites were that intolerant), while a white who was willing to enter the majority black area was assigned the score of 0 (27 percent said they were willing to do so).

Table 7.3 presents these two indexes. The average score for the Discomfort Index fell from 47 to 40, implying that, on average, the first card to produce an "uncomfortable" response from whites in 1976 was the 5 black/10 white neighborhood; sixteen years later, it was the 8 black/7 white diagram. The willingness of whites to enter integrated neighborhoods changed in a similar manner, with the average score declining from 59 to 45.

Two primary determinants of the racial attitudes of whites are their age and their educational attainment. Younger people typically report more egalitarian attitudes about racial issues than older people. While there are many reasons for this, an important one is that younger people attended schools in an era when racial justice and racial equality were taught. Presumably, those who completed their school before the civil rights decade were less frequently taught about the importance of racial justice and equal opportunity. Older persons grew up when Jim Crow policies were enforced by law in the South and by custom in Detroit. Extensively educated whites have more egalitarian attitudes about residential integration than do whites who spent few years in school. Presumably, this results not so much from an exposure to minority students in the classroom as from courses that encourage students to reject generalizations and stereotypes about racial and ethnic groups. (For an analysis of racial attitudes and their determinants, see Schuman et al., 1997).

Table 7.3 classifies whites by five characteristics linked to racial attitudes. Younger whites said they were more comfortable with integrated living than older whites, and also reported a greater willingness to move into mixed areas. Whites who completed college were much more willing to live in integrated neighborhoods than those who had a high school diploma or less.

Higher family incomes, we presumed, would be related to the ac-

TABLE 7.3   *Attitudes of Whites Concerning Racial Residential Integration, Detroit Area, 1976 and 1992*

Characteristics of Respondents	Index of Discomfort with Black Neighbors[a]			Index of Unwillingness to Move into Mixed Neighborhoods[b]		
	1976	1992	Change	1976	1992	Change
Age						
Under thirty-five	41[d]	30[e]	−11*	53[e]	35[e]	−18*
Thirty-five to forty-four	47	34	−13*	56	41	−15*
Forty-five to fifty-four	50	36	−14*	60	45	−15*
Fifty-five to sixty-four	50	45	−5*	65	56	−9*
Sixty-five and over	53	48	−5*	71	58	−13*
Educational attainment						
Less than twelve years	51[e]	46[e]	−5*	64[e]	54[e]	−10*
Twelve years	51	41	−10*	64	50	−14*
Thirteen to fifteen years	39	36	−3*	51	42	−9*
Sixteen or more years	38	29	−9	49	36	−13*
Family income[e]						
Not reported	53	44	−9*	65	49	−16*
Under $20,000	43	39	−4*	55	50	−5*
$20,000 to 39,999	45	35	−10*	57	43	−14*
$40,000 to 59,999	49	38	−9*	61	43	−17*
$60,000 to 79,999	46	38	−8*	61	45	−16*
$80,000 or more	47	32	−15*	58	41	−17*
Gender						
Men	50[d]	39	−11*	61	44	−17*
Women	44	36	−8*	58	45	−13*
Place of residence						
City of Detroit	44	33	−11*	61	45	−16*
Remainder of Wayne County	47	39	−8*	59	46	−13*
Oakland County	46	35	−11*	58	44	−14*
Macomb County	51	40	−11*	61	42	−19*
Total						
Mean	47	40	−7*	59	45	−14*
Standard deviation	33	38		36	35	
Sample size	706	723		706	723	

Source: University of Michigan, Detroit Area Study 1976, 1992.
[a]This index of discomfort ranges from a high score of 100, assigned to those whites who said they would feel "very uncomfortable" should their neighborhood come to have 1 black and 14 white households, to a low of 0, assigned to those whites who said they would feel "very comfortable" should their neighborhood come to have 8 black and 7 white households.
[b]This index of the willingness to enter integrated neighborhoods ranges from a high of 100, assigned to those whites who said they would not consider moving into a neighborhood of 1 black and 14 white households, to a low of 0, assigned to those whites who said they would consider moving into a neighborhood of 8 black and 7 white residents.
[c]In 1991 dollars.
[d]Analysis of variance model reports that residential integration scores differ among categories of this variable at .05 level.
[e]Analysis of variance model reports that residential integration scores differ among categories of this variable at .01 level.
*This change in the residential integration score of whites between 1976 and 1992 was significant at the .01 level.

ceptance of neighborhood integration. That is evident in our data, but the relationship is a weak one and, unlike the relationship of integration to education, not statistically significant. Gender differences were modest but, in every comparison, women were somewhat more accepting of integration then men.

For more than two decades, whites in the city of Detroit have lived in a black-majority municipality.[2] So it is not surprising to find that whites in the city were more comfortable with black neighbors than were whites living in the suburban ring. However, differences in whites' attitudes about integration by their place of residence in 1992 were not large, and city whites were no more willing than suburban whites to say that they would move into an attractive, affordable home in an integrated neighborhood.

Table 7.3 reports that the shift toward more egalitarian attitudes was certainly not limited to specific groups of whites. Rather, there was a widespread pattern of an increasing acceptance of residential integration. To be sure, demographic processes are propelling a further change in white racial attitudes, as younger whites gradually replace older ones. And the shift toward greater educational attainment implies even more acceptance of residential integration in the future. But more is going on. In every comparison, whites in 1992 said that they were less upset by the arrival of blacks in their neighborhood and they were more willing to consider moving into integrated places than had whites in 1976.

A majority of whites (53 percent in 1992) said they would try to move away from one of the integrated neighborhoods pictured on our cards. This implies considerable tolerance, since almost half said they would remain even. However, few neighborhoods will become integrated in the near future. As Thomas Schelling (1971 and 1972) has shown, stable interracial neighborhoods are likely to be rare. The arrival of just a few blacks will lead a small number of whites to move away. If some of those departing whites are replaced by African Americans, the proportion of blacks will rise, leading those whites who were willing to tolerate some—but not very many—black neighbors to leave. If there are many African Americans seeking housing in integrated neighborhoods and only a few areas are open to them, the eventual outcome will be the white-to-black transition that occurred throughout metropolitan America.

Why do many whites try to move away when blacks come to their neighborhoods? Those who said they would try to leave were asked, "Why would you try to move out?" Verbatim responses were recorded and then themes were coded. Forty-one percent mentioned declining property values. This was the most frequently given reason. Examples of such responses are:

The people would be okay, property values might drop. I would want to get out before property values drop off a cliff.

Values of houses go down when blacks move in. It's not right, but you have to go with what everybody else does. For Sale signs would pop up and I can't afford to lose on my house.

I'd like to feel I'm not a racist, but as a homeowner, I'd be concerned that my property value would go down. That seems to be what happens. It's not the African Americans' fault, but the whites' reactions.

The property values explanation frees whites from expressing any racial animosity. Indeed, as the last response indicates, some whites exonerate blacks and blame other whites for the fall in property values. By using this explanation, these respondents may picture themselves as responding appropriately and logically to inexorable market forces, rather than fleeing black neighbors.

Just about as frequently were responses describing negative characteristics of integrated neighborhoods, without directly mentioning a specific negative stereotype about blacks. For example:

Basing this on when I lived in Detroit, when we moved out, a lot of black people moved in. Crime got worse. I don't know if that can be correlated with who lives there, though.

And:

Well, because it's a different race, a different people. I'm not used to them, not because I don't like them [but] because I don't know them.

The third most common theme, expressed by 24 percent of the whites who would try to move out, invoked negative images of blacks, frequently having to do with violence, drugs, or the perceived tendency of African Americans to let their properties run down. Examples of this thinking include the following:

Because then I would feel like the minority. When I think of blacks, I think of drugs, and I don't want my kids around it.

I don't like black men. I'm scared of black people.

I would feel uncomfortable, not safe. Would depend on class of people— normal, American-type of black family wouldn't both me, but most aren't.

This open-ended question was posed to whites after showing them diagrams of integrated neighborhoods, so their explanations were constrained to focus on racial issues.

This analysis gives us insight into what whites think when their cognitive map of their neighborhood includes blacks. A large fraction of whites tell us they would remain even if many blacks came, but the majority say they would try to leave.[3] The primary reason they give for leaving are centered around falling property values and the problems they associate with black neighbors.

The Neighborhood Preferences of Blacks

What about African Americans? Do they prefer segregated neighborhoods? Does segregation persist largely because blacks are unwilling or reluctant to move into white neighborhoods, as Stephan Thernstrom and Abigail Thernstrom (1997) and Orlando Patterson (1997, 43–48) contend? The idea that segregation persists because both blacks and whites prefer to live in their own neighborhoods has a long history, especially among those who believe that discrimination is an irrational impediment that could not long survive in a competitive housing market and those who believe the Open Housing Law ended discrimination (Becker 1957, 78–81; Clark 1986, 1988, 1989, and 1991).

Blacks in our survey were given the set of neighborhood cards shown in figure 7.6. These cards displayed varying racial compositions, ranging from all black to all white, but they are not identical to the cards shown to whites. In pre-tests, we found that virtually no whites would remain in or consider moving into overwhelmingly black neighborhoods. We could ask blacks about moving into all-white neighborhoods, but asking whites about moving into all-black or almost all-black neighborhoods was futile.

African Americans were asked to imagine that they were searching for a home, and found an attractive one in their price range. This home was designated at the center of each neighborhood. They were then asked to rank the neighborhoods from most attractive to the least attractive. To make sure we captured their attention, we asked them to actually put the cards in their preference order.

Blacks clearly preferred racially mixed neighborhoods, but one with a large representation of African Americans. In 1992, 53 percent selected the 7 black/7 white neighborhood as their first choice. Once they moved in, the neighborhood would be majority black. And 22 percent of blacks said the 10 black/4 white neighborhood was their first choice. Only 15 percent selected the all-black area. And, highly consistent with the open-ended responses of blacks about suburbs, just 1.6 percent said that their top choice would be the all-white neighborhood. Figure 7.7 shows the percentage of blacks who rated each neighborhood as their *first* or *second* choice in both 1976 and 1992.

FIGURE 7.6   *Neighborhood Diagrams Used for White Respondents,
1976 and 1992*

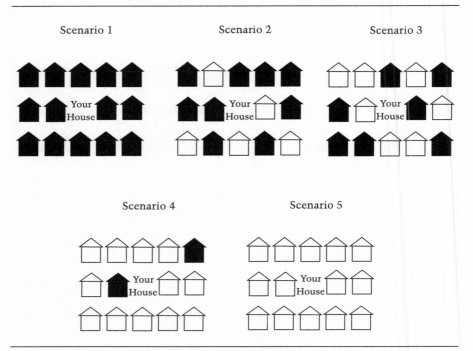

Source: University of Michigan, Detroit Area Study 1976, 1992. For additional information, see Farley et al. 1978, 1993.

Unlike the trend among whites, the residential preferences of Detroit blacks changed little between 1976 and 1992, but the changes were away from integration. There was a significant decline in the proportion who ranked the 12 white/2 black area as their preferred place to live, and a significant increase in the proportion preferring the 10 black/4 white neighborhood. The changes among blacks go in the opposite direction from those among whites.

If residential segregation is to decline, some blacks will have to move into exclusively white neighborhoods, such as those found throughout Detroit's suburban ring. Are blacks willing to be the pioneers who integrate a white neighborhood? Many books describe African Americans who pioneered in southern universities, in major sports, in the military, and on the Supreme Court, but few studies recount the experiences of blacks who pioneer in white neighborhoods.

We gave the cards to African Americans a second time, and asked

FIGURE 7.7 Attractiveness of Neighborhoods of Varying Racial Compositions for Black Respondents, 1976 and 1992

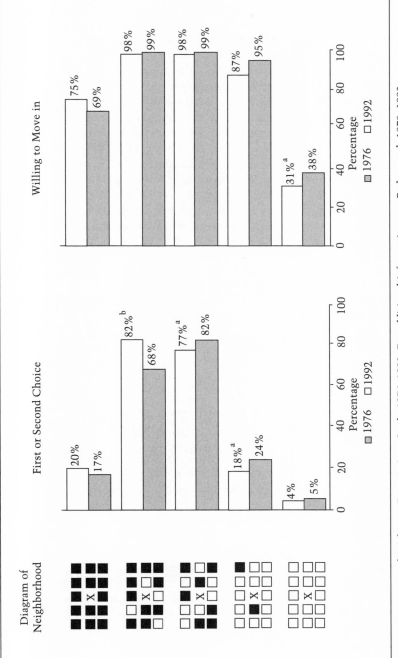

Source: University of Michigan, Detroit Area Study 1976, 1992. For additional information, see Farley et al. 1978, 1993.
[a]Change is statistically significant at .01 level.
[b]Change is statistically significant at .05 level.
1976 N = 404, 1992 N = 750

them to imagine they had searched for and then found an attractive, affordable home in each of the neighborhoods. We then asked them which neighborhoods, ranging from all-black to all-white, they would be willing to enter. This question moves beyond preferences and seeks information about where blacks are willing to live.

Almost all blacks were willing to enter an already-integrated neighborhood, and three-quarters were willing to move into an all-black area, but only a small minority was willing to take the risk of being the first black on an all-white block. Blacks are so favorably disposed toward residential integration that 1 out of 4 was *unwilling* to move into an affordable, attractive home in an all-black area. The major reason—given by 78 percent of blacks whose first choice was integration—had to do with the racial mix itself. Many expressed the idea that there would be little racial hostility in such neighborhoods, that people would get along, and that the demographic mix would be beneficial. African Americans told us that they saw benefits to living with white neighbors, so long as there were other blacks around, but feared being treated with hostility if they were the only black. That fear is deeply rooted in Detroit's contentious racial history.

There were no significant differences between 1976 and 1992 in the willingness of blacks to enter all-black or already-integrated neighborhoods, but there was one notable shift. In 1992, 31 percent said they would be willing to be the African American pioneer on an all-white block, a significant decrease from the 38 percent who said they would have done so sixteen years earlier.

How Widespread Were Changes in Black Attitudes About Residential Integration?

Changes in the preferences of blacks were small, but differed in direction from those among whites. Do such changes typify all groups of blacks? We calculated a score indexing the preferences of blacks based on their rating of the five neighborhoods. If a black respondent put the all-black area at the top and ranked all other areas according to their "blackness," with the all-white area at the bottom, he or she received the maximum score of 100. A black that reversed this ranking by putting the all-white neighborhood at the top and the all-black area on the bottom received the minimum score of 0. High scores on this index represent a preference for high-density black neighborhoods; low scores report a preference for integrated or largely white ones. Table 7.4 presents these scores, along with another important measure: the percentage of blacks who were willing to enter an all-white neighborhood.

TABLE 7.4   *Preferences of Blacks Concerning Racial Residential Integration, Detroit Area, 1976 and 1992*

Characteristics of Respondents	Index of Neighborhood Racial Preference			Percentage Willing to Enter an All-White Neighborhood		
	1976	1992	Change	1976	1992	Change
Age						
Under thirty-five	65	68	+3	39	21	-17^b
Thirty-five to forty-four	61	70	$+9^b$	36	24	-12
Forty-five to fifty-four	62	70	+8	38	26	-12
Fifty-five to sixty-four	61	67	+6	30	30	0
Sixty-five and over	60	67	+7	43	38	-5
Educational attainment						
Less than twelve years	65	70	+5	35	25	-10^b
Twelve years	61	70	$+9^b$	37	31	-6
Thirteen to fifteen years	59	67	$+8^b$	48	25	-23^b
Sixteen or more years	71	65	-5	17	24	+7
Family income						
Not reported	60	71	$+11^a$	37	28	-9
Under $20,000	65	69	+4	38	27	-11^b
$20,000 to 39,999	63	67	+4	43	25	-18^b
$40,000 to 59,999	60	73	$+13^b$	33	29	-4
$60,000 or more	64	59	-6	25	30	+5
Gender						
Men	64	68	+4	33	30	-3
Women	62	69	$+7^b$	39	26	-13^b
Place of residence						
City of Detroit	62	68	$+6^b$	38	27	-11^b
Suburban ring	67	68	+1	19	30	+11
Total						
Mean	63	68	$+5^b$	38	31	-6^a
Standard deviation	24	20		48	45	
Sample size	379	750		379	750	

Source: University of Michigan, Detroit Area Study 1976, 1992.
[a]Change is significant at .05 level.
[b]Change is significant at .01 level.
[c]This index has a maximum value of 100 for respondents who ranked all-black neighborhoods as their first choice and all-white neighborhoods as their last choice. The minimum of zero was assigned to respondents whose first choice was the all-white neighborhood.

The score on this Index of Neighborhood Racial Preference increased by 5 points between the 1970s and the 1990s implying an increased preference for higher density black neighborhoods. This upward shift occurred for all age groups, at most educational levels, at all income levels, and among both men and women. Thus, the shift away from preferring integration was a widespread trend involving all components of Detroit's black population, with the possible exception of the emerging black elite. That is, the index declined among those who had college degrees and those whose families had incomes exceeding $60,000. We also analyzed changes between 1976 and 1992 in the percent of blacks willing to move into an all-white neighborhood. These findings are shown on the right of table 7.4 and are similar to those for the Index of Neighborhood Racial Preference. For almost all groups of African Americans, fewer were willing to be the first black in 1992 than in 1976.

In earlier chapters we described the increasing economic polarization of Detroit's black community since the civil rights decade. The distinctive group in table 7.4 is the black elite, since their preference for residential living increased, while it decreased for all other Detroit-area African Americans. Why is this the case? Recent analyses of in-depth interviews with several hundred middle-class black professionals from across the county report that they recognize both the psychic costs of living in overwhelmingly white areas and the advantages. Quite a few of them were determined to face the discomfort they anticipated to claim for themselves and their families the American symbols of success: a nice home that will appreciate in value, good schools for their children, and a prestigious address (Feagin and Sikes 1994, chap. 6). Findings from Detroit in 1992 support that view: a small shift away from preferring neighborhood integration for most blacks, but a change in the opposite direction among the most highly educated and financially successful.

Is There Still Discrimination in the Detroit-Area Housing Market?

What about racial discrimination in the housing market? Is this a major cause of continued segregation? A household survey cannot assess discrimination. Many respondents had not searched for a home or apartment for years. More important, it is usually difficult to know when one is the victim of discrimination. If a broker shows a client an array of homes, the customer may not realize that being white led the agent to present different options than to a similar black client. And if a prospective buyer is turned down for a mortgage, the lender will never say it was because of skin color or gender.

Audit Studies

Since the Supreme Court upheld the Fair Housing Law (*Jones v. Alfred Mayer* 1968), three types of investigation have been carried out. While there is ambiguity about the exact cause of racial disparities in the housing market, many assert they are the outcome of discrimination, or that discrimination is the most plausible cause (Massey and Denton 1993, Yinger 1999). First, there are audit tests in the sale or rental of housing to see if race makes a difference. Matched pairs of black and white applicants are sent to a broker. Following their meeting with the agent, they fill out detailed questionnaires about the information they were provided, the number of homes or apartments they were shown, their location, whether they were encouraged to come back, what questions they were asked, and exactly how much time the broker spent with them.

One of the first such scientific studies was carried out in Detroit in 1974 and 1975 by Diana Pearce (1979). She randomly selected ninety-seven real estate agents who did business either in the suburbs or in the northwest corner of the central city—an area that was then over-whelmingly white. A white couple and a matched black couple visited each broker. About one-quarter of the black testers were shown homes on their first visit, but three-quarters of the white testers saw homes. Even though testers were matched with regard to financial status and housing requirements, the homes that brokers showed to or discussed with whites were significantly more expensive that those shown to or discussed with blacks. Important for the perpetuation of segregation, homes shown to or discussed with blacks were typically in neighborhoods where there already were black residents or in neighborhoods near predominantly black areas; homes shown to whites were in white neighborhoods. Pearce concluded that the biggest difference was that whites were more often taken to suitable homes on their first visit and were steered to different locations than blacks.

Equal-housing opportunity groups in many metropolises carried out similar audits. (For a summary see Yinger 1995, 48.) They so often reported racial disparities that the federal Department of Housing and Urban Development (HUD) conducted national investigations: the 1977 Housing Market Practices Survey involving 3,264 audits in forty metropolises and the 1989 Housing Discrimination Survey involving 3,800 audits in twenty-four metropolises. The real estate industry challenged the use of testers who were not really seeking homes, asserting entrapment but, in 1982, the Supreme Court (*Havens v. Coleman*) ratified the use of testers and granted them standing to sue offending brokers.

Recent studies typically find little blatant discrimination, such as agents who assert they do not sell or rent to blacks or who encourage minorities to go elsewhere. But the evidence suggests that black home-seekers are typically provided with less information and given different or less advice than whites. Yinger (1995, 5) summarized findings of the most recent investigation by concluding:

> Compared to their white counterparts, African American and Hispanic homeseekers are shown far fewer homes and apartments (and, indeed, sometimes excluded from available housing altogether), given less assistance in finding the homes and apartments that best fit their needs and in finding a mortgage, and are steered to neighborhoods with minority concentration of low home values. (See also, Yinger 1992; Turner 1992)

In 1989, HUD study found that steering and apparent discrimination against black testers who sought to buy was significantly greater in Detroit than in the other twenty-three metropolises. But Detroit's auditors who sought rental units did not experience discrimination or steering above the national average (Yinger 1995, tables A.4 and A.6).

Lending Practices

A second array of studies analyzed lending practices to determine whether blacks and whites had seemingly similar access to credit markets. These are statistical analyses of where lenders did or did not approve mortgages and business loans.

As the nation's population shifted to the suburbs in the 1960s, neighborhood organizations in older cities realized that it was becoming increasingly challenging for inner-city residents and firms to borrow money. Some banks closed offices in declining or minority inner-city neighborhoods, while opening branches in the suburbs. Newspaper reports, among others, began to describe the dearth of regular financial services in older neighborhoods—especially those with poor black residents—and the rise of costly alternative services such as currency exchanges. Civil rights groups asserted that some lenders continued to redline low-income and minority neighborhoods, a practice prohibited by the Open Housing Law of 1968 and the Equal Credit Opportunity Act of 1974.

Community and civil rights groups successfully pressured Congress to take action. In 1975, the Home Mortgage Disclosure Act (HMDA) went on the books and became a potent freedom-of-information law (Canner and Smith 1991). It mandated that federally chartered fiscal institutions keep records of the race of applicants, the location and value of the property they sought to finance, and decisions about their application. They were obligated to make this information public (without naming the applicant) so that local groups could determine whether applications from their neighborhood were turned down at a suspiciously high rate (Squires 1992).

Two years later, Congress enacted the Community Reinvestment Act (CRA), a surprisingly encompassing law that requires federally chartered fiscal institutions to serve the credit needs of all who live in the metropolis where they are located, not just in the more prosperous suburbs. This law specifically mentions that lenders have to meet the credit needs of low- and moderate-income neighborhoods consistent with fiduciary responsibility (Yinger 1995, chap. 10).

These new laws produced several unexpected outcomes. First, reporters in several cities analyzed HMDA data and typically found that banks made few mortgage loans or business loans in minority or low-income neighborhoods. The first major study, "The Color of Money," appeared in the *Atlanta Journal and Constitution* in May 1988 (Dedman 1988). It reported that Atlanta's major banks financed mortgages in census tracts with predominantly African American residents much less often than in economically similar white census tracts. While this is not proof of discrimination, it suggested that fiscal institutions were not meeting the credit needs of the entire metropolis. For more than two years, a coalition of Atlanta neighborhood development organizations had been meeting with bankers to persuade them to set aside a pool of $10 million for minority and low-income neighborhoods. There had been no progress. Within two weeks of the article's publication, local fiscal institutions created the Atlanta Mortgage Consortium and set aside $65 million for previously underserved neighborhoods (Keating, Brazen, and Fitterman 1992; Robinson 1992).

The story played out differently in contentious Detroit. In the spring of 1987, Mayor Coleman Young announced that city dollars would be used to finance the development of downtown hotels, so that Detroit could attract convention business. Skeptical reporters immediately questioned him about why, in a financially strapped city, the taxes of poor residents should be used to build for-profit hotels. He answered that local lenders were unwilling to put up the money for projects in the city. Local bankers denied this, but three investigative reporters working for the *Detroit Free Press*—David Everett, John Gallagher, and Teresa Blossom—decided to figure out who was correct, using HMDA data as well as information about which lenders financed the Renaissance Center, the Joe Louis Arena, and other massive projects.

After a year of work, the *Free Press* published the findings:

- Detroit lenders made mortgage loans about three times as frequently in predominantly white census tracts as in economically comparable black tracts.

- Detroit's fiscal institutions financed a small share of downtown development, apparently confirming Mayor Young's conclusion. Of $560 million in funding for new central-city projects, Detroit's bankers put up only 11 percent. Banks from other cities, especially Cleveland, were more involved in financing large projects in the Motor City.

- Detroit's lenders, compared to those in other Rust Belt cities, had very low participation rates in governmental programs designed to help low-income borrowers such as Small Business Administration or FHA loans and a host of other state and federal loan programs.

- The top executives of Detroit's fiscal institutions were, with few exceptions, white males who lived in the suburban ring.

The reporters carefully avoided any charges of discrimination. Instead, they pointed out that well-established practices failed to meet the credit needs of the city and its residents.

Rather than setting aside monies for apparently underserved areas of the metropolis, Detroit lenders devoted a major effort to demonstrating they were not guilty of discrimination. Their efforts, not surprisingly, stirred up neighborhood advocacy groups who believed they had been poorly treated or overlooked. Eventually, both Congressional and state legislative committees held hearings to explore lending practices in Detroit.

Community groups had the upper hand, but for reasons that no one foresaw when the HMDA and CRA laws went on the books: the shift from local to state and then from state to nationwide banks. Both Michigan and federal law said that how well an institution met its CRA obligation should be taken into account whenever the institution sought to amend its charter.

Within a few months after the *Free Press* series, one of Detroit's larger banks, Comerica, sought to purchase a Toledo bank and, shortly after that, a chain of Texas banks. Its officers knew that public hearings would be held, that neighborhood representatives would poignantly tell how far they had to travel to find a bank, how they were denied loans for home improvements or for their businesses, and how Comerica offered them little help in getting federally backed loans. And then academic experts would produce extensive evidence showing that the bank's loan portfolio was heavy with suburban mortgage and business loans, but light when it came to inner-city loans.

Officers of the banks realized that they could not easily demonstrate that they satisfied their CRA responsibilities. In April 1989, First Federal and the National Bank of Detroit promised to make $61 million available to underserved potential customers. By the end of 1991, Comerica and other Detroit lenders committed to making $2.1 billion available. This was a set-aside of loan money, so only qualified borrowers had access to it, but it promised to bring about a sea change in the availability of financing to central-city residents and businesses (Everett 1992). Unfortunately, there appear to be no studies assessing the consequences of these CRA set-asides, even though they now involve billions of dollars across the nation (Squires 1992).

Mortgage Approvals and Turndowns

A third strategy for detecting racial disparities uses statistical analyses to determine whether black applicants for mortgages are turned down more frequently than ostensibly similar white applicants. Such investigations were facilitated by 1989 amendments to the HMDA law requiring that lenders obtain and make public financial information about applicants, as well as information about race, value and place of property, and the outcome of the application. The most comprehensive investigation of this type is known as the Boston Fed Study. Using data for 1990, Alicia Munnell and her collaborators (1992, 1996) examined information about applicants seeking mortgages from banks supervised by the Boston Federal Reserve. After thoroughly analyzing the information and controlling for relevant variables, they reported that black and Hispanic applicants were roughly 60 percent more likely to be denied a mortgage than were whites. That is, 11 percent of white applicants were turned down, compared with 17 percent of ostensibly similar black and Hispanic mortgage seekers (Munnell et al. 1992, 44). There have been, so far as we know, few similar studies of the practices of Detroit's lenders.

We do not know how frequently discrimination occurs in Detroit's housing market. But anyone who reads Detroit newspapers will see reports of possible discrimination several times a year. Quite frequently, charges are made, a lawsuit is threatened, and then a settlement is reached in which the probable defendant agrees to implement an integration strategy or make a payment to an apparent victim, but he or she does not admit violating any law. Some examples of these press accounts follow:

September 1996   Owners of a 252-unit complex in Allen Park agreed to a $475,000 settlement following charges of discrimination. This was reported to be a record high amount for this type of alleged housing discrimination (*Detroit News*, September 25, 1996).

April 1997 A settlement was reached in a twenty-year-old lawsuit that charged that Hamtramck officials in the mid-1960s rezoned a neighborhood for commercial purposes so as to force black residents out and then denied the black property owners federal relocation monies that the city could have obtained (*Detroit News*, April 10, 1997).

May 1997 A federal jury awarded $130,000 to an African American resident of Detroit, James Stevenson, who sued when he was denied a mortgage (*Detroit News*, May 22, 1997).

October 1997 The Department of Justice filed a suit against a Dearborn broker, Coldwell Banker Prestige, charging that they systematically steered their white clients away from homes in Inkster, the suburb with a 62 percent black population, but one that is seeking to maintain a racial balance (*Detroit News*, October 21, 1997).

November 1997 The owners of Marsten Apartments in Allen Park; Wellington Manor in Woodhaven; and Park Heights in Livonia, agreed to a $200,000 settlement following charges of racial discrimination (*Detroit News*, November 21, 1997).

June 1998 The suburb of Inkster also filed against Coldwell Banker Prestige, asserting that the firm steered its black, but not its white, customers to Inkster (*Detroit Free Press*, June 23, 1998).

February 1999 Oralandar Brand-Williams, Jodi Upton, and Lynn Waldsmith of the *Detroit News* analyzed Detroit area HMDA data for 1997 and reported that upper-income blacks were denied mortgages at more than twice the rate of upper-income whites. Among those with incomes exceeding $64,000 in that year, 14 percent of blacks, compared to 6 percent of whites, were turned down for regular mortgages. For refinance and home improvement loans, the disparity was greater with a rejection rate of 20 percent for upper-income African Americans; 8 percent for whites (February 7, 1999).

June 1999 The Fair Housing Center of Metropolitan Detroit filed suit in 1997, charging that the Henry Ford Retirement Village in Dearborn was perpetuating segregation by exclusively showing white clients in their ads and promotional materials. A settlement was reached, and the owners agreed to spend $469,000 on ads implying that black customers are welcome, and agreed to pay the Fair Housing Center $100,000 (*Detroit Free Press*, June 29, 1999).

Conclusion

Nearly thirty years ago, the National Academy of Sciences (1972) commissioned an investigation into the causes of residential segregation. They described a "web of discrimination" involving brokers, lenders, local governmental officials, developers, and school administrators who effectively reduced the supply of housing available to blacks and confined them to specific segments of the housing market. Segregation has declined very little in metropolitan Detroit since that report was issued. Overt discrimination brought about the racial isolation. Several additional reasons explain its persistence.

First, the stagnation of Detroit's population has produced a low rate of new housing construction. Compared to other metropolises, few developments have been built in Detroit in recent decades. Newer developments are less clearly marked as "for whites only" on the cognitive maps of homebuyers than older suburbs with their histories of hostility to blacks or neighborhoods constructed long before the Fair Housing Law was passed. The results of litigation brought by advocacy groups now require developers to market affirmatively, meaning they must advertise in the black-oriented media. If there were more new developments in and around Detroit, the prospects for increasing the number of racially diverse neighborhoods would be greater than is now the case.

Second, Detroit remains a black-white metropolis. During the 1980s, metropolises in which a second (Latino) or third (Asian) minority grew rapidly, and saw their black-white residential segregation scores drop more than metropolises that remained largely black and white (Farley and Frey 1994). African Americans may take the presence of another nonwhite minority in a neighborhood as a signal that the area is "open" to them. Although whites may move away when blacks move into their neighborhoods, they may be slower to depart if other nonwhites are simultaneously moving in. They will also have a much harder time finding exclusively white neighborhoods to enter. (For a discussion of Latinos and Asians as buffers between whites and African Americans in the housing market, see Bobo and Zubrinsky 1996.)

Third, African American homeowners in the city of Detroit have lost a substantial proportion of their housing equity in recent decades. The demand for housing in the city has fallen as the number of residents dropped by one-half since 1950.

Table 7.5 presents information about homes enumerated as owner-occupied in the censuses of 1980 and 1990, classifies them by age, and shows their owner's estimate of their market value. We report the percentage change in median value taking inflation into account. There was a pervasive decline in real equity for most homeowners—11 percent

TABLE 7.5   *Change in the Value of Owner-Occupied Housing from 1980 to 1990 for Whites in the Suburban Ring and Blacks in the City of Detroit*

Date Home Was Built	White Owners in Suburban Ring			Black Owners in City of Detroit		
	Age Distribution of Homes	Median Value in 1990	Change in Median Value 1980 to 1990	Age Distribution of Homes	Median Value in 1990	Change in Median Value 1980 to 1990
1970 to 1979	21%	$93,150	−20%	1%	$30,650	−20%
1960 to 1969	22	81,700	−15	5	28,550	−24
1950 to 1959	33	66,500	−10	26	29,440	−26
1940 to 1949	13	57,200	−6	31	27,550	−23
Before 1940	11	59,700	+3	37	21,600	−24
Total	100%	$72,550	−11%	100%	$26,350	−23%

Percentage of Metropolitan White Homeowners Living in Suburban Ring		Percentage of Metropolitan Black Homeowners Living in City	
1980	86%	1980	88%
1990	93%	1990	83%

Source: U.S. Department of Commerce 1983, 1993.

Note: These data pertain to homes that were built before April 1980. Homes are classified by the race of owners, and median values are shown by age of housing. While the race of owner was the same in 1980 and 1990, it was not necessarily the same family occupying the home. Medians were derived from the owner's estimates of the home's value. The change in median value takes inflation into account using the consumer price index. For homes represented in this analysis, the nominal median value rose by 41 percent for white owners and 21 percent for black owners, but to keep pace with inflation, a home would have had to have its value increase 99 percent between 1980 and 1990. Amounts are shown in 1990 dollars.

for white owners in the suburban ring but 23 percent for black owners in the city.

Black owners were disadvantaged by segregation since the demand for homes in the city was exceptionally weak. Because they typically lost a higher percent of their equity, African American owners undoubtedly were handicapped when they tried to trade up from one home to another, a trade that might have contributed to declining segregation.

What does the future hold for segregation? On the optimistic side, there is now widespread support for the principle that all have a right to live wherever they wish. When asked about the statement "White people have a right to keep blacks out of their neighborhoods if they want to and blacks should respect that right," 8 of 10 whites in our 1992 study and 9 of 10 African Americans rejected it.

More realistically, however, there is a legacy of past animosity in Detroit that limits the extent of integration. The major declines in segregation recorded in Dallas, Orlando, Phoenix, and Los Angeles in the 1980s seem improbable for metropolitan Detroit. Whites are unlikely to move into the city or into the few suburban neighborhoods with large or growing African American populations. When we told whites to imagine they had found an attractive affordable home in the neighborhoods shown on our cards and asked them which ones they would be willing to move into, their responses are listed in table 7.6.

TABLE 7.6   *Willingness of Whites to Move into Integrated Neighborhoods, Metropolitan Detroit, 1992*

Racial Composition of the Neighborhood	Percentage of Whites Willing to Move There
All white (14 white homes)	96
1 black home, 13 white homes	87
3 black homes, 11 white homes	69
5 black homes, 9 white homes	41
8 black homes, 7 white homes	27

Source: University of Michigan, Detroit Area Study 1992.

As the density of African American neighbors increased, whites' willingness to consider the neighborhood declined. When asked open-ended questions, whites told us they were concerned about property values and crime when African Americans moved to their neighborhoods. Thus, even though whites support the principle of racial equity, they think they have little to gain from residential integration and much to lose.

TABLE 7.7   *Willingness of Blacks to Move into Integrated*
Neighborhoods, Metropolitan Detroit, 1992

Racial Composition of the Neighborhood	Percentage of Blacks Willing to Move There
All white (14 white homes)	31
2 black homes, 12 white homes	87
7 black homes, 7 white homes	98
10 black homes, 4 white homes	98
All black homes (14 black homes)	75

Source: University of Michigan, Detroit Area Study 1992.

African Americans are willing to move into all neighborhoods except those that are exclusively white. Their responses are listed in table 7.7.

Blacks think about integration very differently than whites. We selected the neighborhood card the African American respondents said was their most preferred and asked: "You indicated that this neighborhood would be the most attractive to you. Could you tell me why you think that it is the most attractive neighborhood?" The explanations offered by the 80 percent of blacks who selected a mixed neighborhood as their top choice, seldom focused upon better city services, lower crime rate, or improved schools—only 10 percent cited those as advantages of living with white neighbors. The major reasons—given by 78 percent of African Americans choosing an integrated neighborhood—had to do with the racial mix itself. Many felt that there would be little racial hostility in such neighborhoods, that people would get along, and that the demographic mix would be beneficial. African Americans see benefits to living with white neighbors, so long as some other blacks also live there but fear being treated with hostility if they are the only black residents.

Quite likely the Census of 2000 will reveal that somewhat higher percentage of prosperous metropolitan Detroit's African Americans will be living in the suburban ring, especially in Oakland County. If that integration occurs peacefully and if it involves many different areas, African Americans will increasingly see that a wider array of suburban neighborhoods is open to them. If our survey results are indicative of what people do when they actually search for housing, there will be modest increases in suburban integration.

8

Blacks and Whites: Differing Views on the Present and Future

Popular culture and the media have often portrayed blacks negatively. The most enduring derogatory stereotypes stress the limited intellectual abilities of African Americans, their tendency to speak a nonstandard dialect, their proneness to criminal behavior, and their inability or reluctance to conform to the behavioral norms of middle-class American society, especially those regarding family life. These negative stereotypes provided the rationale for policies that excluded blacks from neighborhoods, kept them off payrolls, and segregated them in the military, even though they volunteered in great numbers for every war, going back to the Revolutionary.

One of the achievements of the civil rights revolution was to thoroughly challenge the use of racial, religious, and gender stereotypes by the media and, later, by the nation's entire population. Before the 1960s, colleges and universities seldom sought black applicants and often turned down those who applied because of the widespread stereotype that blacks could not learn as rapidly as whites. Banks redlined neighborhoods presumably because their officers believed the stereotype that African Americans did not take care of their property, did not pay their bills on time, and had a detrimental effect on property values. And the military rationalized the Jim Crow policy on the grounds that blacks would disrupt white units and would not fight valiantly for this country.

Such practices are examples of statistical discrimination based on stereotypes. As Harry J. Holzer defines it: "Employer discrimination may be *statistical*, if employers perceive lower *average* qualification among particular groups (such as minorities and women) and if they use these group averages to judge *individual* job applicants within those groups" (1996, 90). Employers, lenders, and university admissions officers have used statistical discrimination to deny opportunities to minorities and women. Indeed, this was an efficient and once widely approved practice.

The civil rights revolution of the 1960s encouraged changes in Americans' beliefs and behavior. Ethnic and racial jokes and the pejorative terms that were once commonly used to described Italians, Irish, Jews, and blacks are no longer acceptable. As several prominent people (including Nixon's secretary of agriculture and the general manager of the Los Angeles Dodgers) have learned, you can now be fired for telling insulting jokes or declaring that a race is unfit. Negative stereotypes have greatly disappeared from the media. The civil rights laws of the 1960s, federal programs to implement those laws, and numerous court decisions gradually but effectively outlawed statistical discrimination. Judging individuals on the basis of presumed group characteristics is now seen as offensive and inconsistent with national values. Although more costly; employers, real estate brokers, and admissions officers must now treat each applicant on the basis of his or her merits rather than as a member of a group.

Yet, at every job interview, the personnel officer is aware of the skin color and gender of the applicant, and real estate brokers scan people walking into their offices to make a quick judgment about them as potential customers. When Detroit-area whites were asked about residential integration, we learned that many hold negative views of their potential black neighbors, while the African American respondents expressed considerable apprehension about how they would be treated by suburban whites. Do most whites, or just a small minority, hold negative views about blacks? And do blacks endorse negative stereotypes of whites?

This chapter describes how whites and blacks think about each other, seeks to determine whether both races share the same views about the importance of skin color in Detroit's labor and housing markets, and then explores what programs, if any, blacks and whites might support to guarantee equal racial opportunities.

Endorsement or Rejection of Racial Stereotypes: The Modern Questions

In his famous dissent in the *Plessy v. Ferguson* (1896) ruling that approved state-imposed Jim Crow policies, Justice John Harlan described a color-blind Constitution that neither knew nor tolerated classes of citizens. If we lived in a color-blind society, individuals would have a difficult time generalizing about groups. But that is not the case. Our interviews in Detroit reveal that both races readily generalize about the other.

We determined that the best way to get to understand how blacks and whites thought about each race was to ask whether they endorsed or rejected stereotypes. To be sure, some or many members of a group may have unattractive characteristics, but when we generalize to all or most members of a group, we are using a stereotype. If we are influenced by that negative stereotype—unintentionally or intentionally—we will diminish opportunities for a class or people and will, quite likely, violate a civil rights laws.

We investigated four characteristics that are important when families consider new neighborhoods or when employers choose new workers for their payroll:

- intelligence
- work ethic
- compatibility
- whether or not they speak English well.

We presented the 1,543 respondents in the Detroit survey with cards showing a seven-point scale, and asked them to put their own race and the opposite race at some point on that scale. For example, the scale measuring how the races think about compatibility had:

tends to be hard to get along with anchoring one end of the scale
tends to be easy to get along with anchoring the other end of the scale.

Figure 8.1 shows the questions used. (For a discussion of these scales, see Bobo and Hutchins 1996; Bobo and Kluegel 1993; Bobo and Zubrinsky 1996; Smith 1991).

The rating of races using these cards is an unusual procedure in a face-to-face interview, since respondents are typically forced to pick one answer from a list of four or five possible answers read to them. To get respondents warmed up for these modern stereotype questions, we began with a neutral question: we asked people to rank their own race and the other on a seven-point scale, where 7 meant "tends to be rich" and 1 meant "tends to be poor."[1] Previous chapters described large black-white differences in earnings and employment, so it comes as no surprise to find that 80 percent of whites and 78 percent of blacks placed whites closer to the rich end of this scale than they placed blacks. (Indeed, per capita income for whites in metropolitan Detroit in 1998 was $23,100, but only $13,600 for blacks.)[2]

The factual question about economic status introduced respondents to the measurement of stereotypes.[3] The intelligence question, for ex-

FIGURE 8.1   *Modern Stereotype Questions Asked of Whites and Blacks in the Detroit Area Study*

ECONOMIC STATUS QUESTION

[This was used to introduce respondents to the task of rating races on modern stereotype dimensions.]

Now I have some questions about different groups in our society. I'm going to show you a seven-point scale on which the characteristics of people in a group can be rated. In the first statement, a score of 7 means that you think almost all of the people in that group are rich. A score of 1 means that you think almost everyone in the group is poor. A score of 4 means you think that the group is not towards one end or another and, of course, you may choose any number in between that comes closest to where you think people in that group stand.

Where would you rate whites?
Where would you rate blacks?

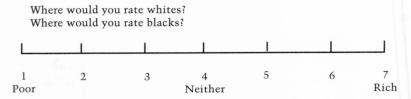

| 1 | 2 | 3 | 4 | 5 | 6 | 7 |
| Poor | | | Neither | | | Rich |

INTELLIGENCE QUESTION

For each group, I want to know whether you think they tend to be intelligent or tend to be unintelligent. Where would you rate (GROUP) on this scale, where 1 means tends to be unintelligent and 7 means tends to be intelligent? A score of 4 means you think that the group is not toward one end or the other and, of course, you may choose any number in between that comes closest to where you think people in that group stand.

Where would you rate whites?
Where would you rate blacks?

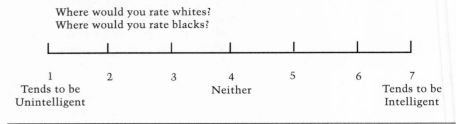

| 1 | 2 | 3 | 4 | 5 | 6 | 7 |
| Tends to be Unintelligent | | | Neither | | | Tends to be Intelligent |

ample, used "tends to be intelligent" at one end of the scale and "tends to be unintelligent" at the other. To get at beliefs about dedication to hard work, the survey used: "tends to prefer to be self-supporting" versus "tends to prefer to live off welfare." Speaking English clearly and correctly is frequently taken as a symbol educational attainment and

FIGURE 8.1   *Continued*

WORK ETHIC QUESTION

For each group, I want to know whether you think they tend to prefer to be self-supporting or tend to prefer to live off welfare. Where would you rate (GROUP) on this scale, where 7 means tends to prefer to be self-supporting and 1 means tends to prefer to live off welfare. A score of 4 means you think that the group is not toward one end or another and, of course, you may choose any number in between that comes closest to where you think people in that group stand.

Where would you rate whites?
Where would you rate blacks?

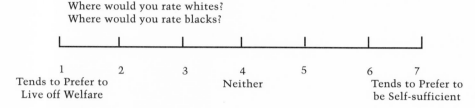

| 1 | 2 | 3 | 4 | 5 | 6 | 7 |

Tends to Prefer to   Neither   Tends to Prefer to
Live off Welfare   be Self-sufficient

COMPATIBILITY QUESTION

For each group, I want to know whether you think they tend to be easy to get along with or tend to be hard to get along with. Where would your rate (GROUP) on this scale, where 1 means tends to be hard to get along with and 7 means tends to be easy to get along with? A score of 4 means you think that the group is not toward one end or the other and, of course, you may choose any number in between that comes closest to where you think people in that group stand.

Where would you rate whites?
Where would you rate blacks?

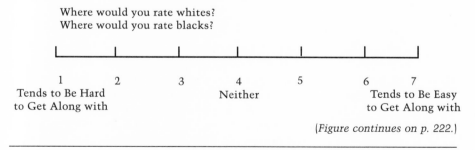

| 1 | 2 | 3 | 4 | 5 | 6 | 7 |

Tends to Be Hard   Neither   Tends to Be Easy
to Get Along with   to Get Along with

(Figure continues on p. 222.)

sophistication. Even in the blue-collar ranks, employers may expect workers to cooperate on projects and express their ideas clearly, so speaking English poorly may be damning in the job interview. The final stereotype question asked whether the race "tended to speak English well" or "tended to speak English poorly." Identical stereotype questions were asked of blacks and whites. Both races evaluated their own race and then went on to evaluate the other on the identical scale.

FIGURE 8.1   *Continued*

SPEAKING ENGLISH QUESTION

For each group, I want to know whether you think they tend to speak English well or tend to speak English poorly. Where would you rate (GROUP) on this scale, where 1 means tends to speak English poorly and 7 means tends to speak English well? A score of 4 means you think that the group is not toward one end or another and, of course, you may choose any number in between that comes closest to where you think people in that group stand.

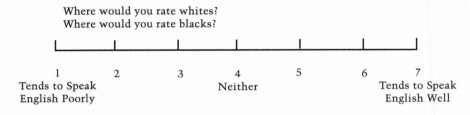

Where would you rate whites?
Where would you rate blacks?

1	2	3	4	5	6	7
Tends to Speak			Neither			Tends to Speak
English Poorly						English Well

Note: These questions were asked in the 1992 Detroit Area Study. this survey also asked white and black respondents to rate Asians, Hispanics, and the most obvious recent immigrant group in Detroit: Arab-Americans. To keep respondents alert, the actual questionnaire used 7 as the positive score for the intelligence and compatibility questions while using 1 as the most positive score for the work ethic and speaking English questions. The sample include750 black and 736 white respondents.

Whites Endorsement of Stereotypes

How widespread among whites are negative evaluations of African Americans? Figure 8.2 shows how whites rates themselves vis-à-vis blacks on each dimension. We took the score each white respondent assigned to whites and subtracted from it the score he or she gave to blacks. (A white who rated whites at 6 on the "tends to be intelligent" scale and blacks at 4, got a score of +2, since the person put whites two points higher than blacks.) Positive values—the maximum was +6—report that whites rate themselves more favorably than blacks, while a score of 0 reveals that the person thought blacks and whites were the same. A few whites (5 percent) rated blacks at a higher point on the "tends to be intelligent" scale than whites, and so they got negative scores. Figure 8.2 shows the distribution of white responses by reporting the differences in the rating whites gave to whites and to blacks.

Many whites reject the stereotype that there are racial differences in intelligence; 43 percent put both blacks and whites at the same point on this scale. But the majority—52 percent of whites—ranked their own race higher than blacks. As figure 8.2 shows, whites on average rated themselves about a full point higher on this scale than blacks, implying that the traditional stereotype about blacks tending to be less intelligent than whites is still held by a majority of whites.[4]

What about a racial difference in the work ethic? Much more than a majority of whites see a racial difference in favor of whites. Almost three-quarters of whites placed their own race closer to the "tends to prefer to be self-supporting" end of the scale than they placed blacks. The average difference was +1.7 points. This is the largest racial difference on any of the items, suggesting that the stereotype of blacks as tending to prefer to live off welfare is alive and well.

One of the oldest stereotypes circulated among whites stresses that one needs to be cautious when dealing with blacks since, if given the opportunity, they will take an unfair advantage. To measure whether whites endorsed such a view, we asked about whether their own race or blacks tended to be easier to get along with.

This is the stereotype item whites were least likely to endorse: 49 percent thought blacks were just as easy as whites to get along with. However, among those who saw a racial difference on this item, four out of five thought whites were easier than blacks to get along with. The average difference was about two-thirds of one point in favor of whites.

White children growing up in the first six decades of this century learned about blacks from the radio and movies. And whether the actors were white or black, they spoke in dialect when playing the role of African Americans: Al Jolson singing Mammie in blackface, Eddie Anderson playing Rochester on the Jack Benny Show, Stepin Fetchit in the movies, Charles Correll and Freeman Gosden in the nation's most popular radio program of the 1930s and 1940s, Amos 'n' Andy. In school many children read the now forgotten Uncle Remus stories of Joel Chandler Harris. There is a rich history of presenting blacks speaking their own version of English (Boskin 1986; Ely 1991).

Figure 8.2 shows that, among whites in metropolitan Detroit, there is still a widespread belief that whites speak the language better than blacks. Only 22 percent of whites placed both races at the same point on this scale. For each of the other stereotypes, a higher proportion of whites thought there was no racial difference. Three whites in four perceived a racial difference in favor of whites, and the average difference score was +1.6 points.

These findings may be interpreted in several ways. There is no sup-

FIGURE 8.2   *How Detroit-Area Whites Rates Whites and Blacks on the Modern Stereotype Items*

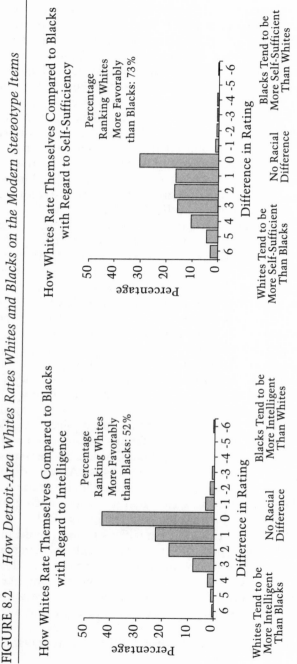

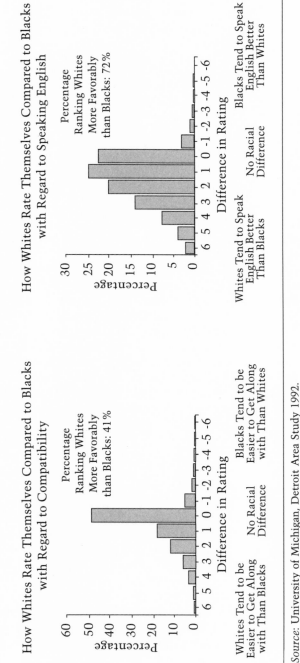

How Whites Rate Themselves Compared to Blacks
with Regard to Compatibility

How Whites Rate Themselves Compared to Blacks
with Regard to Speaking English

Source: University of Michigan, Detroit Area Study 1992.

TABLE 8.1   *How Mean Stereotype Score Varies by Age and*
             Educational Attainment, Whites in Metropolitan
             Detroit, 1992

Age of White Respondent	Mean Stereotype Score	Years of Educational Attainment of White Respondent	Mean Stereotype Score
Under age thirty-five	4.16	Fewer than twelve years	5.34
Thirty-five to forty-four	4.74	Twelve years	5.55
Forty-five to fifty-four	4.87	Some college	5.22
Fifty-five to sixty-four	4.88	College degree	3.13
Sixty-five and over	5.83		

Source: University of Michigan, Detroit Area Study 1992.

port for the idea that all whites hold negative views of African Americans, but neither is there support for the idea that racial stereotypes have disappeared or soon will disappear. Older whites and those with less than a college education were more likely to endorse the stereotypes than younger whites and those with extensive educations. A white respondent who saw the maximum difference on each item would, for all four items, rank whites 24 points higher than blacks, while those who rejected all stereotypes would have a total score of 0. Table 8.1 shows how the endorsement of these modern stereotypes was related to age and educational attainment.

The continuing trend toward greater educational attainment and the cohort replacement process will undoubtedly gradually reduce the endorsement of negative stereotypes by whites.

Blacks

What about blacks? Do they reject stereotypes or hold views contradictory to those of whites? Figure 8.3 provides findings using a similar format. For this analysis, we took the score a black assigned to blacks as a race, and subtracted from it the score assigned to whites. Positive values indicate the black respondent ranked blacks at a more favorable point than whites, while negative value report that the respondent rated whites more favorably.

African Americans reject the stereotype that blacks tend to be less intelligent. Just one half of blacks saw no difference, and the average difference score was −.10. Although in favor of whites, it was not significantly different from 0. It is a different story for the stereotype about the work ethic. It may come as a surprise to learn that African Americans in Detroit shared with whites the view that whites rank higher on this scale. Forty-one percent of blacks rate the races at an identical point, but 46 percent of blacks rated whites as closer to the "tends to prefer to be self-sufficient" end of the scale than they rated African Americans. The racial difference that blacks perceived—.8 point in favor of whites—was half the magnitude of the difference in work ethic that whites perceived. Both races ranked whites higher, but whites thought the difference was twice as large as blacks thought it was.[5]

With regard to tending to be easy or hard to get along with, both races share the view that there is a racial difference and they pretty much agree about its magnitude. What they disagree about is the direction. Whites see whites as considerably easier to get along with than blacks, while blacks see their own race as easier to get along with. This is a strong indication of the racial divide that continues to polarize metropolitan Detroit. It undoubtedly helps explain the preferences both races have to live in neighborhoods where they are numerically dominant.

Blacks also agree with whites that whites tend to speak English better. Almost half the African Americans placed whites at a higher point on this stereotype scale than they did blacks. Once again, the magnitude of the difference as viewed by blacks was about half the magnitude estimated by whites.

While many studies investigate the endorsement and use of stereotypes by whites, few have examined whether blacks endorse them. Detroit-area blacks reject the idea of racial differences in the tendency to be intelligent, but they typically think that blacks are the easier race to get along with. They also share with whites the view that African Americans have a greater tendency to prefer to live off welfare and that blacks tend to speak English less well than whites.

The persistence of negative stereotypes raises questions about what actually happens when blacks seek jobs or try to find attractive, affordable homes. Do white employers, real estate brokers, and lenders understand that they typically think that blacks are harder to get along with then whites, do not speak English as well, and, much more so than whites, prefer welfare to work? Even if they personally reject these stereotypes, do they believe that many other whites, including their white employees and their potential white customers, endorse such stereotypes? Does this influence them when they make decisions or do they realize that, despite their own negative feelings about the capabilities of African Americans, they must judge each applicant and every client individually? When they are selecting employees who must interact with the public, do black employers or personnel officers sometimes give preference to whites, thinking—perhaps without being conscious of it—that whites are more firmly committed to the work ethic and speak better English than black candidates? These negative racial stereotypes may influence who gets a job or which house is shown.

FIGURE 8.3   *How Detroit-Area Blacks Rated Whites and Blacks on the Modern Stereotype Items*

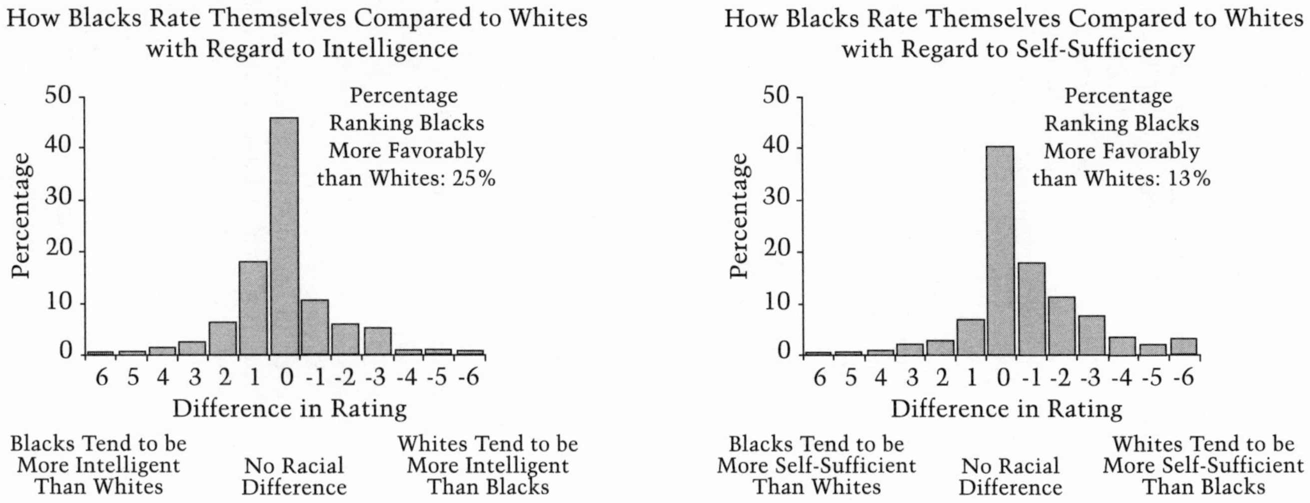

How Blacks Rate Themselves Compared to Whites
with Regard to Intelligence

Percentage
Ranking Blacks
More Favorably
than Whites: 25%

Percentage (y-axis): 50, 40, 30, 20, 10, 0

Difference in Rating (x-axis): 6 5 4 3 2 1 0 -1 -2 -3 -4 -5 -6

Blacks Tend to be
More Intelligent
Than Whites

No Racial
Difference

Whites Tend to be
More Intelligent
Than Blacks

How Blacks Rate Themselves Compared to Whites
with Regard to Self-Sufficiency

Percentage
Ranking Blacks
More Favorably
than Whites: 13%

Percentage (y-axis): 50, 40, 30, 20, 10, 0

Difference in Rating (x-axis): 6 5 4 3 2 1 0 -1 -2 -3 -4 -5 -6

Blacks Tend to be
More Self-Sufficient
Than Whites

No Racial
Difference

Whites Tend to be
More Self-Sufficient
Than Blacks

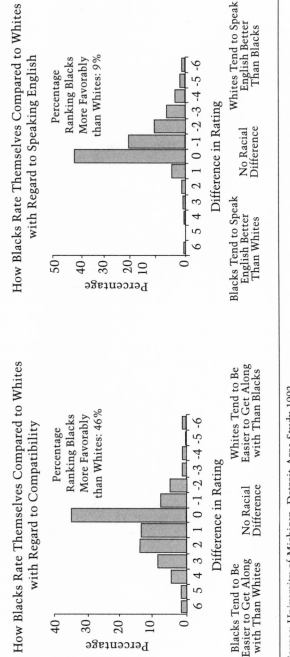

How Blacks Rate Themselves Compared to Whites
with Regard to Compatibility

Percentage
Ranking Blacks
More Favorably
than Whites: 46%

Difference in Rating

Blacks Tend to Be
Easier to Get Along
with Than Whites

No Racial
Difference

Whites Tend to Be
Easier to Get Along
with Than Blacks

How Blacks Rate Themselves Compared to Whites
with Regard to Speaking English

Percentage
Ranking Blacks
More Favorably
than Whites: 9%

Difference in Rating

Blacks Tend to Speak
English Better
Than Whites

No Racial
Difference

Whites Tend to Speak
English Better
Than Blacks

Source: University of Michigan, Detroit Area Study 1992.

How Much Racial Discrimination
Is There? Do Blacks and Whites
Share the Same Views?

Large educational and geographic differences separate the races in metropolitan Detroit. If there is consensus that they result from racial discrimination, there may also be consensus about programs to bring about equal opportunities. On the other hand, if there is a widely shared belief that there is little discrimination and that a lack of hard work accounts for racial differences, there will be little support for programs to provide more effective schools, better jobs, or improved housing for African Americans.

This study found that both races agreed that there was much racial discrimination in the job and housing markets, but there were important differences. Blacks consistently saw more discrimination than whites and, much more often than whites, felt they have lost out because of their skin color. On the other hand, whites thought that reverse discrimination denied them jobs and promotions.

Throughout this century, black men in northern cities have had a much harder time finding and keeping jobs than white men. Even in 1950, when the racial gap in earnings was small, black men had much higher unemployment rates in Detroit (9 percent) than white men (4 percent). One common explanation for this is that African Americans lack the skills that whites have. Another is that employers are reluctant to hire qualified blacks.

To ascertain how people thought about labor market discrimination, we asked respondents how much discrimination hurts the chances of blacks to get good jobs. They could tell us: "a lot," "some," "only a little," or "none at all." Those scores were coded, with a value of 4 assigned to "a lot" and a value of 1 to "none at all," so high scores report the respondent thought there was much discrimination. Figure 8.4 shows the range of responses given by two-thirds of the respondents. The midpoint of each bar reports the average score given by blacks and whites, and its value is reported to the right.

Almost two-thirds of blacks told us there was a lot of labor market discrimination, and the other one-third told us there was some. That is, all but 5 percent of African Americans thought discrimination limited the chances of blacks to get good jobs. Among whites, about one-third said there was a lot of discrimination, and another 45 percent said there was some. So whites, similar to blacks, thought there was extensive labor market discrimination.

Turning to how individuals thought about the consequences of skin color when searching for a home, we found black-white similarities but fascinating differences. These results are also shown in figure 8.4. Both races were asked:

> I'm going to mention several reasons why Black people may miss out on good housing in the Detroit area. I'd like you to tell me how often you think Black people miss out on good housing for each of the reasons I mention. The first reason is because White owners will not rent or sell to Blacks. Do you think that Blacks miss out on good housing because White owners will not rent or sell to Blacks "very often," "sometimes," "rarely" or "almost never"?

Eighty-two percent of whites and 87 percent of African Americans thought that blacks missed out on good housing "very often" or "sometimes" because white property owners would not sell or rent to blacks. Although the difference is statistically significant, it is small and reveals a racial consensus: most Detroiters think that white property owners continue to favor whites over blacks.

Using the identical introduction, we went on to ask: "Do you think blacks missed out on good housing because real estate agents refused to show, sell, or rent to blacks?" The majority of both races agreed that this occurred frequently, but there was a racial difference, as shown in figure 8.4. Sixty percent of whites thought blacks missed out "sometimes" or "very often" because of this practice. Among blacks, however, 85 percent thought brokers discriminated.

Going one step further, we asked: "Do you think blacks miss out on good housing because banks and lenders will not loan money to blacks to purchase a home?" The proportion of whites agreeing that this happened "sometimes" or "very often" declined to 55 percent. But among blacks, 89 percent said banks and lenders caused them to miss out on good housing.

Whites and blacks share the view that African Americans confront discrimination when they deal with individual white owners, but after that, a racial difference emerges. To be sure, whites saw extensive discrimination throughout Detroit's housing market, but they did not see it as so institutionalized and pervasive as blacks did. Whites thought that real estate brokers, banks, and lenders were less likely to discriminate than were white property owners, but blacks presumed they would be treated unfairly at every stage in the housing market.

Perceptions of discrimination in the labor and housing markets were not strongly linked to the age of either blacks or whites, nor to the educational attainment of whites. However, the higher the educational

FIGURE 8.4   *Perceptions of How Much Discrimination Hurts*
Chances of Blacks, Detroit-Area Blacks and Whites

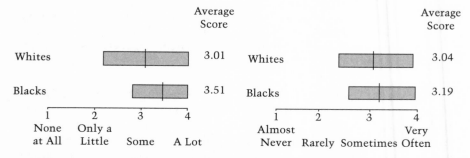

How Much Discrimination Is There
That Hurts the Chances of Black People
to Get Good-Paying Jobs?[a]

Do You Think That Blacks Miss Out on
Good Housing Because White Owners
Will Not Rent or Sell to Blacks?[a]

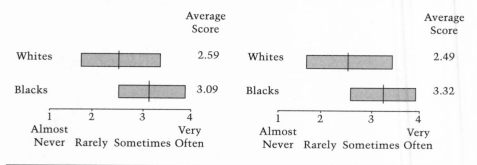

Do You Think That Blacks Miss Out on
Good Housing Because Real Estate Agents
Will Not Show, Sell, or Rent to Blacks?[a]

Do You Think That Blacks Miss Out on Good
Housing Because Banks and Lenders Will Not
Lend Money to Blacks to Purchase a Home?[a]

Note: This figure shows the average (mean) response for whites and blacks for each item using a four-point scale. Data were obtained in the Detroit Area Study 1992, with a sample size of 750 blacks and 736 whites.
[a]Indicates that the racial difference in the belief about discrimination was significant at the .01 level.

attainment of a black, the more likely he or she was to perceive discrimination. This study did not determine whether highly educated blacks are actually targeted for more discrimination than blacks with limited educations, or whether this finding results from extensively educated blacks being more cognizant of unfavorable outcomes they attribute to racial discrimination.

Experiences of Discrimination

Detroit-area blacks think there is much discrimination, and this likely influences how and where they search for jobs and homes. Some undoubtedly challenge discrimination to prove they can overcome it, but more common, we assume, is a decision that it is a waste of time to look for a new job if the employer is going to turn you down, or seek a suburban home if it is going to be difficult to live there.

How many people think they have actually been victimized by discrimination? When investigating experiences of discrimination, we found large racial and gender differences. As expected, blacks were more likely than whites to report losing out because of discrimination.

Those who said they had looked for a job in the last ten years were asked: "Have you even felt at any time in the past they you were refused a job because of your race or ethnicity?" Respondents could answer "yes" or "no." Figure 8.5 shows the findings.

The percent who said they were turned down because of their race or ethnicity was more than five times as great for African Americans as for whites: 40 percent versus 7 percent. On many indicators of labor market achievements, black women fare better vis-à-vis white women than black men fare vis-à-vis white men. For example, in metropolitan Detroit in 1997, adult black women who worked full-time earned 83 percent as much per hour as white women, but black men who worked full-time earned only 76 percent as much per hour as white men. Such differences are consistent with the findings shown in figure 8.5. Black men reported more racial discrimination in getting a job than black women. Nevertheless, a sizable minority of black women felt they had been denied employment because of their skin color. Despite civil rights laws and the "equal employment opportunity" phrase inserted into job advertisements, many Detroit-area blacks think they were victimized by discrimination when they sought work. As the educational attainment of blacks increased, so too did their reports of being victimized. Among those with college degrees, 57 percent thought they had been refused a job because of their race, but among black high school dropouts, it was only 27 percent. When it comes to getting a job, college-educated blacks think the playing field is much less level than do blacks who quit school before their high school graduations.

Perhaps there is more racial discrimination in hiring decisions than in subsequent decisions about pay raises and promotions. Selectively promoting white employees over ostensibly similar African Americans exposes an employer to challenges before the Equal Employment Opportunity Commission and in the courts. To get at perceptions of this type of discrimination, persons who held jobs within the last five years were asked: "Have you ever felt at any time in the past that others at your

Have you ever felt in the past that you were refused a job because of your race or ethnicity?

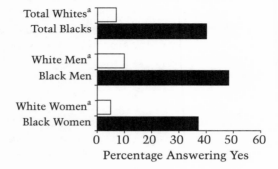

Have you ever felt at any time in the past that others at your place of employment got promotions or pay raises faster than you did because of your race or ethnicity?

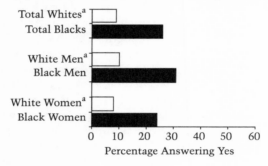

Do you think you have ever been discriminated against when you were trying to buy or rent a house or apartment?

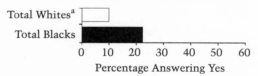

Note: This figure shows the percent saying yes. Data were obtained in the Detroit Area Study 1992, with a sample size of 750 blacks and 736 whites. The question about being refused a job because of race or ethnicity was asked of people who had searched for work in the last ten years. The question about missing out on promotions or pay raises because of race or ethnicity was asked of all persons who had been employed in the last five years. [a]Indicates that the racial difference in the report of discrimination was significant at the .01 level.

place of employment got promotions or pay raises faster than you did because of your race or ethnicity?" When asked about this, Detroit blacks reported less discrimination than when asked about being hired in the first place (see figure 8.5). However, one-third of employed black men and one-quarter of black women felt they had missed out on pay and promotions because of their race. Such treatment was reported rarely by whites—approximately 1 in 14 thought their race or ethnicity had cost them more pay or a better job.

Most people look for new jobs more often than they seek new homes, and that may help explain the next finding: racial differences in the experience of discrimination in the housing market. All respondents were asked: "Do you think that you have ever been discriminated against when you were trying to buy or rent a house or apartment?" We did not specifically mention racial discrimination, but this question immediately followed those asking about which racially mixed neighborhoods respondents would move into, so the context implied racial discrimination. As the bottom panel of figure 8.5 illustrates, about one-quarter of blacks said yes when asked about housing discrimination. Only 10 percent of whites reported such discrimination. If someone told us they had been victimized, we probed for an explanation and heard many reasons. Quite a few thought they had been turned away because they had young children, and some said they were denied because they were single mothers with children. The most common reason given by blacks was discrimination because of race, with over one-tenth of the total sample saying they had been victimized in this way. In comparison, just 9 whites in the sample of 736 said they had been victimized in the housing market because of their ethnicity or race. For whites, the most commonly reported reason was having children.

Reverse Discrimination

Both races agree that there is racial discrimination in the labor market, but their perception of what it is and how it affects them differs greatly. Whites thought blacks were unfairly treated since 76 percent thought there was "a lot" or "some" discrimination hurting the chances of African Americans to get good-paying jobs. But they simultaneously felt that their own chances for getting jobs and promotions were constrained by affirmative action policies. Blacks, on the other hand, thought reverse discrimination occurred infrequently.

Busing to integrate schools was the controversial racial policy of the late 1960s, but in the 1990s, affirmative action became the focus of political activity and litigation. By affirmative action, we mean programs and policies specifying that certain numbers or proportions of qualified

TABLE 8.2   *Perception of the Frequency of Reverse Discrimination in Employment, Metropolitan Detroit 1992*

Response	Whites	Blacks
Very likely that the black gets a job or promotion	19%	9%
Somewhat likely	42	14
Cannot say	14	10
Somewhat unlikely	18	24
Very unlikely the black gets a job or promotion	7	43
Total	100%	100%
Sample size	729	749

Source: University of Michigan, Detroit Area Study 1992.

minorities or women be admitted to training programs or put on payrolls. To understand whether or not people thought affirmative action was common in Detroit's labor market, respondents who had worked in the last five years were asked: "What do you think the chances are these days that a white person will not get a job or promotion while an equally or less qualified black person gets one instead?" The results are listed in table 8.2.

The typical response for whites was "somewhat likely," with more than 6 whites in 10 agreeing that current employment policies favored African Americans over equally or more highly qualified whites. But the typical response from blacks was "very unlikely," and two-thirds of African Americans thought this type of reverse discrimination was not occurring. The majority of whites thought affirmative action put them at a disadvantage in the labor market at least in some circumstances, while the overwhelming majority of blacks reported that affirmative action was not benefiting their race.

We wondered if whites were influenced by media reports of reverse discrimination, and by politicians campaigning against such programs. Or did they have firsthand information about reverse discrimination? For people who said it was "very" or "somewhat" likely that a white person would miss out on a job or promotion to an equally or less qualified African American, we offered a list of five possible reasons they thought this (they could, of course, give us another reason):

- Something that happened to you personally
- Something that happened to a relative, family member, or close friend
- Saw it occurring at work

- Heard about it on the media
- Heard it from another source

Seven percent of whites said they had personally been victimized in the labor market, and another 16 percent said they had a family member, relative, or close friend who lost out to a black because of reverse discrimination.[6] When the sample is limited to those who were actually employed at the time of the survey, one-third of whites thought that equally or less-qualified blacks were hired or promoted at their place of work instead of whites. But among employed blacks, only 1 in 10 said they saw such racial favoritism where they worked. These are among the more striking findings from the survey. Blacks and whites agree about the importance of race in the labor market, but disagree about what is going on. Whites presume that blacks will be the preferred candidates because of their race, while blacks think that happens infrequently and frequently report discrimination against them when they look for jobs.

Explanations for Black-White Differences in Detroit

No scholarly investigation is needed to prove that Detroit blacks typically have worse jobs, lower incomes, and poorer housing than whites. We were interested in knowing how blacks and whites explained these racial gaps so that we might understand what policies they might favor or reject. Do most think these differences result from discrimination, or that African Americans just don't work hard enough to pull themselves up?

The most effective question to obtain information about how people explain racial differences has been asked in national surveys for twenty-five years (Kluegel 1990). It begins with the following noncontroversial statement: "I'm going to mention several reasons why black people have worse jobs, income and housing than white people. I'd like you to tell me whether you strongly agree, somewhat agree, somewhat disagree, or strongly disagree with each reason I mention." Interviewees were then presented with four statements.

- First, black people have worse jobs, income, and housing than white people because of racial discrimination.
- Second, because most blacks have less inborn ability to learn.
- Third, because most blacks don't have the chance for education it takes to rise out of poverty.

- Fourth, because most blacks just don't have the motivation or will-power to pull themselves up out of poverty.

Figure 8.6 lays out the findings. Each bar shows the range of responses given by two-thirds of the sample, with the average score located at the middle of the bar. This summary score is also shown at the right. High scores indicate that the respondent strongly endorsed the explanation.

The majority of Detroit residents agree that racial discrimination is to blame, but, as with previous issues, a much higher percent of blacks than whites thought so: 84 versus 57 percent. The average score for whites was just above the middle of the scale, but for blacks it was toward the top end. Of the four explanations, this is the one that got the strongest endorsement from African Americans. Blacks see discrimination as the primary cause of their status.

Six decades ago, many whites probably explained the limited accomplishments of blacks on the basis of biology and inheritance since when the first national survey in 1942 asked about racial differences in intelligence, the majority of whites denied that blacks were intellectually as capable as whites. Fifty-five percent of whites agreed with the statement that even if they had the same education and training as whites, Negroes would learn less—in the South, the figure was 80 percent of whites (Schuman, Steeh, and Bobo 1985, 124–25; Schuman et al. 1997, 353). The idea of inborn racial differences in intelligence has lost its hold over the years. When we asked Detroiters whether blacks had worse jobs, income, and housing because they had less ability to learn, both races overwhelmingly said no (81 percent of whites and 82 percent of blacks). The percent rejecting this explanation will increase in the future since those who said there was a difference in innate ability tended to be quite old. They had not benefited from recent schooling with its emphasis upon the fundamental equality of racial, ethnic and religious groups.

On the question of whether blacks have the opportunity to get the education required for today's good jobs, whites were evenly split. Blacks, on the other hand, strongly endorsed this explanation, with two-thirds agreeing. From these responses, and from other questions about schools asked in this survey, we found a widespread belief among Detroit blacks that the public school system is doing a poor job of educating their children.

Discrimination and educational institutions are structured components of our society and no matter how hard a person tries, he or she will be able to make no more than modest changes. But everyone can

FIGURE 8.6   *Explanations for Why Black People Have Worse Jobs, Income, and Housing than White People*

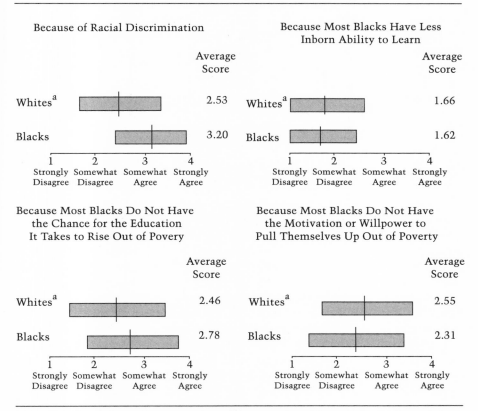

Note: This figure shows the average (mean) response for whites and blacks for each item using a four-point scale. Data were obtained in the Detroit Area Study 1992, with a sample size of 750 blacks and 736 whites.
[a]Indicates that the racial difference in the belief about discrimination was significant at the .01 level.

work a little harder to get ahead. The final choice asked whether black-white gaps came about because African Americans lacked the motivation or willpower to pull themselves into the middle class.

The majority of whites (56 percent) agreed that blacks lacked motivation. Indeed, for whites, this was the most endorsed explanation. One might think that African Americans themselves would reject an explanation focused on personal deficiency in willpower just as strongly as they rejected one focused on an innate inability to learn, but 47 percent agreed with it.

There is considerable racial consensus about why blacks have worse jobs, income, and housing than whites. For the purposes of developing new programs or changing old ones, it is important to look at the differences. Blacks, much more so than whites, endorsed the structural explanations—racial discrimination and the absence of opportunities in education. Whites were just about evenly split with regard to two structural explanations and, while their opinions were divided, they were more likely than African Americans to endorse the explanation focused on the lack of motivation and willpower.

Programs to Reduce Racial Differences

Since the riots of 1967, numerous major efforts have sought to increase opportunities for African Americans in Detroit and to minimize racial differences. Following that violence, local financial and civic leaders formed the New Detroit Committee, which successfully encouraged manufacturing firms and retailers to hire blacks. By spring of 1968, some 28,000 had been put on the payrolls by the "big three," Detroit's utility companies and Hudson's department store (Jacoby 1998, 254; Harris 1982, 169). But a recession at the end of that decade and then macroeconomic trends in the next decade wiped out those gains. The committee also called for the building of a new downtown and successfully encouraged investors to build the Renaissance Center, but this had, at least in the short run, only modest consequences (Jacoby 1998, chap. 8). In the late 1960s and early 1970s, HUD Secretary Romney tried to open up Detroit's suburbs, and the NAACP sought a massive change in public education so that black and white children would learn together in the same classrooms (Wolf 1981). Those efforts were unsuccessful. Today it seems unlikely that those earlier efforts will be repeated, but there is still an interest in programs that might maximize opportunities for blacks in the short run and minimize black-white gaps in the long run.

We wanted to know how Detroit residents felt about such programs, so the survey asked about two: affirmative action in employment and special job training and education for blacks. Not surprisingly, the races disagreed greatly about affirmative action, but were much closer to agreement about education targeted to African Americans.

To determine how people evaluated affirmative action, we asked a question that started by invoking a justification for affirmative action in employment: "Some people feel that because of past disadvantages there are some groups in society that should be given preferences in hiring and promotion. Others say that it is unfair to give these groups special preferences. What about you? Do you strongly favor, favor, neither favor nor oppose, oppose or strongly oppose giving special preferences in hiring and promotion to blacks?"

Figure 8.7 uses vertical bars to report the views of African Americans and whites. A value of 5 points was assigned to those who strongly favored affirmative action in employment and 1 point to those who strongly opposed it. Thus, high scores report the endorsement of affirmative action. The average scores given by whites and blacks are shown, along with the range of scores that includes two-thirds of the respondents.

Blacks overwhelmingly endorsed a program that would give their race preference in the labor market: 31 percent strongly favored it, and another 33 percent favored it. Blacks perceived extensive discrimination in the labor market, and the majority of African American men thought they had lost out on a job in the last decade because of their skin color. So it is no surprise to find that the overwhelming majority of blacks—men and women, young and old, highly educated and not so educated—favored giving African Americans an edge in the competition for jobs.

The responses of whites were not so highly concentrated. About 1 in 5 favored or strongly favored affirmative action. Another one-quarter said they were neutral, but the majority—53 percent—said they were opposed. Educational attainment was only weakly linked to whites' support for affirmative action, but those who dropped out of high school and those with college degrees were more supportive than those with educational attainments in the middle. Older whites were more supportive of affirmative action for blacks than younger whites—a puzzling finding.

Similar to blacks, women as a group fare less well in the labor market than white men, although the reasons for their relative lack of success may be quite different from those explaining the limited achievements of racial minorities. Is support for or opposition to affirmative action solely a matter of the group selected for special treatment, or is it a matter of opposition to affirmative action per se? Will any group favored by an affirmative action policy strongly endorse it? To resolve these issues, we asked about affirmative action for women, changing only the word *women* for *blacks* in the question.

Interestingly, African Americans supported affirmative action for women just about as strongly as they did for themselves: 61 percent favored it, and only 15 percent opposed. Black men did not differ from black women in their strong endorsement of affirmative action for women. Whites opposed affirmative action for women, although, as the

FIGURE 8.7   *Views of Detroit-Area Blacks and Whites About Affirmative Action and Special Training Programs*

Affirmative Action in Employment

Some people feel that because of past disadvantages, there are some groups in society that should be given preference in hiring and promotion. Others say that it is unfair to give these groups special preference. What about you?

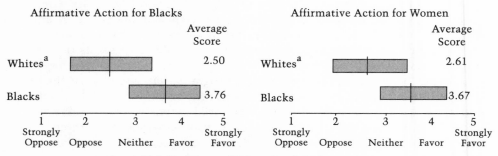

Special Job Training and Educational Assistance

Some people feel that because of past disadvantages, there are some groups in society that should receive special job training and educational assistance. Others say that it is unfair to give these groups special job training and educational assistance. What about you?

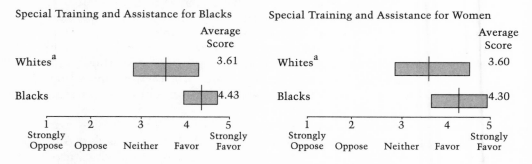

Note: These data were obtained in the Detroit Area Study 1992 from a randomly selected sample of 750 black respondents and 736 whites. This figure presents information for blacks and all others. The average (mean) response is shown along with the range that includes two-thirds of the respondents.
[a]Racial difference in this item is statistically significant at .01 level.

average scores shown in figure 8.7 reveal, their opposition was more muted than in the case of affirmative action for blacks: 53 percent opposed or strongly opposed affirmative action in the labor market for African Americans; 49 percent opposed it for women. Among whites, there average scores shown in figure 8.7 reveal, their opposition was more muted than in the case of affirmative action for blacks: 53 percent opposed or strongly opposed affirmative action in the labor market for African Americans; 49 percent opposed it for women. Among whites, there was a gender gap. White men were significantly more likely than white women to oppose affirmative action in hiring and promotion for women: 45 percent of women were against it, compared with 57 percent of white men.

These findings are consistent with what blacks and whites told us about Detroit's labor market. Blacks thought there was extensive discrimination and overwhelmingly supported affirmative action for both African Americans and women. Most whites thought there was some discrimination in the labor market, but less than blacks saw. And they were much less likely than blacks to favor affirmative action programs in employment although about 20 percent of whites favored affirmative action for both blacks and women.

Whites' opposition to affirmative action and a variety of rulings by the Supreme Court and lower jurisdictions seem to preclude those programs that might rapidly get more blacks onto payrolls and into higher-ranking jobs. A booming economy should boost employment prospects of all groups but there is such an emphasis on skills and advanced training now, that the unskilled and uneducated may fare poorly. A strategy to get blacks into the economic mainstream—perhaps a slower one than affirmative action—would be specialized educational programs and training targeted to blacks. Whites in metropolitan Detroit quite strongly support this.

Building on the affirmative action question described above, we asked: "Some people feel that because of past disadvantages there are some groups in society that should receive special *job training and educational assistance*. Others say that it is unfair to give these groups special job training and assistance. What about you? Do you "strongly favor," "favor," "neither favor nor oppose," "oppose" or "strongly oppose" special job training and educational assistance for blacks?"

Figure 8.7 presents results using a similar scoring system: 5 points were assigned to those who strongly favored special job training and educational assistance, and 1 point to those who strongly opposed. Among blacks there was virtually unanimous support for more job training and educational assistance targeted to their race—only 8 percent opposed such training or were neutral about the issue.

Although whites were significantly less supportive of special job training and education for blacks, the majority did endorse them: 21 percent strongly favored them, and another 40 percent favored them.

These responses imply that few whites would object to training programs targeted to blacks.

As for the issue of women being given job training and educational assistance because of past disadvantages, the pattern of responses was similar to that for affirmative action in hiring and promotions. Blacks overwhelmingly supported special job training and assistance for women, but so too did the majority of whites. There was a significant gender difference on this item. Women would, in the short run, gain more than men from such special programs, and, not surprisingly, women endorsed them more than men. Black women were only a little more enthusiastic about specialized training and education for women than were black men, but white women were much more in favor of such programs than white men. For all of these questions about affirmative action and targeted training, white men were most strongly opposed.

Conclusion

Race, economic class, and geography divide metropolitan Detroit. The area's history is replete with conflicts in these areas. In the recent past, the pervasive upgrading of skill requirements for employment and the massive shift of blue collar jobs from the central city to the suburbs have had adverse consequences for the employment and earnings of less-educated men, particularly African American men.

In addition to population and labor market transformations, racial attitudes and racial beliefs are important in making Detroit what it is today. They influence our thinking when we make decisions about where to live, where to look for a job, and whom to add to the payroll. They influence the choices of political decision-makers. The Civil Rights Revolution and many events linked to it brought about a great change in the racial values of whites—from strong support for racial segregation in almost all areas of public life to strong support for the principle of equal racial opportunities. Many whites also changed their racial practices so racial discrimination and segregation have diminished in some, but certainly not all, areas of public life.

In Detroit, as across the nation, whites almost universally agree that, in principle, African Americans should have the same chance as whites to get jobs, live wherever they can afford, and send their children to the same schools (Schuman et al. 1997, chap. 3; Duncan, Schuman, and Duncan 1973; 97–112). As Meier and Rudwick (1979, chap. 3) remind us, Detroit's factories in the 1940s were battlegrounds about where the color line in employment should be drawn and, as Sugrue (1996, part 3) recounts, the city's neighborhoods were battlegrounds in the next decade. Fortunately, those bitter and sometimes bloody racial conflicts have come to an end in Detroit. The egalitarian values of whites and authoritative civil rights laws ensure that there are few attacks upon the homes of African Americans who move to the suburban ring.

Despite strong endorsement of the ideals of equal treatment for all races, the remnants of traditional racial stereotypes are still present in the thinking of many Detroit area whites—the majority endorse the idea that blacks tend to be less intelligent than whites, are harder to get along with, and prefer more than whites to live off welfare. African Americans are much less likely to endorse these stereotypes, but see whites as difficult to get along with.

African Americans and whites also differ greatly in their perceptions about racial discrimination. Because the metropolis is highly segregated, blacks and whites typically work at different jobs, live in different neighborhoods, earn different incomes, and send their children to different schools. While African Americans acknowledge several other causes of these racial disparities, they emphasize discrimination as the primary one. Blacks generally see whites as favoring their own race and believe that whites structure the labor and housing markets to benefit whites. Whites recognize the impact of continuing discrimination, but tend to blame the lower incomes and poorer jobs of blacks upon a lack of diligence and work ethic. Police Commissioner Edwards, in the 1960s, used the phrase "river of hatred" to describe how whites and blacks felt about each other in his city (Stolberg 1968, chap. 6). The appropriate analogy today might be a "river of mistrust and misunderstanding."

Detroit's labor market is once again generating new jobs at a substantial rate. Given the shifts in racial attitudes, highly educated African Americans and those with special skills now have better opportunities than ever before. But the emphasis upon skills and advanced education means that the current economic expansion has failed to move many of Detroit's African Americans into the middle class.

What are the prospects for reducing racial tensions through public policies? Once again there are great divides between the views of African Americans and whites. African Americans strongly support programs that would reserve some jobs for blacks whereas most whites reject quotas and a significant minority think that reverse discrimination already benefits Detroit's blacks. Whites strongly endorse the principles of equal opportunity but oppose most governmental programs that might rapidly close the racial gap, such as busing to integrate schools, guaranteeing blacks university admissions, or setting aside jobs and contracts for African Americans.

Howard Schuman and his collaborators pessimistically concluded (1997, 327):

There is no real sign that the larger white public is prepared to see norms of equal treatment reconceptualized to support substantial steps toward drastically reducing economic and social inequality in this country.

Crafting policies to minimize racial differences will be challenging, not only because few such programs can be effectively funded and implemented in the current political climate, but also because of overarching racial differences in beliefs about the current operation of society. We are not willing to abandon the search for program and policies that can both reduce racial tensions and the inequalities in housing and labor market outcomes that we have documented. The next chapter describes a set of policies that we think can reduce Detroit's divisions.

9

Revitalizing Detroit: A Vision for the Future

WHAT WILL metropolitan Detroit look like in four or five decades? Certainly it would be a pleasant place to live if everyone who wanted to work could find a suitable job, paying enough to keep his or her family above the poverty line. It would be ideal if Detroit were recognized as a metropolis with good schools—elementary schools where most students scored at or above the national norms and high schools that effectively guided well-trained graduates into careers or career training. Some would go from high school to job-training programs, others to community colleges, while the majority would enter colleges and universities.

This idealized Detroit would also have low crime rates, so that in deciding where to shop, where to go for entertainment, or which park to visit, residents would never need to think about whether it was a safe or dangerous location. Decisions about buying a home or renting an apartment would not be made on the basis of the racial composition of the neighborhood. If secure job opportunities raised incomes and put most residents into the middle class, if the school system were improved, if crime rates were low, and if race became a less salient issue, the present gaps that separate blacks from whites and distinguish those living in the city from those in the suburbs would diminish.

Many readers will consider this vision an impossible dream. They will speculate that the economic situation is likely to remain problematic, and that black-white and city-suburban polarization are likely to remain high. We are not so pessimistic. In 1900, no one could have predicted that Detroit—then a moderately sized manufacturing metropolis—would soon become the nation's fourth largest city, the world's leader in the automobile industry, and the most important center in the world's biggest war. And no one now knows what will develop in the next century.

Nevertheless, any realistic assessment of the future of the metropolis at the end of its third century must consider some of the forces that now diminish its image as a livable metropolis. Three historical factors loom large. First, there are constraints linked to decisions made decades ago about the location of plants, offices, and residences. Much of the housing stock in the city of Detroit is old and unattractive by today's standards, so a significant portion has come to the end of its useful life and remains vacant. That is, in 1990, one housing unit in eleven was vacant in the city. Many of the inner-ring suburbs also have an older housing stock, are rapidly losing population, and will soon face the infrastructure and tax-base problems that bedevil Detroit and many of the nation's older cities. In contrast, in the outer suburban ring, open land is still available for shopping centers, employment complexes, and the large residential lots now popular with prosperous homeowners. Most population growth and, perhaps, most new jobs will likely be located in the far corners of Oakland County, in western Wayne County, and in the neighboring counties that have not traditionally been part of metropolitan Detroit.

Because of the current state of the housing stock and the labor market, the city's population seems likely to continue to decline in the future. How can this be offset? Can the city capitalize upon its riverfront? Are there other opportunities to build attractive housing for the middle class within the city? Can the city once again offer start-up firms and shoppers the opportunities they now find only in the suburbs?

Second, there is the industrial past and its continuing influence. Detroit owes its prominence to the automobile industry. Into the middle of the next century, it is likely that Detroit will still be the international center where American, European, and Asian producers employ thousands of engineers, scientists, financial experts, and patent attorneys. There will undoubtedly be continued employment in this industry at all ranks, although the job openings will favor the highly skilled. When recessions occur, Detroit will likely be hard hit, since at present—as in the past—there are no other major industries to cushion slumps in vehicle production when the business cycle turns sour.

The third historical constraint has been described at length in this book: white distrust of blacks and black distrust of whites. Survey data tell us that many whites still hold negative stereotypes about blacks. This helps explain why some employers are reluctant to hire black workers, why whites generally do not want to live with more than token numbers of black neighbors, and why discriminatory practices in housing and employment continue to be widespread. African Americans consistently report that the playing field is far from level, and that they experience racial discrimination when they search for jobs or buy a home. Our interviews reveal that many, perhaps most, African Americans view Detroit as a color-coded metropolis, with whites holding most of the decision-making power and using it to favor other whites for good jobs and good homes. This racial distrust continues to play itself out when political and economic decisions are made, be they decisions about bus routes, funding for public schools, art museums, or whether black or white firms will run the new gambling casinos.

In addition to these three historical constraints, what will happen in Detroit will depend on the nation's fundamental economic trends, changes in governmental policies regarding cities, and the civic values that Americans hold or reject. Changes in each of these areas will have far more impact than any specific public program or policy that may be implemented in Detroit. A high rate of economic growth is crucial for a manufacturing metropolis such as Detroit, which, unlike many other urban areas, is neither attracting new industries nor seeing high rates of growth across a wide array of industrial sectors.

Governmental policies in the 1960s and 1970s directed substantial federal spending to urban areas, including monies for building the super-highways that stimulated the automobile business and spurred suburban population and employment growth. Federal monies were briefly targeted to rebuild older cities and provide job training for the unskilled, especially in the aftermath of President Johnson's War on Poverty and Great Society Programs. In addition, there was a new willingness in the late 1960s and throughout the 1970s to move the nation rapidly in the direction of equal racial opportunities, in the hopes that equal outcomes would follow. The Office of Federal Contract Compliance and the Equal Employment Opportunity Commission put substantial pressures upon large employers to hire minority workers, while federal courts called for affirmative action programs designed to increase the employment of blacks and women. Some of the programs targeting money to local areas or providing specific opportunities for minorities remain in place, but there has been a major change in the government's role so that many programs were challenged, cut back, then eliminated.

Will there be a new government dedication to rebuilding the infra-structure of urban America, especially those places, such as Detroit, where the minority poor are concentrated? Will tax policies be changed to foster this? In an era of federal budget surpluses, will there be a new commitment of funds to such places? In the 1960s, central cities of the Rust Belt, including Detroit, were seen as particularly deserving of federal support for urban renewal. Now, there is a ring of older suburbs around most central cities with needs as great or greater than those of the big cities. Will we see new efforts to create metropolitanwide solutions, leading to a merger of central-city and suburban services, or even a merger of city and suburban governments? To date, the prospects for such efforts remain dim.

In 1997 President Clinton attempted to begin a national conversation about race, but it did not attract much attention. No one knows whether there will be a serious national discussion about this topic or what direction it might take. Obviously there is a great need for frank discussion of racial issues in Detroit, and we think there are some prospects for beginning such a dialogue. The population is now more highly educated than ever before, implying a greater understanding of the nation's confrontational racial history and of the country's ideals. And, racial relations between the city of Detroit and the surrounding suburbs have been improving, particularly since the election of Mayor Dennis Archer.

The nation is experiencing a dramatic racial and ethnic change, as Latino and Asian populations soar. While metropolitan Detroit is primarily home to whites and blacks, it has gradually attracted some of the new immigration flows. Will this demographic shift and a national debate about race and ethnicity provoke a new idealism about providing equal opportunities?

It is difficult to imagine great support for innovative civil rights laws or for those affirmative action programs that reserve positions for blacks or other minorities. But it may be possible to open a dialogue on the meaning of equal opportunity and what should be done to facilitate it, and a renewed dedication to the removal of barriers to opportunity. If so, race may gradually lose some of its importance as a determinant of socioeconomic success and residential location. Employers might then be more willing to hire African Americans, and both blacks and whites might search for housing without first determining which race dominates the neighborhood.

This optimistic vision for the future will be accomplished only if there are favorable economic and social trends at the national level, along with dozens of small steps taken at the local level. The remainder of this chapter discusses specific policies and practices that might realistically be implemented in the near future to move Detroit forward in the Renaissance process initiated by those who sought to rebuild the city after the riots of 1967.

The Current Policy Context

In late 1999, despite a booming national economy and the lowest unemployment rate in thirty years, poverty and unemployment in central-city Detroit remain high in absolute terms, and especially high in relation to their levels in the surrounding suburbs. In addition, the central city continues to lose population, even though the rate of out-migration may be slowing, and its retail and wholesale trade sectors remain almost nonex-

The Renaissance Center

The riot of 1967 provoked Detroit's financial elite to rebuild downtown starting with the Renaissance Center, which serves as the headquarters for GM. Photo reprinted with permission from the Detroit News Archives © 1996.

istent. Nevertheless, economic prospects for downtown Detroit are better than they have been for decades, based on the large construction projects near the Urban Employment Zone that will provide new stadiums for the Detroit Tigers and the Detroit Lions and facilities for three gambling casinos. The city does have several economic advantages that can facilitate its revival. The headquarters of the world's largest firm, General Motors, is now located in an array of attractive buildings along the riverfront. It is home to Wayne State University, and extensive medical complexes, and there are many city, state, and federal government jobs downtown. The largest suburban county, Oakland, has among the highest per capita incomes in the country. These are promising elements, but the city of Detroit has a long way to go to regain the economic vitality it once enjoyed.

A concentration of poverty, unemployment, crime, and a variety of other social problems in the central city characterize many other older metropolises, especially those where the city was unable to annex the outlying territory that became suburban. But Detroit's population loss and relative economic decline have been much larger than those in most other northeastern and Midwestern central cities, and its crime rate has dropped much less.

As we have emphasized in previous chapters, housing market and labor market processes and outcomes are influenced by racial attitudes in complex ways. Since African Americans arrived in Detroit in great numbers, these interactions have often been negative, with deteriorations in one arena having negative implications in another. Thus, a major goal of the multipronged policy initiative we describe here would be to generate positive interactions across these domains. Consider the following scenario, in which a positive labor market trend leads to positive population flows and favorable changes in racial attitudes.

Labor market policies should, we believe, be specifically targeted at the following goals:

(1)   to increase the skills of job seekers, thereby minimizing the skills mismatch revealed by the labor market data

(2)   to increase the demand for workers with moderate skills and for those who lack college training and raise their earnings so that poverty is greatly reduced

(3)   to increase information and reduce transportation costs to better match job seekers with job openings.

If this happened, poverty and unemployment among central-city residents would fall dramatically. Higher family incomes would contribute to increased demand for housing and other goods and services, further stimulating economic activity in the city and the suburbs. Increased employment and earnings would promote housing renovation and retail activity, thus raising the central-city tax base.

Assume further that another set of policies, using these additional revenues, could be successfully put into place to upgrade the quality of city services, especially with regard to police protection, infrastructure, and public schools. The resulting improvement in Detroit's image might discourage further white and black middle-class flight from the central city. The low housing prices in the city, the reduction in poverty and unemployment, and the improvement of public services and Detroit's image might even encourage some suburban residents to move back to the central city, thereby reducing racial segregation and reducing racial stereotypes about Detroit as a place to live, work, or visit.

Of course, hopes for this kind of urban revival have been a feature of policy debates for the past thirty-five years. And this hypothetical set of ideas is based on many optimistic assumptions, the most important being favorable macroeconomic trends and the implementation of the labor market policies just described. Some grounds for optimism can be found in the experiences of other central cities that have been revitalized. But, more often than not, revitalization has proven to be an elusive goal, and the policies that have been tried thus far have yielded disappointing results. It remains all too true that when one compares almost any American suburb with its central city, one finds a series of persisting inequalities and dichotomies: white-black, economically comfortable-poor, low unemployment-high unemployment, schools with strong reputations-schools with bad reputations, low crime-high crime. We are not so naive as to think that the policy options we advocate could quickly eliminate these divisions and inequalities, but they could certainly moderate them.

The previous chapters documented a long history of racial hostility and residential segregation in Detroit that continues to complicate the policy process and make revitalization efforts more difficult. The white population and many firms began moving to the suburbs in the post–World War II years, and this trend accelerated after the 1967 riots. For half a century or more, Detroit's suburbs have focused on their own spending priorities and their own tax bases, so they have tended to view proposals for metropolitanwide cooperation as a threat to their private interests, at worst, and of little personal benefit, at best. We think that much of this city-suburban polarization is rooted in the traditional racial and economic divide that characterizes Detroit.

Consider, for example, the lack of coordination in public transport policies that makes commuting to the suburbs difficult for many low-income, central-city residents who lack access to automobiles. At the same time, because of the economic boom of the late 1990s, suburban employers are concerned about a labor shortage. One reason why bus transportation from the central city to suburban jobs remains so difficult is that racial mistrust and tensions have prevented the coordination of Detroit's bus lines with those of the surrounding suburbs. Suburban residents express concerns that better public transportation would facilitate a "spillover" of central-city crime into their suburbs, or that their tax dollars would subsidize transportation services that few suburbanites would utilize. They would prefer that public funds be spent on road repair and maintenance in their own suburb or that their taxes be reduced. And central-city residents worry that metropolitanwide governance in any arena might dilute their political power and drastically reduce the number of middle-class jobs available to African Americans. Thus, racial attitudes, the structure of local government financing and political authority, and private economic interests all create barriers that have to be overcome to implement this one particular component of an urban revitalization strategy.

Another public policy mechanism for addressing the spatial employment mismatch is through enhanced antidiscrimination enforcement in the housing market (for example, rental, sales, and mortgage practices) to facilitate racial integration of the suburbs and enhanced enforcement in the labor market (such as employer recruiting, hiring, and promotion practices) to improve access for city residents to suburban jobs. Stepped-up enforcement of antidiscrimination laws in housing and employment, however, might exacerbate racial tensions between the suburbs and the central-city and make it more difficult to move forward with metropolitanwide transportation planning.

We have documented that a major source of Detroit's current economic problems are labor market changes that began in the early 1970s—especially the spread of labor-saving technological innovations and declines in the percentage of employment accounted for by manufacturing industries. These changes have reduced the employment and earnings prospects for less-skilled workers throughout the country, but have had particularly negative effects on residents of the city of Detroit, especially African Americans, because their economic gains in the quarter-century following World War II were based largely on high-paying jobs in the automobile industry. Responding to these labor market changes requires policies to increase the rewards to work for low-skill workers, to raise the educational attainment and skills of the young so that they will have higher wages when they enter the labor force, and to provide jobs of last resort for the most disadvantaged job seekers whom employers are not inclined to hire, even when labor markets are tight.

Similar housing market, labor market, and transportation policy proposals have been put forward by other researchers. Indeed, an indication that the problems confronting Detroit are similar to those of other large cities is found in a recent Report to the President from the Secretary of the Department of Housing and Urban Development, *The State of the Cities, 1998*. Its two key city-specific findings echo our conclusions:

- Despite recent gains, cities still face the triple threat of concentrated poverty, shrinking populations, and middle-class flight that began two decades ago.
- Cities face three fundamental opportunity gaps—in jobs, education, and housing—that are critical to reducing poverty and retaining middle-class families. (iii)

The policy proposals we discuss here, closely linked to those of the HUD report, emphasize the theme that the problems of large cities have been neglected and/or underfunded for too long. We need to implement a comprehensive set of labor market, housing, transportation, educational, and antidiscrimination policies. The specific policy prescriptions are familiar. What is missing is the political will to take bold actions to confront these problems. Many policy options require a substantial infusion of public funds. Yet, as long as "no new taxes" remains the dominant political mantra, it is not likely that major social policy initiatives will soon be implemented.

Some of the specific policies we propose could be pursued with modest additional funds; others would require metropolitan-wide tax sharing or spending districts; others would require an infusion of state or federal funds. Nonetheless, these proposals are conceptually sound, and their benefits will exceed their costs if political will and public funds move them forward. We are not alone in our guarded optimism. A recent issue of *The Brookings Review* was devoted to "The New Metropolitan Agenda." The issue editors (Katz and Bernstein 1998, 7) concluded:

> Finally, metropolitan issues do not invite traditional or simple programmatic responses. There is no "silver bullet" that can be designed and implemented by one level of government or one sector of the economy. To grow differently—to grow in a way that promotes reinvestment and reuse over sprawl, equity and fairness over division, access to opportunity over barriers to mobility—requires the pursuit of integrated public- and private-sector strategies that must be sustained and nurtured over a long time. The effort has an immense way to go, but at least it has begun.

An Urban Policy Agenda

Our analysis has shown that skills, space, and race all matter in the labor market, and that race matters greatly in the housing market. Our proposed public policies attempt to break down these barriers. We group the policy options into four categories: labor market supply-side strategies, mobility strategies, labor market demand-side strategies, and antidiscrimination strategies.

Labor Market Supply-Side Strategies

In the long run, improving educational attainment and labor market skills is the highest priority and offers the best prospects for raising employment and earnings and closing both the city-suburban and black-white gaps in socioeconomic status. In the late 1960s, a young man graduating from high school had an excellent chance of finding a job in metropolitan Detroit that provided good wages and benefits. In the late 1990s, many high school graduates earn less than the poverty line. Thus, it is critical that we invest more in young people to reduce the high rates of school dropout in the inner city, raise the skills of high school graduates, and increase enrollment of young people from low-income families in community and four-year colleges.

In *Teaching the New Basic Skills: Principles for Educating Children to Thrive in a Changing Economy*, Richard Murnane and Frank Levy insist that high schools teach their graduates the skills required to get and keep a middle-class job, including: the ability to read at the ninth-grade level or higher; the ability to do math at the ninth-grade level or higher; the ability to solve semistructured problems where hypotheses must be formed and tested; the ability to work in groups with persons of various backgrounds; the ability to communicate effectively, both orally and in writing; and the ability to use personal computers to carry out simple tasks like word processing (32). They observe that, across the nation, "close to half of all 17-year-olds cannot read or do math at the level needed to get a job in a modern automobile plant" (35). Notice that this list of skills is highly consistent with what Detroit employers told us they were looking for when they hired their most recent workers. All high school graduates should possess the cognitive skills, computer skills, and social interaction skills that employers demand of entry-level workers.

Unfortunately, these skills and abilities and achievements are not being learned by many low-income students in public schools in Detroit and other large central cities, where students score well below the national averages on standardized tests. And employers told us that many high school graduates lack the "new basic" skills. In part, this deficiency is due to the fact that central-city schools are underfunded relative to suburban schools. And in order to achieve the same educational outcomes as suburban schools, central city schools would need greater revenues per student, because their costs tend to be higher. Compared to suburban school districts, central-city schools have older buildings that require more maintenance, enroll more disadvantaged students who require additional attention and services, and have difficulty recruiting and retaining qualified teachers.

Apart from finances, central-city school districts in Detroit and other large central cities have been plagued by bureaucratic inefficiencies and other administrative impediments. Such schools would still have difficulty delivering the educational services needed to prepare their students for the demands of today's workplace, even if they received additional funding. Michigan's legislature drastically reorganized the administration and control of the city's school system generating high expectations for reform of education. Murnane and Levy describe model schools and how they have managed to reduce dropout rates and raise the skills of their high school graduates. If the new administrators

of Detroit's schools adopt such innovative models, they will successfully change the image of the schools. Murnane and Levy conclude that
for most schools to produce graduates with the new basic skills "will
require dramatic departures from current practice" (222). In addition to
funding problems, many central-city school districts, including Detroit's, have not been able to implement even those structural reforms
that do not require additional spending. This may be changing as the
new administration of public schools in Detroit has a mandate to pursue
fundamental reform.

In addition to improving school performance, other supply-side
strategies should focus on easing the school-to-work transition through
a system of apprenticeships with suburban employers for high school
students after school and during the summers. Such programs would
provide work experience for young job entrants and teach them about
the kinds of jobs available in the suburbs and the kind of skills needed
for success in the labor market. They will also break down informational barriers, by providing suburban employers with an opportunity to
learn about the skills and abilities of central-city residents. Experience
in such a program might make firms more willing to hire a worker who
differs from their current workforce. Because these apprenticeships will
operate on a temporary basis, it would be easier to terminate apprentices
who do not work out than to terminate a regular employee. Thus, firms
might hire more central-city high school graduates as apprentices and
then as regular employees if they prove worthy.

Mobility Strategies to Link Firms and Workers

Mobility strategies, like supply-side strategies, have been widely discussed for the past thirty-five years. However, as with public education,
there are few success stories. Three approaches have been tested: moving central-city residents to homes in the suburbs; moving firms back to
central-city locations; and transportation policies that take firm and residential location as given and that facilitate commuting of central city
workers to suburban jobs.

Moving Central-City Residents to the Suburbs   The first mobility
strategy addresses the spatial mismatch in the labor market by attempt-
ing to "open up" the suburbs. Access to less-skilled jobs, especially
those in small firms and those located off transportation routes, would
be increased if greater numbers of low-income, especially minority, central-city residents could obtain affordable housing in the suburbs. These
residential relocation policies seek to raise employment and earnings

prospects for two generations. Commuting costs are reduced, and information about and access to job vacancies increase. If these programs are successful, adults will have better labor-market outcomes. And their children will have access to higher-quality suburban schools. Presumably, they will learn more in school and be more likely to pursue an advanced degree.

The Gautreaux program has specifically documented these kinds of gains for both parents and children. It resulted from a 1976 Supreme Court consent decree in a lawsuit brought by some Chicago public housing residents against the U.S. Department of Housing and Urban Development, who charged that city and federal policies deliberately and unconstitutionally concentrated the black poor in isolated public housing projects (see Rosenbaum 1995). The settlement gave more than five thousand public housing residents and those on waiting lists in 1981 the option of housing subsidies to rent on the housing market outside the projects, either in the city of Chicago or its suburbs.

Some former housing project residents used the subsidies for housing in inner-city neighborhoods, while others selected suburban neighborhoods where few minorities lived. There were modest employment gains for the parents who moved from the projects to the suburbs, as opposed to other areas in the city of Chicago, but enormous educational gains for the children. For example, 20 percent of the interviewed children who attended city schools dropped out before getting a high school degree, whereas only 5 percent of those attending suburban schools dropped out. And 54 percent of the suburban high school graduates enrolled in higher education, compared with only 21 percent of the city high school graduates.

The Clinton administration implemented a ten-year demonstration program modeled on the Gautreaux program. It was designed to test the hypothesis that impoverished families moving out of neighborhoods of concentrated poverty will see measurable improvements in economic and educational outcomes. The Moving to Opportunity (MTO) Program, originally proposed during the Bush administration, began in five metropolitan areas in the early 1990s. MTO aims to move low-income families with children from high-poverty areas (census tracts with a poverty rate of 40 percent or more) to low-poverty areas (with rates of 10 percent or less). It provides participating families with vouchers to be used on the regular housing market. In addition, applicants are provided with considerable assistance in their housing search and counseling about their housing options (Goering and Feins 1997).

Unfortunately, the program expansion to additional metro areas sought by the Clinton administration was rejected by Congress, in part because of opposition from white suburban residents who objected to the prospect of even small numbers of poor and minority families moving into their neighborhoods (Yinger 1995, 235–36). This is yet another example of the negative interplay between hostile racial attitudes and public policies designed to break down the spatial concentration of poverty in the central city.

Given the success of the Gautreaux Program, and promising early findings from MTO (Katz, Kling, and Liebman 1997), Detroit philanthropic organizations, fair housing advocacy groups, and socially active businesses could contribute modest amounts of funds to undertake a similar program in the Detroit area.

Moving Firms to the Inner City Labor-market supply-side strategies are designed to reduce the skills mismatch between what employers need to fill their vacant jobs and the skills of unemployed city workers. Other policies, taking the skills of inner-city residents as fixed at least in the short run, attempt to encourage firms to expand employment for the disadvantaged in inner-city neighborhoods. The goal is both to reduce spatial mismatches and to revitalize neighborhoods.

Proposals to promote economic development in lagging regions have a long history in the United States, ranging from the War on Poverty's proposals for economic stimulation in Appalachia to the Clinton administration's Empowerment Zones and Enterprise Communities. Such economic development policies typically provide tax subsidies to encourage firms to expand employment in certain geographic areas. One problem is that some firms may bring jobs to these areas, but not hire local residents, in part because the subsidies have been structured in ways that allow them to change the location of their activities without changing the nature of their workforce. And, as our employer interviews demonstrate, firms have decreased their overall demand for less-skilled workers over the past several decades.

The research consensus suggests that the public costs for each new job created in this manner are quite high (see Ladd 1994 and Gramlich and Heflin 1998) because some subsidies actually encourage firms to use more capital equipment rather than less-skilled workers and because tax subsidies are often not attractive to small or start-up firms that do not yet have much of a tax burden. Nonetheless, such programs have been politically popular, garnering more bipartisan political and business support than many other policies reviewed in this chapter. They are viewed as appropriate governmental subsidies for businesses, as they are expected to increase employment and tax revenues in lagging areas.

For example, the Committee for Economic Development's report, *Rebuilding Inner-City Communities: A New Approach to the Nation's Urban Crisis* (1995), calls on "business, government and private philanthropy to take a more integrated approach to urban improvement, focusing on community-building and enlisting neighborhood residents and local institutions as partners." Many of the report's goals address the problems we have been discussing: expand inner-city employment and retail trade, upgrade housing, improve public safety, and eliminate discrimination in jobs, credit, and housing.

Dennis Rondinelli, James Johnson Jr., and John Kasarda (1998) suggest that urban economic development policies should focus not only on bringing existing firms back to the city but also on developing the business skills of inner-city entrepreneurs. They distinguish between the labor market supply-side strategies (discussed earlier) that would raise the skills of the inner-city workforce—education and literacy training, family and child development, drug and crime prevention—and technical assistance for minority-owned businesses and inner-city entrepreneurs who run the firms that are most likely to hire inner-city residents. This would involve providing assistance in business practices and helping to link these firms to the wider business community in order to improve the survival rate of minority business enterprises. As we showed in previous chapters, minority employers are more likely than white employers to hire minority workers. Thus, this strategy, if successful, would increase both assets of minority firms and minority employment.

All these goals are embodied in the Urban Empowerment Zone legislation. Detroit was selected as one of only six Urban Empowerment Zones awarded late in 1994, but it is still too early to evaluate whether it will be successful in simultaneously bringing new employers to the city and increasing the employment of central-city residents. Tax credits are available for capital projects, employment, social services, and other community development activities. The goal is to geographically concentrate a set of federal initiatives to generate positive spillovers that promote revitalization, while encouraging business development and minority employment. The construction of two new stadiums and three gambling casinos in downtown Detroit will create new jobs for both the highly skilled and those whose work skills are modest.

Reducing Transportation Costs Transportation policies take both firm and residential location as fixed, and hence are less costly than programs that seek either to move central-city residents closer to suburban jobs or to encourage firms to move close to inner-city residents.

Many low-income African American residents of Detroit do not have access to a car and, not surprisingly, those lacking vehicles seldom search for work in the far outlying suburbs, where job growth is fastest. Transportation issues are particularly important in metropolitan Detroit, where there is no rail or subway system and an underdeveloped bus system. The motor capital of the world is the most appropriate place to experiment with programs that would subsidize automobile ownership or encourage vanpools—much less costly strategies than building mass transit systems. For example, in a study of single-mother welfare recipients in an urban Michigan county, about two-thirds of those who had access to a car and a driver's license were working at least twenty hours per week, compared with only 45 percent of those who lacked access to a car and/or license (S.K. Danziger et al. 2000). This suggests a role for policies that subsidize automobile ownership, or encourage vanpools or metrowide transportation systems.

Mark Alan Hughes (1995) has long advocated this kind of employment strategy. Historically, low-income residents in Detroit and other cities have tended to live close to the factories where they worked, but the suburbanization of employment and the emergence of central cities as service centers have contributed to a spatial mismatch. He argues that transportation policies that foster mobility to jobs can provide city residents with "access to economic opportunity without sacrificing community networks such as extended family and institutional affiliations. . . . City governments retain voters who have received the benefits of the strategy" (288). He advocates policies to connect inner-city residents with suburban employers searching for workers and to facilitate access to these firms by coordinated ride sharing, vanpools, subsidized automobile purchase, and other means.

In 1996, the Clinton administration instituted the Bridges to Work demonstration in five cities. It attempts to connect inner-city job seekers with job placement, transportation, child care, and other supportive services, and is an example of the kind of mobility strategy that might be used in Detroit.

Labor Market Demand-Side Strategies

Despite rapid economic growth in the 1990s, there is much to be done to improve the employment prospects and earning levels of the less-skilled residents of Detroit. Through no fault of their own, they face much bleaker labor market prospects than did their counterparts from 1940 through the 1960s, when Detroit was booming. Our survey reveals that many inner-city residents want to work and are willing to take minimum-wage jobs, but do not have the skills that employers are demanding. We discuss two demand-side strategies here: employer subsidies, which are included as part of the Empowerment Zone policies, and low-wage public service jobs of last resort.

Employer Subsidies If firms are unwilling to hire the less skilled at the minimum wage, then direct subsidies that lower hiring costs might induce them to do so. The existing evidence on employer subsidies is modestly promising. Lawrence Katz (1998), in a comprehensive review, concluded that "wage subsidies combined with training and job development are effective in improving the earnings and employment of disadvantaged adults, particularly welfare recipients" (46). He further notes that "wage subsidies for less skilled workers are likely to be more effective when utilized in conjunction with labor market intermediaries that help provide some training, placement services and job retention services" (49).

This implies that a wage subsidy that is part of the Urban Empowerment Zone package may yield positive results for inner-city residents. That is, a program of wage subsidies tied to job training will likely be popular with both employers and the unskilled workers themselves. Such programs, linked to Empowerment Zones, will be more targeted geographically than previous subsidies and will be accompanied by federal funds to subsidize additional training and social services, including child care (see Engberg 1996). The Empowerment Zone employer wage credit provides tax relief of 20 percent of the first $15,000 of wages and training expenses for each employee who both lives and works in the zone. This may be particularly beneficial when labor markets are tight (as was the case in the late 1990s). Employers may be more willing to hire less-skilled workers because they can use the $3,000 for some combination of tax relief or worker training. A small start-up firm with little tax liability could use the funds to send the worker to a special training course, for example.

Targeting residents of empowerment zones offers a way to increase minority employment in the context of opposition to affirmative action programs. Our survey results also imply that there would be support for programs targeted to raising skills, especially if the emphasis is on training workers for vacant jobs.

Employment of Last Resort While employer subsidies may help some less-skilled workers living in the Empowerment Zone, there remains a need for low-wage jobs of last resort for those living elsewhere, and for many inner-city residents when labor markets are slack. Public service employment programs (PSE) have a long history in the United States, but they are not politically popular. President Reagan terminated the last large federally sponsored program when he eliminated the Comprehensive Employment and Training Act (CETA) in the early 1980s.

We propose that the federal government should select a number of distressed cities, including Detroit, for a demonstration project that would offer transitional low-wage jobs of last resort to poor inner-city residents. The jobs would be subsidized by the federal government—for example, they might pay 80 percent of the costs—but the positions would be administered by nonprofit or community-based organizations or by local governmental agencies. The goal would be to have the workers perform tasks that are socially beneficial, but for which there is little effective labor demand. We envision workers providing labor-intensive public services that would be valued in poor communities and that are provided in more affluent communities: monitoring of playgrounds, neighborhood maintenance, and assisting the elderly, for example.

Graduated job ladders would provide rewards to workers who succeeded on the job, but wages would be lower than the worker would receive in the private sector, thereby providing an incentive to take an available job. Employees who failed to meet performance standards would be dismissed. Those hired might be limited to a year to two of public employment, after which time they should have acquired some of the experience and skills needed to get a private-sector job.

The jobs we are proposing are offered as a safety net to poor people who want to work but cannot find a private-sector or public-sector job. They are particularly needed now that welfare reform has placed time limits on the cash social safety net because it appears that some welfare recipients, despite a great pressure to do so, cannot find and keep a job (Danziger 1999).

Antidiscrimination Strategies

Despite much progress on some fronts, there is still not a level playing field when it comes to race. Federal and state laws ban racial discrimination in all areas of public life, but enforcement is lax.

We recommend several strategies for reducing racial tensions. First, civic organizations, civil rights groups in Detroit, and governmental leaders should regularly stress racial integration as a goal. The organizations that promote our health use effective advertising campaigns to remind us not to smoke, to exercise regularly, to drink moderately, and to practice safe sex. Millions of Americans regularly get medical tests that, just forty years ago, were rarely performed. Death rates are down and continue to fall. There should be a similar campaign pointing out that blacks and whites are welcome to live wherever they find good housing, and to compete equally for both central-city and suburban jobs. This advertising campaign should stress the advantages of integrating schools, neighborhoods, and workplaces and the continuing costs of racial discrimination and segregation.

Second, private organizations in Detroit should expand the extent of testing for racial and gender discrimination in the labor and housing markets. Fortunately, the blatant types of racial discrimination that were once widespread have all but disappeared. Indeed, many employers note their commitment to nondiscrimination in job advertisements, and every real estate broker's office posts a statement about dedication to equal opportunities. But less obvious types of racial discrimination continue to maintain Detroit as one of the most segregated places in the nation: reluctance of some brokers to show black and white home seekers the same housing, the unwillingness of some underwriters to provide home insurance to units located in minority neighborhoods, the tendency of some suburban police officers to stop young male drivers who are black much more frequently than those who are white.

The hiring patterns revealed by the data we gathered from employers suggest that establishments located in the distant suburbs, particularly small establishments that serve mostly white customers, continue to prefer white applicants over African Americans. This implies a need to strengthen enforcement of existing equal employment laws, and ensure that all establishments abide by them. Indeed, there is a complementarity between the kinds of mobility or transportation policies designed to improve the access of inner-city blacks to suburban establishments, and antidiscrimination enforcement that ensures that applicants are treated fairly once they apply for these jobs.

Also, while the problem of discrimination is, presumably, somewhat less severe in the context of the tight labor markets of the late 1990s (as many employers are desperate to find qualified workers), it will likely become more serious again when the economy falters. We believe that employers would be less likely to discriminate if they thought an applicant might be a participant in an audit study. Thus, we recommend that audit studies by civil rights and civic organizations be expanded.

We believe that regular reporting of the fundamental social and economic trends that are reshaping metropolitan Detroit could also reduce racial tensions. In the absence of accurate information, it is easy for presumptions about racial progress or deterioration in race relations to go unchallenged. Federal and state statistical agencies regularly gather extensive data about employment trends, earnings, and crime, while the Census Bureau prepares local area population estimates and conducts a monthly survey of labor market issues. For the most part, these data are not readily available to the public or the press, so they seldom inform discussion of public policies.

Philanthropic organizations, civic organizations, and Detroit's major industries could commission the preparation of a comprehensive, biannual "Report on Metropolitan Detroit." This would lay out the major social, economic, and demographic trends in an informative, nonpartisan manner. From time to time, surveys, similar to those used in this volume, might be commissioned to provide an accurate picture of important economic changes and race relations. Research institutes, major newspapers, and universities have the expertise and facilities needed to prepare reports that can inform the public and provide the basic information needed to assess existing public policies and develop new ones.

A Final Word

Detroit has been divided along geographic, racial, and class lines for many decades. While a prosperous but small black economic elite has emerged in the post–civil rights era, on most economic measures black-white gaps remain as large today as they were a quarter-century ago. The policies we propose, if successfully implemented, should gradually reduce inequalities in educational attainment, employment, occupational achievement, and earnings. They will thus contribute to the revitalization of the entire metropolis, with particularly great gains for the city of Detroit. Without a comprehensive urban redevelopment and anti-poverty strategy, it is likely that the divisions we have described will continue and, if macroeconomic trends turn unfavorable, worsen.

July 24, 2001, will mark the 300th anniversary of the arrival of Antoine de Lamothe Cadillac at that narrow point in the river that is now the city of Detroit. This anniversary should stimulate interest in both Detroit's history and its continuing revitalization prospects. Perhaps the attention that will be focused on this anniversary will generate the commitment and the will to move these strategies forward and diminish Detroit's racial, spatial, and economic divide.

ployees. Within an establishment, there may be some overrepresentation of higher-turnover jobs, though comparisons between these occupations and those that appear in the Census of Population of 1990 show few large differences (Holzer 1996).

8. Because most of the variables presented in this table and those that follow are dichotomous, the standard error on the mean is the square root of $P^*(1-P)/N$, where P is the mean and N is the sample size. Standard errors on most of the means listed in table 4.2 are in the range of .02 to .03. The standard error on the difference in means between central-city and suburban samples is the square root of the sum of squared standard errors of each. Most of the differences between central city and suburbs in the variables discussed in the text are significant at the .05 level or better.

9. Indeed, Bushway (1996) presents evidence suggesting that African Americans have relatively better employment outcomes in states that reduce the amount of uncertainty about such activity by making data on criminal records of individuals more easily obtainable by employers.

10. See Murnane and Levy (1996) for thorough descriptions of the kinds of analytical skills that are needed on noncollege jobs in order to achieve relatively higher wages. See Newman and Lennon (1995) for more evidence on this issue.

11. Simulated mismatch rates for these groups in Detroit are 18 to 29 percent for African Americans, 20 to 31 percent for welfare recipients, and 33 to 50 percent for high school dropouts. We include both actual and potential job seekers in our sample, the latter including any adults who do not report themselves to be retired, students, disabled, or homemakers.

12. At any point in time, a sampling of spells in progress overrepresents long-duration spells and misses short-duration spells, which can be captured only by looking at a sample of completed spells. Even though the spells in progress are incomplete, the "length" bias will usually outweigh the "truncation" bias associated with incomplete spells, causing the latter to look longer than a sample of completed spells. This point was originally made by Kaitz (1970) with regard to unemployment spells, and was applied more recently by Bane and Ellwood (1994) with regard to poverty spells.

13. The fact that lower skills contribute to the lower earnings and employment of young African Americans even after controlling for educational attainment, has recently been stressed by Ferguson (1993) and Neal and Johnson (1996), among others.

14. For the latter measures, we use the ratio of means in the table rather than the means of ratios for each firm, where the latter would have given equal weight to firms regardless of size. Also, we

note that the sample sizes on which the applicant questions are based are smaller than those for new hires, as we began asking separate questions for black male and female applicants after the survey first went into the field.

15. These findings appear regardless of whether we use the racial composition of new hires or of employees overall in the numerator of these ratios.

16. If the ratio of the percent of new hires to the percent of applicants from a particular group is above 1 at a firm, this indicates a relatively greater inclination to hire from that group, whereas a ratio below 1 indicates some disinclination to hire them, whether due to their limited skills, discrimination, or other factors. The weighted sum of the ratios across groups (weighted by the percent of all applicants from each group) should be 1, assuming that there is no measurement error in any of the variables.

17. Indeed, data presented in the next chapter show that gaps in skills between African Americans and whites appear to be lower among those who live and/or work in the suburbs than among those in the central city, providing further support for the notion that the lower tendency of suburban employers to hire black applicants reflects discriminatory behavior.

18. Distance from downtown Detroit was calculated by computing the distance from the central point in each municipality to a central point downtown (the corner of the Lodge Freeway and Grand Avenue), using maps. Percent white in the population was calculated from the 1990 Census of Population, while percent black among customers was calculated from employer reports.

19. The total lack of white hires in retail trade establishments in the central city represents the small percentage of applicants who are white, as well as a small sample of firms in which none of the most recent hires were white. Sample sizes in manufacturing and retail trade for the city of Detroit in table 4.6 and for some of the smaller municipalities in table 4.7 were small (20 or fewer); but the racial differences discussed in the text are generally significant at the .10 level or better. Because each observation in this chapter represents an establishment rather than an individual worker, the data are grouped, and thus measured with less error than data on a comparably sized sample of individuals.

20. All three of these variables have significant effects on black applicant rates in regressions that we have run. Because the percent of customers who are black can be measured at the firm level, it can explain differences within municipalities as well as between them.

21. After completing the sampling, the number of firms generated from the households was 425, while the number from SSI listings was 380. Each source of firms has advantages and disadvantages.

For instance, the SSI listings may miss new firms that are not yet listed in directories or do not yet have phones. The household listings may underrepresent the employers of less-educated workers, some of whom seemed less able or willing to give an accurate listing of their employer's name and address.

22. The distribution of firms across size categories in the SSI group were chosen as follows: 25 percent from firms with 1 to 19 employees; 50 percent from firms with 20 to 99 employees; and 25 percent from firms with 100 or more employees. This distribution approximates the fractions of employment found in these firm size categories in the EOPP Survey of Firms in 1982.

23. We thus use DAS sampling weights on firms generated by DAS respondents; along with an additional weight of roughly 2 for firms generated by college graduates because these were only generated in the half of the sample that came from the DAS.

Chapter 5

1. Population estimates or sample sizes are also included in this table and those that follow, so that standard errors can be calculated on categorical variables. Racial or geographic differences discussed in the text are virtually always significant at the .05 level or better.

2. Higher wages for commuters from the suburbs to the central city are a standard finding in the literature (Madden 1985). Lower wages in the central city, especially for less educated and/or minority workers, have been found by Straszheim (1980).

3. The lack of compensation for the commuting time of blacks is consistent with other findings in the literature (Holzer, Ihlanfeldt, and Sjoquist 1994).

    The census of 1990 reported the following weekly earnings (in 1997 dollars) for white and black men aged twenty-five to sixty-four in metropolitan Detroit:

One-Way Commute Time	Weekly Earnings in 1989	
	White Men	Black Men
One to nine minutes	$961	$697
Ten to nineteen minutes	1,091	809
Twenty to twenty-nine minutes	1,098	877
Thirty to thirty-nine minutes	1,136	842
Forty to forty-nine minutes	1,171	789

Source: U.S. Department of Commerce 1993.

4. These results are from regressions of the log of hourly wages on commute times, with controls included for education and age.

5. This conclusion assumes that most central-city residents who do not report the use of cars to travel to work do not have access to them. The alternative possibility is that they have access, but do not use a car to travel to nearby work. Of central-city residents in 1990 who worked in the suburbs, 97 percent of whites and 89 percent of blacks used cars or vans to get to work.

6. Among whites aged twenty-five to seventy-four, and living in the city of Detroit in 1990, 20 percent reported having an associate's degree or higher. Among whites living in the ring, it was 31 percent.

7. Details are available from the authors.

8. The modestly higher skill requirements of blue-collar jobs located in the suburbs than in the city documented in the last chapter suggests that skill differences play some role in the lower access of African Americans to suburban jobs, while the differences in application and hiring rates across employers in the two locations clearly suggest the importance of the "space" and "race" factors.

9. The effects of "social isolation" on behaviors such as crime, welfare recipiency, and teen pregnancy—which are themselves likely to reduce current or future employability—are stressed in Wilson (1987), and Massey and Denton (1992).

10. The housing and racial attitudes of whites are also likely to be reinforced by factors such as high crime rates among inner-city blacks, thus leading to even greater barriers to good schooling and jobs for African Americans who remain in the city.

11. The importance of automobiles for search and commuting was explored in Holzer, Ihlanfeldt, and Sjoquist (1994). But we can more convincingly argue here that automobile usage is exogenous with respect to search (as opposed to employment) outcomes, as location of search is unlikely by itself to affect whether an individual can afford to buy an automobile.

    The decisions made over the decades in Detroit make the metropolitan area exceptional for the very limited reliance its workers have on public transportation, as indicated by the figures below,

Metropolitan Area	Percentage of Employed Persons Using Public Transportation
Atlanta	5.2
Boston	14.0
Chicago	15.9
Detroit	2.1
Los Angeles	6.3
New York	45.6
Washington	13.7

Source: U.S. Department of Commerce 1993.

274

which indicate the percent of employed workers in each metropolis who relied on public transit in 1990 (U.S. Department of Commerce 1993).

12. As usual, the direction of causality here may run in the opposite direction: blacks may perceive an area as being more friendly as a result of having searched there and dispelled some of their negative perceptions. But the percentage that have searched in each area are not large enough to account for the broad impressions among blacks of relative friendliness in each community.

13. The data measure only the incidence of job search in each area for individuals over the previous ten years, rather than its frequency or intensity. It is quite likely that African Americans who have searched at least once in both Warren and Southfield have done so more much frequently or more intensively in Southfield, since they perceive it to be a relatively friendlier area.

14. A similar result appears in Holzer, Ihlanfeldt, and Sjoquist (1994), in which blacks and/or central-city residents do not respond to greater metropolitan decentralization of jobs with search or commuting over a wider geographic area. Fear of hostile responses, as well as general lack of information or connections in those areas, may be behind these results.

15. There has been some evidence of labor force withdrawals among less-educated white and black males in response to declining wages, though this factor does not seem to account for a large fraction of the difference in employment outcomes between the two groups.

16. The sample sizes for whites and blacks that have searched in the past thirty days become relatively small in tables 5.5 and 5.6. Nonetheless, the differences discussed below are generally significant at the .10 level or better.

17. A comparable or higher rate of search activity among young black than white searchers has also been observed in Holzer, Ihlanfeldt, and Sjoquist (1994). Of course, if our surveys disproportionately fail to capture nonemployed and nonsearching young blacks, these results may not generalize to those parts of the population.

18. Previously received wages are likely to be somewhat higher than offered wages, since the lowest of the latter are eliminated from the sample when they fall below the reservation wages of individuals. This will tend to bias the ratio of reservation to received wages toward 1, particularly for groups where this ratio would otherwise be relatively high; thus, differences between the groups may be understated by differences in these ratios. Because many individuals do not report previously received wages, we attribute the wages of others in the respective group to these individuals.

19. Both of these papers use data from the National Longitudinal Survey of Youth (NLSY), though the latter paper contains many more recent panels than the former.

20. The effect of an increase in the relative reservation wage on nonemployment should depend on the elasticities of labor demand for various groups. Estimated elasticities for all less-educated young workers are generally 1 or less (for example, Hamermesh 1993), though for specific subgroups like young blacks they might be higher. Thus, the reservation wage differences between whites and blacks might account for something on the order of 10 to 30 percent of the racial difference in nonemployment durations, whereas the observed racial differences are much higher than that (Holzer 1986).

21. The low representation of black males in our sample at least raises this disturbing possibility. The unwillingness of young blacks involved in gangs and other illegal activities to consider mainstream employment options, especially at low wages, is apparent in Taylor (1990).

22. Holzer (1986) also finds that the relatively high reservation wages of blacks could explain up to 30 to 40 percent of their higher unemployment durations, and somewhat less of their higher unemployment rates. Clearly, this leaves the majority of the differential due to other factors.

23. The subjective attitudes documented in tables 5.6 and 5.7 are no doubt measured with considerable error, and are likely to be highly correlated with unobserved skill differences of the respondents. For an analysis of how personnel managers in fast food restaurants in Manhattan assess soft and hard skills and why they generally prefer Latino or foreign-born applicants to native-born African Americans, see Newman (1999, chap. 8).

Chapter 7

1. Most Detroit-area blacks live in the central city (83 percent in 1990), while most whites live in the ring (92 percent in 1990). We presumed that distribution would give whites an advantage with regard to knowing about suburban locations. Our findings support that view. When asked about Warren, 21 percent of blacks, compared with 13 percent of whites, said they "did not know." For Troy, it was 24 percent of blacks and 10 percent of whites. For three suburbs—Dearborn, Warren, and Troy—blacks had a significantly higher percent saying "don't know," but there was no significant racial difference in the knowledge of Southfield or Taylor. However, when the respondent's age, tenure, education, gender, household in-

come, and race were entered into a model explaining whether or not the respondent "knew" a suburb, the only significant racial difference involved Southfield. Black respondents were *less likely* to give the "don't know" response for Southfield than whites, suggesting that this prosperous suburb with its unique racial composition is well known in the Detroit black community (Krysan 1999a, table 1).

2. Using data from the census of 1990 about block groups, we determined the average percent black in the neighborhood of the typical central city and the typical suburban white. Block groups average 559 residents. For whites living in the city, blacks made up an average of 36 percent of their neighborhood's population. For whites living in the suburban ring, it was only 3 percent. Central city whites going about their neighborhoods have much more contact with African Americans than do suburban whites.

3. In both 1976 and 1992, Detroit-area whites who said they would try to leave if blacks moved to their neighborhood were asked the open-ended question. Krysan (1999b) coded the themes for both years and analyzed changes over time. There was a significant decrease—from 31 to 24—in the percent of whites invoking a specific negative stereotype about blacks. This is consistent with many studies that report decreases in whites' use of traditional racial stereotypes (Schuman et al. 1997, chap. 3). There was a significant increase—from 29 to 41—in the percent of whites who explained their potential departure in terms of the more racially neutral explanation of property value decline.

Chapter 8

1. The modern stereotype cards used with Detroit-area respondents varied with regard to whether a positive or negative characteristic was at the left or right end of the scale. They alternated from one stereotype to the next, so as to encourage the respondent to think carefully about his or her rating. For purposes of illustration and statistical analysis, the coding was changed for all items, so that 7 became the most positive score and 1 the most negative.

2. According to the Census Bureau's March survey, 28 percent of the metropolitan black population in 1999 lived in households with incomes below the poverty line. For whites, it was 9 percent. At the other point income distribution, 16 percent of blacks but 34 percent of whites lived in households with incomes exceeding five times the poverty line (U.S. Department of Commerce 1999).

3. While whites and blacks in Detroit agree that whites are financially better off, there is a racial difference in the perception of the economic gap, with blacks seeing the larger gap: blacks typically placed whites 2.0 points ahead of their own race on this 7-point scale.

Whites typically placed their race only 1.6 points ahead of blacks, implying that whites see a much smaller economic gap.

4. A summary of the distribution of whites on these stereotype items is shown below:

Item	Percentage Rating Whites More Favorably	Percentage Rating Both Races the Same	Percentage Rating Blacks More Favorably
Economic status	80	15	5
Intelligence item	52	43	5
Work ethic item	67	30	3
Compatibility item	41	49	10
Speaks English item	72	22	6

Source: University of Michigan, Detroit Area Study 1992.

5. A summary of the distribution of African American responses on these stereotype items is shown below:

Item	Percentage Rating Blacks More Favorably	Percentage Rating Both Races the Same	Percentage Rating Whites More Favorably
Economic status	6	16	78
Intelligence item	25	46	29
Work ethic item	13	41	46
Compatibility item	46	36	18
Speaks English item	9	43	48

Source: University of Michigan, Detroit Area Study 1992.

6. As a check on consistency, note that 7 percent of currently or recently employed whites reported being victimized by reverse discrimination on the job. This is consistent with the 7 percent of whites who had searched for a job in the last decade and reported having lost a job because of their race or ethnicity, and the 9 percent of those recently employed whites who thought they were passed over for raises or promotions because of their race or ethnicity.

1948–1972." *Brookings Papers on Economic Activity.* Washington, D.C.: Brookings Institution.

———. 1976. *Black Elite: The New Market for Highly Educated Black Americans.* New York: McGraw-Hill.

———. 1992. "Crime and the Employment of Disadvantaged Youth." In *Urban Labor Markets and Job Opportunities,* edited by R. Peterson and W. Vroman. Washington, D.C.: Urban Institute Press.

Frey, William H. 1994. "Minority Suburbanization and Continued 'White Flight' in U.S. Metropolitan Areas: Assessing Findings from the 1990 Census." *Research on Community Sociology* 4: 15–42.

———. 1995. "The New Geography of Population Shifts." In *State of the Union: America in the 1990s,* edited by Reynolds Farley. New York: Russell Sage Foundation.

Garreau, Joel. 1991. *Edge City: Life on the New Frontier.* New York: Doubleday.

Georgakas, Dan, and Marvin Surkin. 1975. *Detroit: I Do Mind Dying: A Study in Urban Revolution.* New York: St. Martin's Press.

Gilpin, Alec R. 1970. *The Territory of Michigan.* East Lansing: Michigan State University Press.

Goering, John, and Judie Feins. 1997. "The Moving to Opportunity Social 'Experiment': Early Stages of Implementation and Research Plans." *Poverty Research News* 1(2): 4–6.

Goering, John, and Ron Wienk, eds. 1995. *Mortgage Lending, Racial Discrimination, and Federal Policy.* Washington, D.C.: Urban Institute Press.

Goldin, Claudia. 1990. *Understanding the Gender Gap: An Economic History of American Women.* New York: Oxford University Press.

Good, David L. 1989. *Orvie: The Dictator of Dearborn: The Rise and Reign of Orville L. Hubbard.* Detroit: Wayne State University Press.

Graham, Lawrence Otis. 1999. *Our Kind of People: Inside America's Black Upper Class.* New York: HarperCollins.

Gramlich, Edward, and Colleen Heflin. 1998. "The Spatial Dimension: Should Worker Assistance Be Given to Poor People or Poor Places?" In *Generating Jobs: How to Increase Demand for Less-Skilled Workers,* edited by Richard Freeman and Peter Gottschalk. New York: Russell Sage Foundation.

Greenberg, Stanley B. 1996. *Middle-Class Dreams: The Politics and Power of the New American Majority.* New York: Random House.

Hacker, Andrew. 1992. *Two Nations: Black and White, Separate, Hostile, Unequal.* New York: Scribner's.

Hain, Ellwood. 1978. "Sealing Off the City: School Desegregation in Detroit." In *Limits of Justice: The Courts' Role in School Desegregation,* edited by Howard I. Kalodner and James J. Fishman. Cambridge, Mass.: Ballinger Publishing.

Hamermesh, Daniel. 1993. *Labor Demand.* Princeton, N.J.: Princeton University Press.

Hamill, Pete. 1999. *Diego Rivera.* New York: Harry N. Abrams, Inc.

Harrigan, Patrick. 1997. *The Detroit Tigers: Club and Community: 1945–1995*. Toronto, Ont.: University of Toronto Press.

Harris, William H. 1982. *The Harder We Run: Black Workers Since the Civil War*. New York: Oxford University Press.

Hart, Kevin D., Stephen J. Kunitz, Ralph Sell, and Dana B. Mukamel. 1998. "Metropolitan Governance, Residential Segregation, annd Mortality among African Americans." *American Journal of Public Health* 88(3): 434–38.

Havens v. Coleman. 1982. 455 U.S. 363.

Heckman, James, and Brook Payner. 1989. "Determining the Impact of Federal Antidiscrimination Policy on the Economic Status of Blacks." *American Economic Review* 79(1): 138–77.

Heckman, James J., and Peter Siegelman. 1992. "The Urban Institute Audit Studies: Their Methods and Findings." In *Clear and Convincing Evidence: Measurement of Discrimination in America*, edited by Michael Fix and Raymond J. Struyk. Washington, D.C.: Urban Institute Press.

Helper, Rose. 1969. *Racial Policies and Practices of Real Estate Brokers*. Minneapolis: University of Minnesota Press.

Henrickson, Wilma Wood, ed. 1991. *Detroit Perspectives: Crossroads and Turning Points*. Detroit: Wayne State University Press.

Herrera, Hayden. 1983. *Frida: A Biography of Frida Kahlo*. New York: Harper & Row.

Hersey, John. 1968. *The Algiers Motel Incident*. New York: Alfred A. Knopf.

Hesslink, George K. 1968. *Black Neighbors: Negroes in a Northern Rural Community*. Indianapolis: Bobbs-Merrill.

Hirsch, Barry, and David MacPherson. 1994. "Wages, Racial Composition and Quality Sorting in Labor Markets." Working paper. Florida State University.

Hivert-Carthew, Annick. 1994. *Cadillac and the Dawn of Detroit*. Davisburg, Mich.: Wilderness Adventure Books.

Holzer, Harry. 1986. "Reservation Wages and Their Labor Market Effects for White and Black Male Youth." *Journal of Human Resources* 21: 157–77.

———. 1989. *Unemployment, Vacancies, and Local Labor Markets*. Kalamazoo, Mich.: W.E. Upjohn Institute for Employment Research.

———. 1991. "The Spatial Mismatch Hypothesis: What Has the Evidence Shown?" *Urban Studies* 28(1): 105–22.

———. 1996. *What Employers Want: Job Prospects for Less-Educated Workers*. New York: Russell Sage Foundation.

Holzer, Harry, and Sheldon Danziger. 2000. "Are Jobs Available for Disadvantaged Workers in Urban Areas?" In *Urban Inequality in the United States: Evidence from Four Cities*, edited by Lawrence Bobo, Alice O'Connor, and Chris Tilly. New York: Russell Sage Foundation.

———. 1996. "Spatial Factors and the Employment of Blacks at the Firm Level." *New England Economic Review* (May/June): 65–82.

Holzer, Harry, and Keith Ihlanfeldt. 1998. "Customer Discrimination and Employment Outcomes for Minority Workers." *Quarterly Journal of Economics* 113(3): 835–67.

Holzer, Harry, Keith Ihlanfeldt, and David Sjoquist. 1994. "Work, Search and Travel Among White and Black Youth." *Journal of Urban Economics* 35(3): 320–45.

Hughes, Langston. 1940. *The Big Sea*. New York: Alfred A. Knopf.

Hughes, Mark Alan. 1995. "A Mobility Strategy for Improving Opportunity." *Housing Policy Debate* 6(1): 217–97.

Hughes, Mark, and Julie Sternberg. 1992. "The New Metropolitan Reality: Where the Rubber Meets the Road in Antipoverty Policy." Washington, D.C.: Urban Institute Press.

Ihlanfeldt, Keith. 1997. "Information on the Spatial Distribution of Job Opportunities Within Metropolitan Areas." *Journal of Urban Economics* 41(2): 218–42.

Ihlanfeldt, Keith, and David L. Sjoquist. 1998a. "Intrametropolitan Variation in Earnings and Labor Market Discrimination: An Analysis of the Atlanta Labor Market." *Southern Economic Journal* 55: 123–40.

———. 1998b. "The Spatial Mismatch Hypothesis: A Review of Recent Studies and Their Implications for Welfare Reform." *Housing Policy Debate* 9(4): 849–892.

Irons, Peter. 1999. *A People's History of the Supreme Court*. New York: Viking.

Jackson, Kenneth T. 1967. *The Ku Klux Klan in the City: 1915–1930*. New York: Oxford University Press.

———. 1985. *Crabgrass Frontier: The Suburbanization of the United States*. New York: Oxford University Press.

Jacoby, Tamar. 1998. *Someone Else's House: America's Unfinished Struggle for Integration*. New York: Free Press.

Jargowsky, Paul. 1996. *Poverty and Place: Ghettos, Barrios, and the American City.* New York: Russell Sage Foundation.

Jenkins, Bette Smith. 1991. "Sojourner Truth Housing Riots." In *Detroit Perspectives: Crossroads and Turning Points*, edited by Wilma Wood Henrickson. Detroit: Wayne State University Press.

Johnson, Charles S. 1943. *Patterns of Negro Segregation*. New York: Harper & Brothers.

Johnson, James Weldon. 1968. *Black Manhattan*. New York: Atheneum. (Orig. pub. 1930.)

Jones v. Alfred H. Mayer Co. 1968. 392 U.S. 409.

Juhn, Chinhui, Kevin Murphy, and Brooks Pierce. 1993. "Wage Inequality and the Rise in the Returns to Skill." *Journal of Political Economy* 101(3): 410–42.

Kain, John F. 1968. "Housing Segregation, Negro Employment, and Metropolitan Decentralization." *Quarterly Journal of Economics* 82(2): 175–97.

———. 1992. "The Spatial Mismatch Hypothesis Three Decades Later." *Housing Policy Debate* 3: 371–462.

Kaitz, Hyman. 1970. "Analyzing the Length of Unemployment Spells." *Monthly Labor Review* 93: 11–16.

Kasarda, John D. 1985. "Urban Change and Minority Opportunities." In *The Urban Underclass*, edited by Paul E. Petersen. Washington, D.C.: Brookings Institution.

———. 1989. "Urban Industrial Transition and the Underclass." *Annals of the American Academy of Political and Social Sciences* 501: 26–47.

———. 1993. "Entry Level Jobs, Mobility, and Urban Minority Unemployment." *Urban Affairs Quarterly* 19(1): 21–40.

———. 1995. "Industrial Restructuring and the Changing Location of Jobs." In *State of the Union: American in the 1990s*, edited by Reynolds Farley. Vol. 1. New York: Russell Sage Foundation.

Katz, Bruce, and Scott Bernstein. 1998. "The New Metropolitan Agenda: Connecting Cities and Suburbs." *Brookings Review* 16(4): 4–7.

Katz, Lawrence. 1998. "Wage Subsidies for the Disadvantaged." In *Generating Jobs: How to Increase Demand for Less-Skilled Workers*, edited by Richard Freeman and Peter Gottschalk. New York: Russell Sage Foundation.

Katz, Lawrence, Jeffrey Kling, and Jeffrey Liebman. 1997. "Moving to Opportunity in Boston: Early Impacts of a Housing Mobility Program Mimeo. Harvard University, Department of Economics.

Katz, Lawrence, and Kevin Murphy. 1992. "Changes in Relative Wages, 1963–87: The Role of Supply and Demand Factors." *Quarterly Journal of Economics* 107(1): 35–78.

Katzman, David M. 1973. *Before the Ghetto: Black Detroit in the Nineteenth Century*. Urbana: University of Illinois Press.

Keating, W. Dennis. 1994. *The Suburban Racial Dilemma: Housing and Neighborhoods*. Philadelphia: Temple University Press.

Keating, Larry E., Lynn M. Brazaen, and Stan F. Fitterman. 1992. "Reluctant Response to Community Pressure in Atlanta. In *From Redlining to Reinvestment: Community Responses to Urban Disinvestment*, edited by Gregory D. Squires. Philadelphia: Temple University Press.

Keyes v. Denver School District No. 1. 1973. 413 U.S. 189.

Kinder, Donald O., and David O. Sears. 1981. "Prejudice and Politics: Symbolic Racism versus Racial Threats to the Good Life." *Journal of Personality and Social Psychology* 40: 414–31.

Kirschenman, Joleen. 1991. "Gender Within Race in the Labor Market." Mimeo. University of Chicago.

Kirschenman, Joleen, and Kathryn M. Neckerman. 1991. "We'd Love to Hire Them, But . . . : The Meaning of Race for Employers." In *The Urban Underclass*, edited by Christopher Jencks and Paul E. Peterson. Washington, D.C.: Brookings Institution.

Kluegel, James R. 1990. "Trends in Whites' Explanations of the Black-White Gap in Socioeconomic Status, 1977–1989." *American Sociological Review* 55(4): 512–25.

Klueger, Richard. 1975. *Simple Justice*. New York: Alfred A. Knopf.

Krueger, Alan, and Lawrence Summers. 1987. "Reflections on Inter Industry Wage Structure." In *Unemployment and the Structure of Labor Markets*, edited by Kevin Lang and Jonathan Leonard. New York: Basil Blackwell.

Krysan, Maria. 1999a. "Community Undesirability in Black and White: Racial Differences in Cognitive Maps and Their Role in Residential Segregation." Mimeo. Pennsylvania State University, Department of Sociology.

———. 1999b. "Whites Who Say They'd Flee: Who Are They and Why Would They Leave?" Mimeo. Pennsylvania State University, Department of Sociology.

Kusmer, Kenneth L. 1976. *A Ghetto Takes Shape: Black Cleveland: 1870–1930*. Urbana: University of Illinois Press.

Ladd, Helen. 1994. "Spatially Targeted Economic Development Strategies: Do They Work?" *Cityscape* 1: 193–211.

LaVeist, Thomas A. 1989. "Linking Residential Segregation to the Infant Mortality Race: Disparity in U.S. Cities." *Social Science Review* 73(2): 90–94.

———. 1993. "Segregation, Poverty and Empowerment: Health Consequences for African-Americans" *Milbank Quarterly* 71(1): 42–64.

Lee, Barrett A., and Peter B. Wood. 1991. "Is Neighborhood Racial Succession Place-Specific?" *Demography* 28(1): 21–40.

Leonard, Jonathan. 1990. "The Impact of Affirmative Action Regulation and Equal Opportunity Law on Black Employment." *Journal of Economic Perspectives* 4(4): 47–63.

Levine, David Allan. 1976. *Internal Combustion: The Races in Detroit: 1915–1926*. Westport, Conn.: Greenwood Press.

Levy, Frank. 1987. *Dollars and Dreams: The Changing American Income Distribution*. New York: Russell Sage Foundation.

Levy, Frank, and Richard J. Murnane. 1996. "With What Skills Are Computers a Complement?" *American Economic Review* 6(2): 258–62.

Lichtenstein, Nelson. 1995. *The Most Dangerous Man in Detroit: Walter Reuther and the Fate of American Labor*. New York: Basic Books.

Litwack, Leon F. 1961. *North of Slavery: The Negro in the Free States: 1790–1860*. Chicago: University of Chicago Press.

Madden, Janice. 1985. "Urban Wage Gradients: Empirical Evidence." *Journal of Urban Economics* 18: 291–301.

Maloney, Thomas N., and Warren C. Whatley. 1995. "Making the Effort: The Contours of Racial Discrimination in Detroit's Labor Markets, 1920–1940." *Journal of Economic History* 55(3): 465–93.

Marnham, Patrick. 1998. *Dreaming with His Eyes Open: A Life of Diego Rivera*. New York: Alfred A. Knopf.

Massey, Douglas, and Nancy Denton. 1993. *American Apartheid: Segregation and the Making of the Underclass*. Cambridge, Mass.: Harvard University Press.

Mayer, Albert J. 1960. "Russell Woods: Change Without Conflict: A Case Study of Neighborhood Transition in Detroit." In *Studies in*

Housing and Minority Groups, edited by Nathan Glazer and Davis McEntire. Berkeley: University of California Press.

McEntire, Davis. 1960. *Residence and Race: Final and Comprehensive Report to the Commission on Race and Housing*. Berkeley: University of California Press.

McGreevy, John T. 1996. *Parish Boundaries: The Catholic Encounter with Race in the Twentieth-Century Urban North*. Chicago: University of Chicago Press.

McLanahan, Sara, and Gary Sandfeur. 1994. *Growing Up With a Single Parent: What Hurts, What Helps*. Cambridge, Mass.: Harvard University Press.

McRae, Norman. 1991. "The Thornton Blackburn Affair." In *Detroit Perspectives: Crossroads and Turning Points*, edited by Wilma Wood Henrickson. Detroit: Wayne University Press. (Orig. pub. 1966.)

Mead, Lawrence, 1986. *Beyond Entitlement: The Social Obligations of Citizenship*. New York: Basic Books.

———. 1992. *The New Politics of Poverty*. New York: Basic Books.

Meier, August, and Elliott Rudwick. 1979. *Black Detroit and the Rise of the UAW*. New York: Oxford University Press.

Meyer, Katherine Mattingly, ed. 1971. *Detroit Architecture: A. L. A. Guide*. Detroit: Wayne State University Press.

Michigan Employment Security Commission. 1997. *Michigan Statistical Abstract: 1996 Edition*. Ann Arbor: University of Michigan.

Milliken v. Bradley. 1974. 418 U.S. 717.

Mirel, Jeffrey. 1981. *The Rise and Fall of an Urban School System: Detroit, 1907–1981*. Ann Arbor: University of Michigan Press.

Moss, Philip, and Chris Tilly. 1995. "Soft Skills and Race." Working Paper, Russell Sage Foundation.

Munnell, Alicia H., Lynn E. Broener, James McEneaney, and Geoffery M. B. Tootell. 1992. "Mortgage Lending in Boston: Interpreting the HMDA Data." Working paper 92-7. Boston: Federal Reserve Bank of Boston.

Munnell, Alicia H., Geoffrey M. B. Tootell, Lynn E. Browne, and James McEneaney. 1996. "Mortgage Lending in Boston: Interpreting HMDA Data." *American Economic Review* 86(1): 25–53.

Murnane, Richard J., and Frank Levy. 1996. *Teaching the New Basic Skills*. New York: Free Press.

Myrdal, Gunnar. 1944. *An American Dilemma: The Negro Problem and Modern Democracy*. New York: Harper & Brothers.

National Academy of Sciences. 1972. *Freedom of Choice in Housing: Opportunities and Constraints*. Report of the Advisory Committee to the Department of Housing and Urban Development. Washington, D.C.: National Academy of Sciences Printing and Publishing Office.

National Advisory Commission on Civil Disorders. 1968. *Report of the National Advisory Commission on Civil Disorders*. Washington: Government Printing Office. (Known as the Kerner Commission report, after its chair, Governor Otto Kerner.)

Neal, Derek, and William Johnson. 1996. "The Role of U.S. Pre-Market Factors in Black-White Wage Differences." *Journal of Political Economy* 104(5): 869–95.

Newman, Katherine S. 1999. *No Shame in My Game: The Working Poor in the Inner City*. New York: Russell Sage Foundation/Knopf.

Newman, Katherine S., and Chauncy Lennon. 1995. "Finding Work in the Inner City: How Hard Is It Now? How Hard Will It Be for the AFDC Recipients?" Mimeo. Columbia University.

Patterson, Orlando. 1997. *The Ordeal of Integration: Progress and Resentment in America's Racial Crisis*. Washington, D.C.: Counterpoint.

Pearce, Diana. 1979. "Gatekeepers and Homeseekers: Institutional Patterns in Racial Steering." *Social Problems* 26 (February): 325–42.

Peterson, Ruth D., and Lauren J. Krivo. 1993. "Racial Segregation and Urban Black Homicide." *Social Forces* 70(4): 1001–26.

———. 1999. "Racial Segregation, the Concentration of Disadvantage, and Black and White Homicide Victimization." *Sociological Forum* 14(3): 465–93.

Petterson, Stephen Mark. 1997. "Black-White Joblessness Among Young Men: The Limits of Cultural Explanations." *American Sociological Review* 62(August): 605–13.

Plessy v. Ferguson. 1896. 163 U.S. 537.

Polednak, Anthony P. 1991. "Black-White Differences in Infant Mortality in 38 Standard Metropolitan Statistical Areas." *American Journal of Public Health* 81(11): 1480–82.

———. 1992. "Poverty, Residential Segregation, and Black/White Mortality Ratios in Urban Areas." *Journal of Health Care for the Poor and Underserved* 4(4): 363–73.

Quadagno, Jill. 1994. *The Color of Welfare: How Racism Undermined the War on Poverty*. New York: Oxford University Press.

Rice, Roger L. 1968. "Residential Segregation by Law: 1910–1917." *Journal of Southern History* 24 (May): 179–99.

Rich, Wilbur C. 1989. *Coleman Young and Detroit Politics: From Social Activist to Power Broker*. Detroit: Wayne State University Press.

Rivera, Diego (with Gladys March). 1960. *My Art, My Life: An Autobiography*. New York: Citadel Press.

Robinson, Carla J. 1992. "Racial Disparity in the Atlanta Housing Market." In *The Housing Status of Black Americans*, edited by Wihelmina A. Leigh and James B. Stewart. New Brunswick, N.J.: Transaction Publishers.

Rondinelli, Dennis, James Johnson, Jr., and John Kasarda. 1998. "The Changing Forces of Urban Economic Development: Globalization and City Competitiveness in the 21st Century." *Cityscape* 3(3): 71–105.

Rosenbaum, James. 1995. "Changing the Geography of Opportunity by Expanding Residential Choice: Lessons from the Gautreaux Program." *Housing Policy Debate* 6(1): 231–69.

Ruggles, Steven, and Matthew Sobek. 1997. *Integrated Public Use Mi-*

crodata Series. Vers. 2.0. Mimeo. University of Minnesota, Department of History, Historical Census Projects.

Rybczynski, Witold. 1998. *A Clearing in the Distance: Frederick Law Olmsted and America in the Nineteenth Century*. New York: Scribener.

Schelling, Thomas C. 1971. "Dynamic Models of Segregation." *Journal of Mathematical Sociology* 1: 148–86.

———. 1972. "A Process of Residential Segregation: Neighborhood Tipping." In *Racial Discrimination in Economic Life*, edited by A. H. Pascal. Boston: D.C. Heath.

Schuman, Howard, Charlotte Steeh, and Lawrence Bobo. 1985. *Racial Attitudes in America: Trends and Interpretations*. Cambridge, Mass.: Harvard University Press.

Schuman, Howard, Charlotte Steeh, Lawrence Bobo, and Maria Krysan. 1997. *Racial Attitudes in America: Trends and Interpretations*. (Rev. ed.) Cambridge, Mass.: Harvard University Press.

Sears, David O. 1988. "Symbolic Racism." In *Eliminating Racism: Profiles in Controversy*, edited by Phyllis A. Katz and Dalmas A. Taylor. New York: Plenum.

Shapiro, Herbert. 1988. *White Violence and Black Response: From Reconstruction to Montgomery*. Amherst: University of Massachusetts Press.

Shogan, Robert, and Tom Craig. 1964. *The Detroit Race Riot: A Study in Violence*. Philadelphia: Chilton Books.

Smith, Suzanne E. 1999. *Dancing in the Street: Motown and the Cultural Politics of Detroit*. Cambridge, Mass.: Harvard University Press.

Smith, Tom W. 1991. "Ethnic Images." *GSS Technical Report No. 19*. Chicago: University of Chicago, National Opinion Research Center (January).

Spear, Allan H. 1967. *Black Chicago: The Making of a Negro Ghetto: 1890–1920*. Chicago: University of Chicago Press.

Squires, Gregory D. 1992. "Community Reinvestment: An Emerging Social Movement." In *From Redlining to Reinvestment: Community Responses to Urban Disinvestment*, edited by Gregory D. Squires. Philadelphia: Temple University Press.

Stanton, Mary. 2000. *From Selma to Sorrow: The Life and Death of Viola Liuzzo*. Athens: University of Georgia Press.

Stolberg, Mary M. 1998. *Bridging the River of Hatred: The Pioneering Efforts of Detroit Police Commissioner George Edwards*. Detroit: Wayne State University Press.

Strazheim, Mahlon. 1980. "Discrimination and the Spatial Characteristics of the Urban Labor Market for Black Workers." *Journal of Urban Economics* 7: 119–40.

Sugden, John. 1997. *Tecumseh: A Life*. New York: Henry Holt.

Sugrue, Thomas J. 1995. "Crabgrass-Roots Politics: Race, Rights, and the Reaction Against Liberalism in the Urban North, 1940–1964." *Journal of American History* 82(Sept.): 551–78.

———. 1996. *The Origins of the Urban Crisis: Race and Inequality in Postwar Detroit*. Princeton, N.J.: Princeton University Press.

Takaki, Ronald T. 1979. *Iron Cages: Race and Culture in 19th Century America*. Seattle: University of Washington Press.

Taylor, Carl S. 1990. *Dangerous Society*. East Lansing: Michigan State University Press.

Tentler, Leslie Woodcock. 1990. *Seasons of Grace: A History of the Catholic Archdiocese of Detroit*. Detroit: Wayne State University Press.

Thernstrom, Stephan, and Abigail Thernstrom. 1997. *America in Black and White: One Nation, Indivisible: Race in Modern America*. New York: Simon & Schuster.

Thomas, June Manning. 1997. *Redevelopment and Race: Planning a Finer City in Postwar Detroit*. Baltimore, Md.: Johns Hopkins University Press.

Thomas, Richard W. 1992. *Life for Us Is What We Make It: Building Black Community in Detroit: 1915–1945*. Bloomington: University of Indiana Press.

Tootell, Geoffrey M. B. 1996. "Turning a Critical Eye on the Critics." In *Mortgage Lending, Racial Discrimination, and Federal Policy*, edited by John Goering and Ron Wienk. Washington, D.C.: Urban Institute Press.

Turner, Margery Austin. 1992. "Limits on Neighborhood Choice: Evidence of Racial and Ethnic Steering in Urban Housing Markets." In *Clear and Convincing Evidence: Measurement of Discrimination in America*, edited by Michael Fix and Raymond Struyk. Washington, D.C.: Urban Institute Press.

Tygiel, Jules. 1983. *Baseball's Great Experiment: Jackie Robinson and His Legacy*. New York: Oxford University Press.

U.S. Department of Commerce, Bureau of the Census. 1918. *Negro Population in the United States: 1790–1915*. Washington: U.S. Government Printing Office.

———. 1921. *Fourteenth Census of the United States: 1920. Population*, vol. 2. Washington: U.S. Government Printing Office.

———. 1922. *Fourteenth Census of the United States. Population*, vol. 2. Washington: U.S. Government Printing Office.

———. 1932. *Fifteenth Census of the United States: 1930, Population* III, Part 1. Washington: U.S. Government Printing Office.

———. 1935. *Negroes in the United States: 1920–1932*. Washington: U.S. Government Printing Office.

———. 1943. *Sixteenth Census of the United States 1940, Population*, vol. II, part 3. Washington: U.S. Government Printing Office.

———. 1952. *Census of Population: 1950*, vol. 2, pt. 22. Washington: U.S. Government Printing Office.

———. 1963. *Census of Population: 1960*, vol. 1, no. 24. Washington: U.S. Government Printing Office.

———. 1972. *Census of Population: 1970*, vol. 1, pt. 24. Washington: U.S. Government Printing Office.

———. 1973a. *Census of Population: 1970*, Subject report, PC (2)-6D. Washington: U.S. Government Printing Office.

———. 1973b. *Census of Population: 1970*, vol. 1, part 24. Washington: U.S. Government Printing Office.

———. 1975a. *Historical Statistics of the United States: Colonial Times to 1970*. Washington: U.S. Government Printing Office.

———. 1975b. *Statistical Abstract of the United States, 1975–1998*, Series 148–150. Washington: U.S. Government Printing Office.

———. 1983. *Census of Population and Housing: 1980*. Public Use Microdata Sample. Washington: U.S. Government Printing Office.

———. 1991. *Census of Population: 1990*, CP2-24. Washington: U.S. Government Printing Office.

———. 1992a. *Census of Population and Housing: 1990*. Summary File Tape 3A. Washington: U.S. Government Printing Office.

———. 1992b. *Census of Housing*. CH-1-24. Washington: U.S. Government Printing Office.

———. 1993. *Census of Population and Housing: 1990*. Public Use Microdata Sample. Washington: U.S. Government Printing Office.

———. 1994. *County and City Data Book*. Washington: U.S. Government Printing Office.

———. 1995. *County Business Patterns: 1993*, Series CBP-93. Washington: U.S. Government Printing Office.

———. 1996. *Current Population Survey*. Public Use Microdata Sample of the 1995 Annual Demographic File. Washington: U.S. Government Printing Office (March).

———. 1997. *Current Population Survey*. Public Use Microdata File. Washington: U.S. Government Printing Office (March).

———. 1998. *Current Population Survey*. Public Use Microdata Sample of the Annual Demographic File. Washington: U.S. Government Printing Office (March).

———. 1999. *Current Population Survey*. Public Use Microdata File. Washington: Government Printing Office (March).

———. Various years. *Census of Manufacturers: Report for Michigan, 1947–1992*. Washington: U.S. Government Printing Office.

U.S. Department of Housing and Urban Development. 1999. *The State of the Cities 1998*. Washington: Office of Policy Development and Research.

U.S. Department of Labor, Bureau of Labor Statistics. 1989. *Employment, Hours and Earnings, States and Areas, 1972–1987*. vol. II, bull. 2232. Washington: U.S. Government Printing Office.

———. 1994. *Employment, Hours and Earnings, States and Areas, 1987–1992*. vol. II, bull. 2411. Washington: U.S. Government Printing Office.

———. 1999. *Employment and Earnings*. vol. 46, no. 8. Washington: U.S. Government Printing Office.

———. 2000. *Employment and Earnings*. vol. 47, no. 1. Washington: U.S. Government Printing Office.

U.S. National Center for Health Statistics. Various years. *Vital Statistics of the United States, 1972–1998*. Washington: U.S. Government Printing Office.

Vose, Clement E. 1959. *Caucasians Only: The Supreme Court, the NAACP and the Restrictive Covenant Cases.* Berkeley: University of California Press.

Warren, Donald. 1996. *Radio Priest: Charles Coughlin: The Father of Hate Radio.* New York: Free Press.

Washington, Forrester. 1991. "Police Brutality." In *Detroit Perspectives: Crossroads and Turning Points,* edited by Wilma Wood Henrickson. Detroit: Wayne State University Press. (From the essay "The Negro in Detroit, 1926.") (Orig. pub. in 1983)

Watkins, Steve. 1997. *The Black O: Racism and Redemption in an American Corporate Empire.* Athens: University of Georgia Press.

Weaver, Robert C. 1946. *Negro Labor: A National Problem.* New York: Harcourt, Brace and White, 1983.

White, Walter, and Thurgood Marshall. 1943. "What Caused the Detroit Riots? An Analysis." New York: National Association for the Advancement of Colored People. In *Detroit Perspectives: Crossroads and Turning Points,* edited by Wilma Wood Henrickson. Detroit: Wayne State University Press.

Widick, B. J. 1989. *Detroit: City of Race and Class Violence,* rev. ed. Detroit: Wayne State University Press. (Orig. pub. in 1983)

Wilson, William Julius. 1978. *The Declining Significance of Race: Blacks and Changing American Institutions.* Chicago: University of Chicago Press.

———. 1987. *The Truly Disadvantaged: The Inner City, the Underclass, and Public Policy.* Chicago: University of Chicago Press.

———. 1996. *When Work Disappears: The World of the New Urban Poor.* New York: Alfred A. Knopf.

Wolf, Eleanor P. 1981. *Trial and Error: The Detroit School Segregation Case.* Detroit: Wayne State University Press.

Woodford, Frank B., and Aruthus M. Woodford. 1969. *All Our Yesterdays: A Brief History of Detroit.* Detroit: Wayne State University Press.

Yinger, John. 1992. "Access Denied, Access Constrained: Results and Implications of the 1989 Housing Discrimination Study." In *Clear and Convincing Evidence: Measurement of Discrimination in America,* edited by Michael Fix and Raymond Struyk. Washington, D.C.: Urban Institute Press.

———. 1995. *Closed Doors, Opportunities Lost: The Continuing Costs of Housing Discrimination.* New York: Russell Sage Foundation.

———. 1998. "Housing Discrimination Is Still Worth Worrying About." *Housing Policy Debate* 9(4): 893–927.

Zunz, Olivier. 1982. *The Changing Face of Inequality: Urbanization, Industrial Development, and Immigrants in Detroit: 1880–1920.* Chicago: University of Chicago Press.

Index

Numbers in **boldface** refer to figures and tables. Numbers in *italics* refer to photographs.

59–65, **64,** 109, **125,** 127–37, **129,** 143; manufacturing industry location, 23–25, 59–65, **64;** policies to address, 253–54, 257–61

sports, Detroit professional, 12, 48–49, 151, 181, 251

St. Louis, MO, **162,** 163, 169

Stanzione, Giuseppe, 157–58

The State of the Cities, 1998, 254

statistical discrimination, 217

steering by real estate professionals, 208

stereotypes: endorsement or rejection of, 218–32, **224–25, 228–29;** explanations of black-white differences, 237–40; negative racial, 217–18, 244–46, 248–49; programs to reduce racial differences, 240–44; as remaining prevalent, 245. *See also* racial issues

Stevens, Henry, 154

streetcars, 25

STRESS unit (Stop Robberies, Enjoy Safe Streets), 47

strikes against black employment, 83–84

suburbs and suburban ring: application vs. hire rate, 118–24, **122;** black suburban residence, 169–72, 176; vs. central city as turning point for metropolitan Detroit, 45–52, **50,** 171–73; desirability of, 178, 185–88; development of, 9; economic status, 49–50, **50,** 169–72; employment in, 63, **64,** 110–18; historical industrial construction in, 8; moving central city residents to, 257–59; residential and workplace locations, 127–37, **129,** 143; residential segregation, 10, 154–61. *See also* metropolitan Detroit

Sugrue, Thomas, 3, 65, 70, 104, 149, 151, 163, 244

supply-side policy strategies, 255–57

Supreme Court: Constitution as colorblind, 218; Fair Housing Law, 207; Gautreaux program, 258, 259; public school busing, 3; residential segregation, 146, 152

Survey Sampling incorporated (SSI), 124

surveys utilized, 4–5

Sweet, Dr. Ossian, 144–45

Sweet, Henry, 145

TANF (Temporary Assistance for Needy Families), 77

task performance and hiring criteria, 113–16

tax incentives, 259, 260

Taylor, MI: black perception of welcome, 135, 136; residential description and perception, **180,** 181, 182, **183, 186,** 187, 188, 192–96, **193;** suburban blacks, 169

teachers in Detroit public schools, 83

team player skills as important to employers, 141, **142**

technological automation and productivity in auto industry, 57, 59

Tecumseh, 16

Temporary Assistance for Needy Families (TANF), 77

Tenerowicz, Rudolph, 150

Thernstrom, Stephan and Abigail, 201

Tilly, Chris, 141

Title VII, Civil Rights Act (1964), 73, 123, 159

tolerance of minorities in neighborhood, 32, 33, 179–88, 191, 196–201, **198**

top earners, descriptions of, 98–99

Townsend, Francis, 29

training and hiring requirements, 115

transportation: commuting, 111, 128, **129,** 130, 132; job searches, 134, 138; public, 24–25, 111, 253, 257–61; reducing cost for, 252

travel distance and job searches, 134–35

Treaty of Detroit (1948), 7

Troy, MI: application and hiring, 121, **122;** black perception of welcome, 135, 136; job search in, **133,** 134;